THE BEST IN TENT CAMPING:

NEW ENGLAND

---

*A Guide for Car Campers Who Hate RVs, Concrete Slabs,
and Loud Portable Stereos*

THE BEST IN TENT CAMPING:

NEW ENGLAND

A Guide for Car Campers Who Hate RVs, Concrete Slabs, and Loud Portable Stereos

1st Edition

Lafe Low

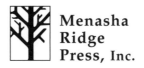

Menasha
Ridge
Press, Inc.

This is for my son Devin, my best camping buddy ever.

Copyright© 2002 by Lafe Low
All rights reserved
Printed in the United States of America
Published by Menasha Ridge Press
Distributed by the Globe Pequot Press
First edition

Library of Congress Cataloging-in-Publication Data

Low, Lafe, 1962–
   The best in tent camping, New England : a guide for campers who hate
RVs, concrete slabs, and loud portable stereos / Lafe Low.—1st ed.
      p.   cm.
   ISBN 0-89732-327-0
   1. Camping—New England—Guidebooks.   2. Camp sites, facilities,
etc.—New England—Guidebooks.   3. New England—Guidebooks.
4. New England—Guidebooks. I. Title.

GV191.42.N3 L69 2002
917.404`05—dc21

                                                        2002024446

Cover design by Grant Tatum
Cover photo of Acadia National Park by COMSTOCK

Menasha Ridge Press
P.O. Box 43673
Birmingham, Alabama 35243
www.menasharidge.com

CONTENTS

NEW ENGLAND

NEW ENGLAND

MAP LEGEND
AND KEY

WHITE WOLF

Campground name
and location

Table Rock

Other nearby
campgrounds

NATIONAL FOREST   NATIONAL PARK

Public lands

0   1   2
MILES

Approximate
scale

64

Interstate
highways

40

U.S.
highways

120 49

State roads

22

Other
paved roads

Unpaved
roads

4WD

Jeep
roads

80 80

U.S. Forest Service
and County roads

Railroads

⊙ Asheville

City
or town

Ward Lake

Ocean, lake,
or bay

Swift Creek

River or stream

Political
boundary

Bridge or tunnel

Cliff or outcropping

Falls or rapid

Food

Historical site

House or cabin

Lighthouse

Lodging

Marina or boat ramp

Mine or quarry

Museum

Observatory

ORV area

Park office

Picnic area

Spring

Stable or ranch

Summit
3312 or lookout

Ski area

Maine

1. Baxter State Park Campgrounds
2. Blackwoods Campground
3. Bradbury Mountain State Park
4. Camden Hills State Park
5. Lamoine State Park
6. Lily Bay State Park
7. Mount Blue State Park
8. Mount Desert Campground
9. Orr's Island Campground
10. Peaks-Kenny State Park
11. Rangeley Lake State Park
12. Seawall Campground
13. Sebago Lake State Park
14. Warren Island State Park

New Hampshire

15. Bear Brook State Park
16. Big Rock Campground
17. Blackberry Crossing Campground
18. Covered Bridge Campground
19. Dolly Copp Campground
20. Dry River Campground
21. Hancock Campground
22. Jigger Johnson Campground
23. Lafayette Campground
24. Mont Monadnock State Park
25. Passaconaway Campground
26. Pawtuckaway State Park
27. Pillsbury State Park

Vermont

28. Allis State Park
29. Branbury State Park
30. Chittenden Brook Recreation Area
31. Coolidge State Park
32. Gifford Woods State Park
33. Grout Pond Recreation Area
34. Half Moon State Park
35. Jamaica State Park
36. Lake St. Catherine State Park
37. Mount Ascutney State Park
38. Mount Moosalamoo Campground
39. Quechee Gorge State Park
40. Smugglers Notch State Park
41. Thetford Hill State Park
42. Underhill State Park

Massachusetts

43. Beartown State Forest
44. Clarksburg State Park
45. Granville State Forest
46. Harold Parker State Forest
47. Mohawk Trail State Forest
48. Mount Greylock State Reservation
49. Myles Standish State Forest
50. Nickerson State Park
51. Savoy Mountain State Forest
52. Windsor State Forest

Connecticut

53. Devil's Hopyard State Park
54. Housatonic Meadows State Park
55. Macedonia Brook State Park
56. Rocky Neck State Park
57. Selden Neck

Rhode Island

58. Burlingame State Park
59. Fort Getty Recreation Area
60. George Washington Management Area

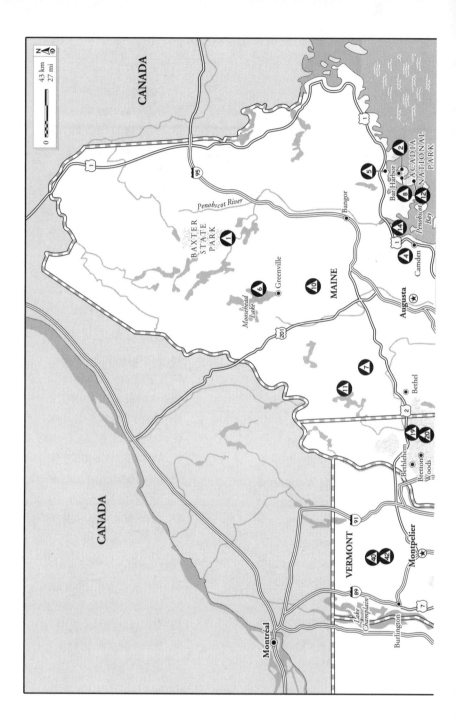

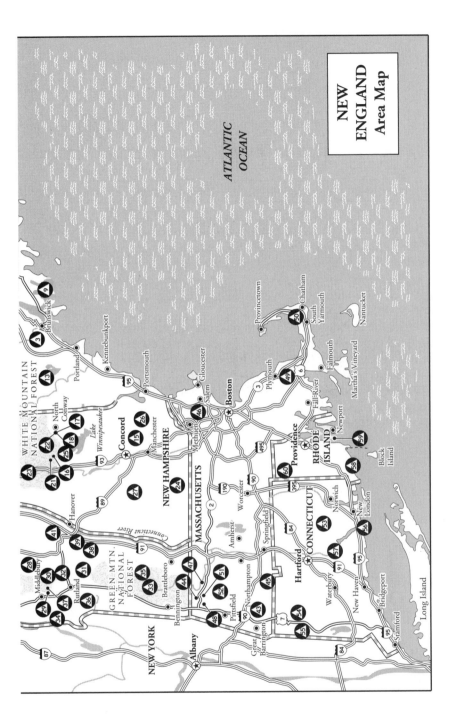

NEW
ENGLAND
Area Map

ACKNOWLEDGMENTS

While I wrote the words and drove the miles in preparing this book, I enjoyed the tremendous benefit of support and inspiration from many people. Most of all, I would like to thank my family and my parents (all three of them!), Douglas and Linsey Low and Larry Howard, for their endless encouragement, understanding, love, and patience, especially while I dragged them around to these campgrounds.

To the innumerable state park rangers and volunteers I chatted with at campgrounds all over New England, as well as the friendly folks at the private campgrounds I visited, I tip my hat to you. I'll be back soon, when I can stay a few days and relax!

Finally, none of this would ever have been possible without the unfailing drive and boundless determination of my Subaru wagon. The green machine rocks! I put more miles on the Scooby Doo while researching this book than I would in two or three years of normal life (note the distinction between book research and normal life).

PREFACE

New England is a remarkable region. Nowhere else in the United States are you so close to the ocean, the mountains, lakes, and rivers. Drive a few hours and the landscape and the scenery will change as rapidly and dramatically as the weather.

I have lived in New England all my life, moving around and experiencing life in almost all of the six New England states. (Rhode Island is the only New England state whose license plate hasn't graced my vehicle at one point or another.) I am also somewhat of a creature of habit. Over the years, I have found spots where I can experience the solitude, wonder, and awesome beauty of the wilderness, and I keep going back to those same spots. I suppose there's a comfortable cloak of familiarity, but in cruising along to familiar territory, I've been blowing by some other incredible areas.

By running all over the place to research this book, I discovered some magical spots I might never have found otherwise, and for that I am thankful. The absolute solitude of camping on the shores of Benedict Pond at Beartown State Forest, the isolation and deep wilderness beauty at several Pillsbury State Park campsites, the natural cathedral of site 21 at Branbury State Park, these are places that gave me chills when I first found them. Now, I'll return to these spots for a longer visit. When you have the chance to visit these places, I hope you have an equally memorable experience. Enjoy the ride.

THE BEST IN TENT CAMPING:

NEW ENGLAND

*A Guide for Car Campers Who Hate RVs, Concrete Slabs,
and Loud Portable Stereos*

INTRODUCTION

A Word about This Book and New England Tent Camping

There are literally hundreds of campgrounds in New England. Winnowing down the list to 60 was no easy task. That said, this book is a guide to 60 of the best for tent camping. There are plenty of wonderful campgrounds and campsites out there that didn't make it into the book, but are still well worth checking out.

In developing the list of campgrounds to explore here, I took into account numerous factors, one of which was accessibility. I wanted to profile campgrounds that offer a peaceful wilderness experience and are also accessible enough for a quick escape. Of course, there are some pristine, incredibly remote campsites carved out of the wilderness of northern Maine, northern New Hampshire, and tucked away on islands in several New England lakes that aren't included in this book—yet. They may be in future editions, so stay tuned.

One other thing you'll no doubt notice is that most of the campgrounds profiled here are either state park or national forest campgrounds. That's no accident, as these campgrounds tend to provide much more of a wilderness experience. It's probably a simple matter of economics. Many private campgrounds cater to the RV crowd because, quite frankly, they spend more money when they visit. RV campers need hookups, which cost money, and they tend to stay for long periods of time. So you can't fault private campground owners for striving to attract RV campers.

There are some notable exceptions, however. The Mount Desert Campground leaps to mind. While the properties neither exclude nor bend over backwards to bring in the land yachts, the simple factor of the rugged, waterfront topography will limit the size and quantity of RVs. The Orr's Island Campground is another tenter-friendly private campground. There is an interesting dichotomy here. There are certainly rows of RVs that you can't help but notice as you enter the campground. Keep driving over to the tent-only area, and you'll know why I chose to profile these beautiful, windswept, secluded campsites.

I hope you'll be able to visit many of the campgrounds profiled in this book and will agree that they are among the region's best.

How to Use This Book

As you pull into your chosen campground, you breathe a sigh of relief. Having sorted through your options, you've selected a destination, and now you've found it. You're here. Time to relax. Well, not quite yet. You still have to choose your site, so check out the descriptions provided here of the individual sites and sections of the campground. Pick up a site map as you register at the campground. Only you will know what factors are important to you, like spaciousness, solitude, scenery, or proximity to a beach, boat launch, or rest room. Armed with the campground profiles in this book, a campground map, and a friendly word of advice from the ranger or campground host, you can't go wrong!

Of course, this guidebook will be far more useful if you know how to find what you're looking for. Before selecting a campground to visit, look over the following descriptions of the profiles' organization, content, and criteria.

Site Descriptions

I have endeavored to give you a sense of how each site feels. Is the site surrounded by forest? What type of forest —the dense, cool feel of evergreens or the breezy, open feeling of maple or birch groves? Is there a view? Is the site far enough from neighboring sites? Are there any particular characteristics unique to the site? These are some of the questions I like to answer in the site descriptions.

While the campground ratings will help give you a barometer of the campground as a whole, every campground here has sites of varying sizes, varying degrees of solitude, and varying scenery. By detailing which parts of the campground are more conducive to tent camping and which sites in particular help you feel as if you're deep in the wilderness, I have tried to help steer you in the best direction possible.

The Rating System

For each campground, there's a rating from one to five for each of the following categories: beauty, site privacy, site spaciousness, quiet, security, and cleanliness/upkeep. This was often a tough call, as there are different sections within the campgrounds that may warrant different ratings.

So the ratings you'll see at the beginning of each profile are representative of the campground as a whole. While you may see a 3 or 4 for privacy overall, you can probably bet on a couple of sites tucked off in the far reaches of the campground that clearly rate a five or more.

Beauty

This factor may seem obvious, but is often elusive, or at the very least, subjective. What appeals to one camper may not appeal to another. I prefer campgrounds and campsites that are set deep within the woods. The greater sense of natural solitude a campsite provides, the better it is, at least in my view.

Speaking of views, many of the campgrounds profiled here, and certainly many of the individual sites within these campgrounds, are perched right along the shores of a lake, a pond, or even the ocean. These campsites are off the charts when it comes to site beauty. If there was a six-star rating, sites like those situated along the waters of Moosehead Lake, Half Moon Pond, and Somes Sound would easily deserve it. There are also many sites at campgrounds in close proximity to the water that, while they may not be right on the shore, provide dramatic water views. These sites too are among some of the most spectacularly scenic.

Site Privacy

When you set off for a camping trip, the last thing you want is to feel as if you're piled up on top of your neighbors. Even in campgrounds where the sites aren't huge, if they are encircled by a relatively dense forest and arranged with a sensitive eye toward privacy, you can find a site that puts you in your own slice of the forest.

Site Spaciousness

Some of the campsites I've seen in New England are just barely big enough for your tent, a picnic table, and a fire ring. Others are large enough to build a house on. I don't typically need a lot of room when I'm camping, but I don't want to pitch my tent right next to the picnic table. This rating will give you an idea of how much elbow room you can expect when you set up camp.

Quiet

This is another factor that is particularly important to me. I like campsites that are very well isolated, secluded from neighboring sites and the rest of the campground. So I find it especially distracting if there is a persistent drone of cars and trucks blasting by on a nearby road, the steady whine of powerboats zipping by on a lake, or (worse yet) the sounds of portable TVs and radios.

You can rest assured I paid close attention to the noisiness of these campgrounds. In some cases, there are parts of a campground that are close to a main road, while the rest of the campground is separated by enough distance and enough forest to block out the road noise.

Security

It's a shame that this even has to be a factor, but one must be practical. I've never had anyone steal or rummage through my stuff at any of the campgrounds mentioned here, but there are some that feel "safer" to me than others. The size of the campground and proximity to urban areas are the primary aspects I considered when making my security determinations. Be prudent, even when it looks like there's no one around. It's not a bad idea to lock up your car and your bike when you retire to your tent for the night. A little bit of precaution can go a long way toward making sure you go home with all your gear.

Cleanliness/upkeep

Most of the campgrounds profiled here scored highly on the cleanliness scale. This is true for a couple of reasons. First, I think that most people who enjoy the idea of spending a night in the woods are also inclined to take good care of the forest and their campsites. Second, many state parks make extraordinary efforts to keep their campsites well maintained. When you see the park rangers or other staff about the campground, take a moment to say "Hi" and thank them for keeping the campground clean.

Of course, all of this depends on you doing your part as well. Even though campgrounds are heavily traveled and well-worn spots, do what you can to leave no trace. Pack out everything you packed in (and even a little more if you find something). Please don't pile your trash in the fireplace or try to burn things that won't burn or things that emit dangerous fumes.

Even at the cleanest of campgrounds and campsites, whenever I find a stray piece of paper, bottle cap, or cigarette butt (especially the latter), I always take a moment to reach down and pick it up to dispose of properly. If everyone is mindful to be as gentle with the forest as possible, it will remain pristine for generations to come. Every time you pick up a bit of trash in the woods, consider it doing a favor for your children or grandchildren, even if you don't have any yet!

Key Information

This is the nuts and bolts section of the campground profiles: how to contact the campground, when it is open, the number of sites and how they are assigned, and so on. Unless otherwise noted, fees are given on a per site, per night basis. If you have any special needs or requirements, check here first. Do you feel more comfortable camping where you can make reservations? Do you have a dog that you want to bring along? Do you really like to have a beer or a glass of wine with your dinner? Check here for any rules and regulations that might not agree with your camping style.

Reservations

Most of the campgrounds described here take reservations for most of their sites. Camping is an increasingly popular activity, so if you're sure where you want to go and for how long, it's probably not a bad idea to call ahead and reserve a site.

That's one of the reasons I tried to be as specific as possible in my site descriptions. If you've never been to a particular campground, I wanted to give you as clear an idea as possible of how a site will feel in terms of surrounding, spaciousness, and location within the campground. You can then reserve a site with confidence.

Camping Tips

Gear Checklist and Packing

There's a lot of gear associated with camping: your tent, sleeping bag, cooking stuff, flashlights, clothes—it can get overwhelming pretty fast. I'm not a terribly organized person, but I try to keep all my camping gear packed in nice, neat little piles. That way, I rarely forget anything. Nothing is worse than setting up your site and realizing you've forgotten something critical, like your tent stakes or a flashlight!

I keep all my cooking gear bundled up in a milk crate. Right on top of that, I have my stove. With both of those items, plus my tent, sleeping bag, and sleeping pad, I'm at least 90 percent packed.

Of course, everyone's needs and preferences are different, but it does help to write down a list of essential camping gear, plus a few things to make the trip more comfortable or enjoyable. My version of the essentials is listed in Appendix A.

Food Safety

Anywhere in New England, there will be critters making their way around the forest as you sleep. Do yourself and them a favor and be careful about how you store your food.

Besides making a mess and depriving you of your next meal, when critters get into your food they become that much more comfortable around human beings. They will return for another snack. These animals can later become aggressive or dangerous, requiring their elimination or relocation, and you don't want to be responsible for that.

This is particularly true of black bears, which are generally shy and reclusive. They'll go out of their way to avoid human contact. However, once they know there is readily available food in a particular area, such as a campground frequented by sloppy campers, they return bolder each time.

Store your food out of the way or in animal-proof containers. The best thing to do is after you're done with dinner and have cleaned up, put your cooler and any containers of food back in your car. Anything that smells like food should be stored out of reach as well. This means any utensils or cookware, napkins, or any clothes upon which you may have spilled food. Additionally, it's surprising what scents animals find attractive, so stashing soaps and toiletries isn't a bad idea either. Any food or anything with a strong scent should spend the night in your car.

Weather Preparation

Even during the summer, it's prudent to pack a fleece jacket and a waterproof jacket. I don't know for sure, but it seems like on at least half of the occasions where I find myself outside in a tent, it rains. I think the camping gods start chuckling every time they see me grab my tent.

Anyway, it's a good idea to be prepared for any kind of potential weather. That doesn't mean bring your snowshoes in August, but by all means do bring a warm jacket and something water-resistant. The weather in New England can and does change faster than the scenery as you drive from Cape Cod to the Berkshires. Have something warm, have something dry. You'll be much more comfortable and safe.

Also, even if it's been a bright, sunny day, foul weather can blow in at any time, and frequently does. I've been tempted on many nights to ignore the rain fly on my tent and just leave it in the car. This can be a bad idea, especially if it starts raining at 2 a.m. Be ready and you'll be happy.

Canoe and Kayak Camping

Several of the campgrounds profiled here are accessible only by canoe or kayak. While this poses several logistical and packing challenges, the rewards of absolute solitude and camping right on the water are well worth any extra effort.

There are a few important safety factors to consider when canoe or kayak camping. First and foremost, you need to be comfortable with your paddling skills before you add the weight of camping gear to your boat. Don't plan a camping trip as your first experience paddling a canoe or kayak.

With a sea kayak, try to stow all your gear in the sealed bulkheads. It may be tempting to strap your tent or sleeping pad to the deck, but anything protruding above deck level will make your kayak less stable. Besides catching the wind, it also raises the boat's center of gravity. Keep all your gear below decks.

Most touring kayaks have a fore and aft storage compartment. Try to spread out your gear evenly. Even if all your gear will fit in the aft compartment, spread it out among both to ensure that your kayak floats level. Once you've packed your boat, take it for a test float. Get it into water deep enough that it floats freely. If it looks like you're riding a wheelie or about to do a nose dive, you need to redistribute your gear. The same goes for side to side balance. If your kayak seems to be listing to one side or the other, try to redistribute your gear so that the boat floats level. Keep those same principles in mind when stowing gear in a canoe. Try to balance to load in the center of the canoe, and evenly distributed fore and aft.

Having said all that, you can pack an amazing amount of gear in a canoe or kayak. Prior to packing up for the first group trip I ever went on, we divided the group gear. I stowed the group gear in my aft compartment and my personal gear in the forward compartment and still had plenty of room in each.

There are a few things you can do to make your canoe or kayak camping trip a bit more convenient. For your first dinner at your island campsite, prepare something in advance, freeze it in a Tupperware container, then when dinnertime arrives, all you have to do is heat it up and you're ready to eat. Also, any gear that you haven't been able to store in a dry bag, you should wrap tightly in a large, plastic garbage bag. Anything you store in the bulkheads or open in your canoe can and most likely will get a bit wet. There's nothing worse than reaching for a jacket or vest to wear and finding it damp and soggy.

The Campfire Awaits

There's nothing like a night spent outside. The soft crackle of a campfire, the flickering light thrown about the forest, the satisfaction of the day's travels, and the anticipation of tomorrow's adventures. It's a potent combination.

Hopefully, the camping tips provided here and the descriptions of the campgrounds that follow will steer you toward a memorable experience. Pick a state, read the profiles, pack the car, and hit the road! New England is a vast and diverse region. There are campgrounds profiled here from the farthest northern reaches of Vermont, New Hampshire, and Maine to the seashores of Connecticut and Rhode Island, and everything in between. Some are familiar haunts, some are unexpected hidden gems, all are spectacular. Wherever you choose to go camping in New England, from the sandy bluffs of Nickerson State Park to the deep woods of Beartown State Forest, from the absolute solitude of Warren Island to the cool, crisp mountain air of Underhill State Park, you're in for a memorable and magical trip.

MAINE

BAXTER STATE PARK

Millinocket

Forever wild—those words of Percival Baxter were perfectly chosen to describe the character of Baxter State Park. The remoteness, size, and grandeur of the park are profound. He also meant those words to describe the stewardship of Baxter State Park. His intent was to keep the park undeveloped. Today, the park is managed as a wildlife preserve first and a recreation resource second.

At more than 200,000 acres, Baxter State Park is a huge place. There are actually nine campgrounds within the park. Truth is, no matter where you end up in Baxter State Park, you're bound to have a remote wilderness experience. Seven of the campgrounds you can reach by driving. The other two are hike-in areas. Camping in these areas requires a bit of additional effort, but the solitude and splendor are well worth it. If you're camping in Baxter State Park, by all means enjoy the convenience of the car-camping areas, but try to spend at least one night at Chimney Pond or Russell Pond, or even one of the many truly remote wilderness campsites that are spread throughout the park.

Upon entering the massive park through the Togue Pond Gate along the park's southern border, the first campground you'll come to is Abol Campground. Abol has 9 tent sites and 12 lean-tos, which can each accommodate four people. Abol Campground is situated at the trailhead

CAMPGROUND RATINGS

Beauty:	★★★★★
Site Privacy:	★★★★★
Site Spaciousness:	★★★★
Quiet:	★★★★★
Security:	★★★★★
Cleanliness/upkeep:	★★★★★

A night spent camping in Baxter State Park, especially in one of the remote sites, is a true wilderness experience.

MAINE

for the Abol Trail, one of the routes to the summit of Katahdin, so this is one of several popular spots for hikers with designs on summiting the park's centerpiece peak.

Further up the Nesowadnehunk Tote Road that encircles the perimeter of the park is Katahdin Stream Campground. This campground has 10 tent sites, 12 lean-tos that can fit anywhere from 3 to 5 people, and a bunkhouse with room for 6. From here, hikers can head to the summit of Katahdin on the Hunt Trail, which is part of the Appalachian Trail. You can also easily get to the Owl Trail and the Grassy Pond Trail heading east.

Just to the east of Katahdin Stream you'll find Daicey Pond Campground. You get there by continuing north and west on the Tote Road, then heading south just before the Foster Field Picnic Area. You could also hike there from Katahdin Stream Campground (or vice versa) on the Grassy Pond Trail.

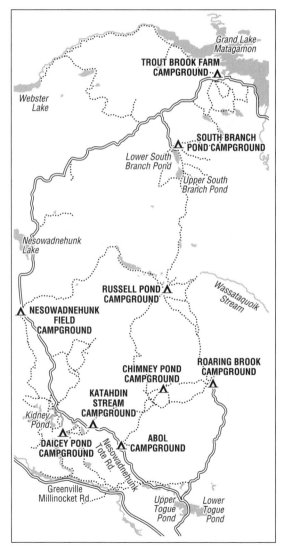

The Daicey Pond Campground doesn't have any tent sites, but does have a pair of lean-tos and 11 cabins with 2 to 4 beds each. The Appalachian Trail goes right through the campground. There's also a trail that encircles Daicey Pond and leads to the short Lost Pond Trail, which takes you out to the still and secluded waters of Lost Pond.

Continuing north on the Nesowadnehunk Tote Road along the western border of the park brings you to Nesowadnehunk Field Campground. Here there are 12 tent sites, 11 three-and four-person lean-tos, and 2 group sites. From here, you could easily get to the Doubletop Trail, a sturdy hike that takes you up and over Doubletop Mountain and offers outrageous views of Katahdin.

Taking Roaring Brook Road off to the right from the Togue Pond gatehouse brings you first to Roaring Brook Campground. There are 10 tent sites (4 of which are walk-in sites), 12 lean-tos that accommodate anywhere from 2 to 6 people each, and a bunkhouse with room for 12. From here, you have plenty of hiking options. Follow the Sandy Stream Pond Trail to the Turner Mountain Trail to hike up Turner Mountain. You could also head west on the Helon Taylor Trail to reach Katahdin.

Head west on the Chimney Pond Trail from Roaring Brook Campground and you'll come to Chimney Pond Campground. This is a remote and supremely beautiful spot. There are no tent sites

To get there: To get to the Togue Pond gatehouse, follow the Baxter State Park Road northwest from the intersection of Routes 11 and 157 in Millinocket. To get to the Matagamon Public Landing gatehouse, take Route 1 North to Route 159 North to Grand Lake Road. Follow Grand Lake Road to the gatehouse.

KEY INFORMATION

Baxter State Park
64 Balsam Drive
Millinocket, ME 04462

Operated by: Maine Department of Conservation, Bureau of Parks & Lands

Information: Baxter State Park, (207) 723-5140

Open: May 15–October 15, except Chimney Pond and Russell Pond, which open June 1, and Nesowadnehunk Field and Trout Brook Farm, which open May 23.

Individual sites: 84 tent sites, 65 lean-tos, 5 bunkhouses, and 11 cabins spread throughout 9 campgrounds.

Each site has: Fire ring, picnic table

Site assignment: Reservations strongly recommended; otherwise first come, first served

Registration: At gatehouse as you enter the park and with ranger as you enter a campground

Facilities: Pit toilets, water spigots

Parking: At sites

Fee: $8 vehicle fee to enter park, $6 per person (min. of two people—$12 fee—per site)

Restrictions:

Pets—No pets allowed

Fires—In established fire rings only

Alcoholic beverages—Not allowed

Vehicles—Parking at sites only

here, but there are 9 lean-tos that can each handle 4 people and a bunkhouse that can fit 12. At least your tent is one less thing to carry.

Besides being remarkably scenic, Chimney Pond Campground is a perfect base camp from which to summit Katahdin. You have your choice of the Saddle Trail, Cathedral Trail, or Didley Trail. Any of these hikes are steep and strenuous, so plan ahead and be prepared.

Also from the Roaring Brook Campground, follow the Russell Pond Trail to Russell Pond Campground, another incredibly remote and wild camping area. There are 4 tent sites, 4 lean-tos that can accommodate anywhere from 4 to 8 people, and a bunkhouse for 12. This campground is also situated within a hub of hiking trails. There are several long hiking trails, including the Russell Pond Trail and the Northwest Basin Trail (which leads to the North Peaks Trail) to the south, the Pogy Notch Trail to the north, and the Wassataquiok Lake Trail to the west. These are all fairly long hikes, so plan and pace yourself carefully, especially if you're doing a round-trip day hike from the campground. If you're looking for a shorter hike from Russell Pond Campground, try the Ledge Falls Trail, Grand Falls Trail, or Lookout Trail.

Entering the park from the northeast at Matagamon Gate Public Landing will get you close to Trout Brook Farm and South Branch Campgrounds. From the gatehouse, follow the road west to Trout Brook Farm Campground. This campground is set aside for tent campers, with 18 tent sites and no lean-tos or bunkhouses. From here, you can also hike in to any of a number of remote, wilderness campsites. To the south, follow Five Ponds Trail to sites spread out along Littlefield Pond, Billfish Pond, and Long Pond. To the north, the lengthy, multi-day Freezeout Trail brings you to remote campsites and lean-tos along Second Lake, Webster Brook, and Webster Lake.

From Trout Brook Campground, continue west on the road to The Crossing picnic area. Then head south on South Branch Road to find South Branch Campground, with 21 tent sites, 12 four-person lean-tos, and a bunkhouse for 6. This campground is located at the northern tip of Lower South Branch Pond. From here, you can hike the short and sweet Ledges Trail or the Middle Fowler Trail.

There are also several excellent hikes to nearby peaks, including the North Traveler Trail, which leads up the mountain of the same name; the Howe Brook Trail, which follows its namesake brook past two dramatic waterfalls; and the Center Ridge Trail, which brings you to the summit of The Traveler. To the west of Upper and Lower South Branch Ponds, the South Branch Mountain Trail takes you up and over Black Cat Mountain. These hikes aren't super long, but they are super steep. Never underestimate the intensity of the hiking anywhere within Baxter State Park.

Baxter State Park is a popular destination, and there are a finite number of campsites in and around the park. You could wing it by not making reservations, but you might end up disappointed or driving way out of your way to find an open site. If you do get jammed, there are several private campgrounds just outside the park that provide a backup plan, but do yourself a favor and make a reservation. The peace of mind will be well worth it.

BLACKWOODS CAMPGROUND

Bar Harbor

For such a huge campground, most of the sites at Blackwoods still retain a cozy atmosphere. The three-lane paved road (two lanes in, one out) accessing the campground might make you wonder what you're getting into, but rest assured, this is a wonderful place to pitch a tent.

For one thing, Blackwoods Campground is situated just off the Park Loop Road that winds its way around Acadia National Park. Better still, from your campsite it's a short walk to the ocean, Sand Beach, Thunder Hole, Otter Cliff...the list goes on. Also, the campground rests on the mostly flat forest floor beneath a loosely spaced forest canopy of mixed pine, balsam, hemlock, and hardwoods. The open forest lets lots of light filter through to the campground floor on sunny days, and the cool breeze from the nearby ocean assures your comfort.

Blackwoods is separated into two main loops. Loop A has 160 sites and Loop B has 154 sites, plus several group sites available by reservation only. The place is big! Blackwoods accepts reservations from June 15 to September 15. Making a reservation for an in-season trip is not a bad idea, as Acadia National Park receives hordes of visitors during the summer and Blackwoods is likely to be full on most weekends.

Outside of those dates, it's first come, first served. About 50 campsites on the A Loop are open year-round if you've come to Acadia to snowshoe or cross-country ski on the

CAMPGROUND RATINGS

Beauty:	★★★★
Site Privacy:	★★★★
Site Spaciousness:	★★★★
Quiet:	★★★★
Security:	★★★★★
Cleanliness/upkeep:	★★★★★

Set between the still of the forests and mountains of Acadia National Park and the thundering surf of the Atlantic, Blackwoods Campground is indeed in a dramatic location.

MAINE

massive network of carriage roads that wend their way in and around the park. Camping during the winter is usually free, unless a ranger at the main station informs you differently. I've visited Blackwoods most often in the off season; there has never been a fee, and I've always felt like I had the place to myself.

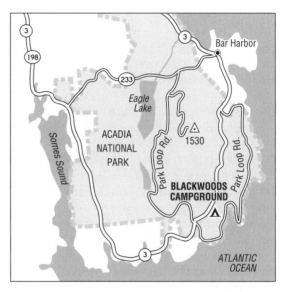

Looking at the 160 sites within the A Loop, there are several areas that are especially conducive to quality tent camping. The first subloop, with sites 3, 4, 5, 7, and 10–19, has loosely spaced sites beneath a rich forest canopy. The sites have a welcoming blanket of pine needles, which make a soft, aromatic bed for your tent and sleeping bag.

The next loop contains sites 2, 6, 8, 9, 22, 27, 29, 32, 33, and 34, which are also loosely spaced. These two loops are quite close to the path leading down to the cliffs—an extra bonus. After the day crowds have cleared out, you've had your fireside dinner, and the campfire has died down, grab a flashlight and a mug of tea (or whatever suits your mood) and wander down the path and across the Park Loop Road to watch the surf crashing incessantly against the cliffs. That's a sight and sound combination of which I never tire.

Further up the larger part of the A Loop, the sites off to the left of the outer loop offer a nice sense of seclusion. Look for sites 104–108, 124–131, and 144–151. In truth, though, most of the sites within the sweeping expanse of the A Loop will offer you a nice spot for your tent.

Over in the B Loop, there are several areas where the sites are set apart from each other. The crossroad at the far end of the B loop sets off sites 141, 143, 147, 150, 153, and 154. These are the sites I'd look for first within the B Loop.

Taking the second or third left from the main outer loop will bring you to sites numbered in the high 60s and low 70s. Sites 65–73 have a good amount of elbow room between one another. Site 45 is also stuck onto the far end of this loop. It's right on the main outer loop, but if you set up well within the site, you'll be fine.

There are also several group sites on the left side of the B Loop. G4 and G5 offer the most space, although G5 is right across from the rest rooms. Each group site has room for 15–20 campers, but by reservation only. There's an amphitheater between the A Loop and B Loop, where rangers present evening slide shows and interpretive programs. Check at the campground entrance ranger station to find out what's on the schedule.

If you end up pitching your tent at the north end of the A Loop, you'll be close to the South Ridge hiking trail, leading to the summit of Cadillac Mountain. Wherever you land at Blackwoods, or even if you stay elsewhere in or near Acadia National Park, a trip to the summit of Cadillac is one thing you won't want to miss. From the mountain, you'll have a sweeping, panoramic view that defies cliches, platitudes, and expletives! Here's a tip: the sunsets are phenomenal, so much so that one per day may not be enough. Situate yourself along the Park Loop Road to watch the sunset. The instant it dips below the horizon, hop in your car and boogie up to the summit of Cadillac Mountain and watch it again!

To get there: From Ellsworth, follow Route 3 onto Mount Desert Island. Follow Route 3 to Route 102/198. Stay on Route 198 when it turns left, and follow this to Route 233. Follow Route 233 to the entrance to Acadia National Park on the left. Enter the park and follow the Park Loop Road to Blackwoods Campground on the right.

KEY INFORMATION

Blackwoods Campground
Maine Highway 3
Bar Harbor, ME 04609

Operated by: National Park Service

Information: Acadia National Park
P.O. Box 177
Bar Harbor, ME 04609
(207) 288-3338

Open: Year-round with reduced facilities mid-September through mid-May

Individual sites: 160 in A Loop, 154 in B Loop, 5 group sites in B Loop

Each site has: Fire ring with grate, picnic table

Site assignment: Reservations strongly recommended during season; otherwise first come, first served

Registration: Pay at ranger station at entrance to park; for reservations, call (800) 365-2267 (CAMP) or visit www.reservations.nps.gov

Facilities: Flush toilets, water spigots

Parking: One vehicle per site, additional parking available

Fee: $15 per site

Restrictions:

Pets—On leash or in cage at all times

Fires—In fire rings only

Alcoholic beverages—At sites only

Vehicles—One per site

Other—Quiet hours 10 p.m.–7 a.m., checkout by 10 a.m.

BRADBURY MOUNTAIN STATE PARK
Pownal

Despite its location, Bradbury Mountain State Park is an exceptionally quiet campground. You're not far from the bustling towns of Yarmouth and Freeport, or from Portland (Maine's cultural and social, if not political, capital), but you feel as if you're deep in the wilderness.

There's a bit of road noise from Route 9 that is sporadic, but the fragrant evergreen scent wafting through the loose forest is constant. The forest is a mix of 70- to 80-foot pines and spruce, mixed with plenty of younger deciduous trees. There's an open, airy character to the forest that lets sunlight brighten the campground floor and breezes blow through the sites.

Pick your campsite, and the ranger will come by to register you. Sites 1, 7, 14, 26–29, 35, 36, 38, and 40 are first come, first served. All other sites can be reserved. There's a campground host site on the right as you enter the campground, in case you have any questions. On a map, it looks like sites 1 and 2 were thrown out into the forest (more on that later) and replaced by the campground host site. When you see sites 1 and 2, I think you'll agree that was a great trade.

All of the sites have a good, hard sandy surface that holds on to tent stakes. Sites 6 and 7 are moderately spacious. The forest in this corner of the campground is mostly young maples and other deciduous trees. There's an old stone wall running along

CAMPGROUND RATINGS

Beauty:	★★★★
Site Privacy:	★★★★
Site Spaciousness:	★★★★
Quiet:	★★★★★
Security:	★★★★
Cleanliness/upkeep:	★★★★

The cool breezes and sunlight filtering through the trees add to the peaceful sense of Bradbury Mountain State Park.

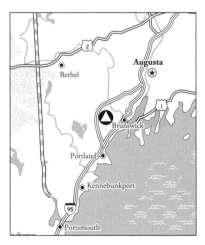

MAINE

the back of these sites, left over no doubt from when this was agricultural land at the turn of the century.

The open character of the forest here provides lots of light and nice breezes, but consequently not as much privacy as would a densely forested campground. Sites 8 and 9 are very spacious, but open to each other and to the road. Sites 15 and 16 are very open to each other. They almost look like one extremely large, sandy spot. They would make a good pair of sites for a larger group or family needing two sites side by side. There's an old stone wall running behind site 15 as well.

The individual sites differ in size, and are so marked on the campground's map, as is the practice at all Maine state parks. The sites at Bradbury Mountain, however, are similar when it comes to their level of privacy. There's only a mild sense of seclusion afforded by relatively light undergrowth.

If you're looking for site 1, you'll find it curiously cast off near site 15. I suspect this site was moved when the rangers set up the campground host site. It doesn't really matter how it got there, just that it did, because the current site 1 is remarkably secluded. It's a hike-in site reserved only for tent campers. The trail leading into the site is located next to site 15. It's about a 100-foot walk on a flat, sandy path to the site, which gives it a true wilderness sense of seclusion. This site is incredible. I love it.

The site itself is set within loosely spaced mixed forest with very little undergrowth. There's a very open, breezy character to the forest here as well, but you're so secluded from the rest of the campground that the sense of privacy is complete. There's a bench built from logs right next to the stone fire ring. From this site, you can look around 360°and all you'll see is the forest. Site 1 at Bradbury Mountain State Park offers a sense of seclusion equal to a backpacking site way off in the backcountry.

Site 2, which must have been moved as well, is another supremely secluded walk-in site. This site shares all the characteristics and accolades of site 1, although it is actually a bit further into the woods. I didn't venture all the way out to the site the last time I visited this campground, because there was already someone there and I didn't want to intrude on their forest experience. However, since I only saw their tent after starting down the path, one can imagine the site enjoys another 360° view of nothing but woods. Perfect.

You might want to avoid sites 17 and 18, as these sites are right next to the shelter/pavilion. Site 19 is huge, but also has a very open feel. As it's exposed on two sides to the campground's loop road, site 20 feels too open for me. Site 21 is a bit more secluded. It's set at the corner of the campground road with a decent amount of space between it and site 19. It looks like you could drive right through site 22. It's very open to site 20, as well as being on the inside corner of the campground road.

Sites 23 through 26 are all very spacious. These sites are set along the edge of an open grassy area. Within this small

> **To get there:** Follow Route 9 North through Pownal. Continue heading north, following signs to the campground. You'll pass the other side of Bradbury Mountain State Park before you come to the campground on the right, if you're heading north.

KEY INFORMATION

**Bradbury Mountain State Park
528 Hallowell Road
Pownal, ME 04069**

Operated by: Maine Department of Conservation, Bureau of Parks & Lands

Information: Bradbury Mountain State Park, (207) 688-4712

Open: Year-round

Individual sites: 41 sites

Each site has: Fire ring and picnic table

Site assignment: First come, first served or by reservation

Registration: At ranger station as you enter the campground

Facilities: Pit toilets, water spigots, recycling station

Parking: At sites

Fee: Maine residents, $9; nonresidents, $11

Restrictions:

Pets—On leash only

Fires—In established fire rings only

Alcoholic beverages—Not allowed

Vehicles—Parking at sites only

Other—No visitors after sunset, quiet hours 10 p.m.–7 a.m.

field, you see the fire pits and picnic tables that belie the other sites. It's a nice area, very open to the sky and framed by a dense wall of mixed deciduous and coniferous trees. It looks like a scene from Winnie the Pooh's 100 Acre Wood! The wall of woods at the back of the sites is also filled in with undergrowth, providing a dense barrier against Route 9.

If you're going to grab a site near this small field, go for site 27, which is set off from the field a bit within a dense grove of mixed young and old deciduous trees. The only drawback to this cluster of sites is that this side of the campground is closer to Route 9, so there is some occasional road noise.

Sites 29 and 30 are tiny, but are surrounded by a bit more undergrowth and feel more secluded. Site 31 is slightly larger and more open, but still nicely set off by the undergrowth encircling the site. The forest on this side of the campground is more dense and has thicker undergrowth.

The forest opens over sites 32 through 36. Site 37 is huge. It's very open to the sky and framed by loose birch and maple trees. There's also a big pile of sand to the right of the site. They were doing a bit of site restoration when I was there.

Set off from the other sites and surrounded by a bit more undergrowth, site 38 is close to the bathrooms. Site 39 is quite spacious and covered by a canopy of maples for a nice shady feel, while 40 is tiny but still feels nicely secluded, as it is set right within a dense pine grove.

Within a delightful maple and birch grove, site 41 is moderately spacious and looks like another scene from the 100 Acre Wood. This site is right next to, and I mean right next to, sites 20 and 22. This troika of sites is in a charming loose grove of deciduous trees, but the sites are very open to each other.

Even though many of the sites here seem exposed to one another, you still won't feel as if you're piled on top of your neighbors. Although you'll certainly be able to see your fellow campers, the sites are generally spacious and spaced far apart enough to offer a modicum of elbow room.

You will have to drive down the road a bit to get to the rest of Bradbury Mountain State Park and the hiking trails, but it's not too far and it's definitely worth the trip.

CAMDEN HILLS STATE PARK
Camden

The campground at Camden Hills State Park makes it into this book by virtue of its location alone. You know what they say about real estate. The campground is nestled at the foot of Mount Battie and on the shores of Penobscot Bay. The whole area is as fine a place as you could possibly hope to find for hiking, climbing, biking (both on and off the road), and sea kayaking.

Fortunately, the campground is also well worth a stay on its own merits. Camden Hills State Park is deceptively large. As you enter the park from Route 1, all you can see is the ranger station, the Mount Battie Auto Road, and a large open field off to the right. You may even spot a (gasp) RV! Don't back up the car—this place definitely deserves closer examination. Venture a bit further into the park, and you'll find the wilderness atmosphere you seek.

There are two main loops and a mini-loop within the campground. The first is just off to the right as you enter the park. This loop is home to most of the sites at Camden Hills. Although the sites here are closer together, there are still quite a few that provide a sense of solitude. Within this primary loop, sites 3–10, 14, 20–24, 35, 37, 39, and 49 are some of my favorites. These seem best suited for pitching a tent. The sites themselves are slightly smaller, and make nice, cozy spots to camp. These tent-friendly sites are grouped together.

CAMPGROUND RATINGS

Beauty:	★★★★
Site Privacy:	★★★★
Site Spaciousness:	★★★★
Quiet:	★★★
Security:	★★★★
Cleanliness/upkeep:	★★★★

Whether your taste in outdoor adventures tends toward hiking, biking, paddling, or climbing, you've come to the right place. The campground is juxtaposed to mountains, lakes, and the ocean.

MAINE

Most of the larger sites, where the land yachts make safe harbor, are also off on their own.

The mini-loop that has sites 103–105 also offers good tent sites. The next loop, just past the mini-loop, has fewer sites than the first loop, with lots of space in between. When you first arrive at Camden Hills, drive this loop and check out sites 70, 74, 76–78, 84–86, and 91–93. The outer loop road that brings you to sites 71–81 also leads to the trailhead for the Mount Megun-

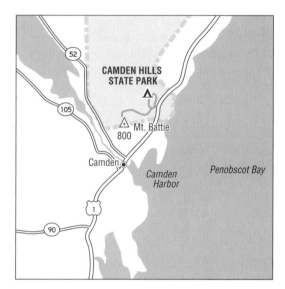

ticook trail, a moderate hike about one mile and one hour in length.

The sites at Camden Hills are cut out of fairly dense mixed deciduous and coniferous forest. In spots where the pine needles outnumber the leaves, visitors are treated to an amazing olfactory gift. When the conditions are just right, you can smell the musty balsam perfume of the forest and the briny tang of the ocean in the same breath. And there's more Camden Hills State Park right across the street (that street being Route 1, so be careful).

The town of Camden's slogan is "Where the Mountains Meet the Sea." Nowhere is that theme more concretely embodied than at the state park. To the west of Route 1 are the campground and Mount Battie. East of Route 1, you'll find a small network of hiking trails and a picnic area settled within the woods right on the shores of Penobscot Bay. Few things are more soothing than watching the waves endlessly crashing over the rocks.

When (or should I say "if") you tire of hanging around the campground or the ocean side of the park, there are numerous hiking trails, literally right at your feet. Take your pick. There are trails for all abilities and interests, and virtually all lead to sweeping views of Penobscot Bay or nearby Lake Megunticook. Start off with a quick jaunt up Mount Battie. From the campground, the only way up is the paved auto road, but if you're heading into town anyway, you can go up the auto road then down the Mount Battie Trail, which drops you off at a small trailhead and parking area. This trail is only half a mile long, but a steep section requires some hand over hand scrambling. Best to take another route if it has recently rained.

The Ski Shelter Trail is a hike everyone in your group can enjoy. An old fire road that leaves from the campground, it passes by a massive stone hearth, all that remains of an old ski shelter. This is a great spot to stop for a snack, a gulp of water, and perhaps a photo or two. You can follow the Ski Shelter Trail all the way to the Youngtown Road, a distance of about three miles. You could also head off on one of several bisecting trails.

For one such foray, try the Bald Rock Trail. After you've passed the stone hearth, keep going for another 30 minutes or so until you see the trail heading off to the right. The Ski Shelter Trail will be going downhill at this point. The Bald Rock trail is short and a little steep, but leads to a large, flat rock outcropping with a commanding view of Penobscot Bay and the islands.

There's enough to do in and around Camden to fill an entire guidebook. Ask the cordial park rangers for a recommendation or just take off on your own and explore. Just set aside plenty of time, because when it's time to leave, you'll swear you haven't been there long enough.

To get there: Follow Route 1 North through Camden. Proceed another couple of miles to the state park on the left. There is a park entrance on the right (the ocean side), but the campground is on the left.

KEY INFORMATION

Camden Hills State Park
Route 1
Camden, ME 04843

Operated by: Maine Department of Conservation, Bureau of Parks & Lands

Information: Camden Hills State Park, (207) 236-3109 (May 1–October 15) or (207)236-0849 (October 16–April 30)

Open: Camden Hills State Park is open year-round; campground is open May 15–October 15

Individual sites: 112 sites

Each site has: Fire ring with grate, picnic table

Site assignment: By reservation or first come, first served (all but 23 sites can be reserved)

Registration: At ranger check-in station as you enter park

Facilities: coin-operated showers, flush toilets, picnic area

Parking: Plenty of parking at separate lots and at most sites

Fee: Maine residents, $13; non-residents, $17

Restrictions:

Pets—Dogs on leash, no pets on beaches

Fires—In fire rings only

Alcoholic beverages—At sites only

Vehicles—One per site

Other—Check out by 11 a.m.

LAMOINE STATE PARK

Ellsworth

What do you do when Acadia National Park is packed? Head a bit further north to Lamoine State Park, which is just far enough away to escape the glance of Acadia area campers and travelers during the summer. There's a very open sense to most of the sites at Lamoine State Park, but they overlook the waters of Frenchman Bay toward Bar Harbor.

The view of the ocean and the cool ocean breezes, even on the muggiest summer afternoons, give Lamoine State Park an easy combination of pastoral serenity and oceanside appeal. The whole gestalt here is that of being on a wind-swept, coastal bluff—which you are! It's a bit different than the wooded campgrounds to which I usually gravitate, but nevertheless wild and beautiful.

The campground loop road encircles the campground and is intersected by several short roads parallel to the seashore. The sites on the outer edge of the loop as you enter the campground, including sites 21–29, are very spacious, very open sites set on a grassy surface and separated by short stands of trees and shrubs. There's a sunny, breezy, open sense to these sites, but not much privacy. On the other side of the campground road, even-numbered sites 20 and up are a bit more secluded, but still have an open feel. The only trouble here would be if an RV stopped in nearby—you would have it right in view. Otherwise, the

CAMPGROUND RATINGS

Beauty:	★★★★
Site Privacy:	★★★
Site Spaciousness:	★★★
Quiet:	★★★★
Security:	★★★★
Cleanliness/upkeep:	★★★★

During the thick of summer, when Acadia is mobbed, head a bit further north to Lamoine State Park to reclaim the solitude for which Maine is renowned.

MAINE

sites themselves are exposed but comfortable and nice.

A big beech tree grows right up through the center of site 19. This proud old guardian of the site gives it a comfortable feeling and a nice canopy of shade. The site is a beautiful, medium-sized site encircled by a dense wall of undergrowth. Sites 16–18 are very open, but are also secluded from each other by short stands of deciduous trees and solid undergrowth. The backs of these sites open to a huge field and the group camping area. This is a great field for stargazing.

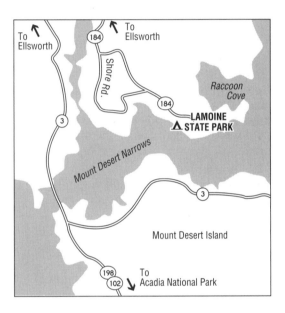

Moving down this side of the campground, there's more of a sense of solitude to sites 13, 14, and 30. These sites are set along the outer edge of the campground loop road. Site 14 is a bit close to the bathroom building, but is encircled by dense, deciduous forest.

Set within a loose grove of spruce and backed into the mixed forest, site 12 is a very open site, but it has a delightful wooded grove feel. It's a bit open to the road and situated right at a campground road intersection, but it's quite spacious and has a comfortable, charming character. Site 30 is small, but also tucked down off the road and nicely isolated by virtue of its location.

Heading back toward the campground entrance on one of the intersecting roads brings you to the lower numbered sites, including sites 11 and 10, which have an exposed feel, but they are secluded on the sides. Site 10 abuts a small field and is near the rest rooms, so it feels a bit too open for me. Sites 7–9 are moderately spacious and isolated from each other. However, site 6 is wide open and right at the corner intersection of the campground road. It's right across from site 5, which also lacks privacy.

The dense, low forest isolates sites 3 and 4 on the sides, but these sites are open to each other across the road. Site 1 is in an open field and definitely not secluded enough for me, but if you want to catch the strongest breezes, this is the spot. Site 2 is right across the road from site 1 and is somewhat isolated by a patch of dense woods and undergrowth, but it is open in the front to the road and the pasture of site 1.

There are a number of wide open field sites in the center of the campground at Lamoine State Park, including sites 35–39 and 60. These sites don't provide much of a sense of privacy. Although site 36 is somewhat isolated on the sides, the others all have a very open character. They're also fairly close to, and within view of, the shower building.

It may be small, but site 33 is nicely secluded, despite being situated on the corner of the campground road. The site is carved out of a mixed deciduous forest of maples, birch and dense undergrowth. Site 32 is a great site. It's very secluded and set off from the other sites as well as surrounded by dense, low forest. There's a scraggly spruce hanging over the site as well, providing shade and companionship to the campsite.

Even though it's on a corner of the campground road, site 31 is quite spacious and also nicely set off. It's surrounded by dense woods and separated from the road by a narrow stand of trees.

To get there: Follow Route 1 North through Ellsworth. At the junction of Route 1 and Route 184, follow Route 184 south to the park.

KEY INFORMATION

Lamoine State Park
RR 2, Box 194
Ellsworth, ME 04605

Operated by: Maine Department of Conservation, Bureau of Parks & Lands

Information: Lamoine State Park, (207) 667-4778

Open: May 15–October 15

Individual sites: 61

Each site has: Fire ring, picnic table

Site assignment: First come, first served or by reservation

Registration: At ranger station as you enter the campground

Facilities: Hot showers, flush toilets, water spigots

Parking: At sites

Fee: Maine residents, $13; non-residents, $17

Restrictions:

Pets—On leash only

Fires—In established fire rings only

Alcoholic beverages—At sites only

Vehicles—Parking at sites only

Site 40 is tiny, but cozy, and very secluded. This site is set off the road, carved out of very dense forest of short deciduous trees and dense undergrowth. There's an exceptionally secluded feel to this site.

Site 41 is wide open to the road, but secluded from its neighbors. You're getting closer to the water here, so there are tantalizing views of the bay through the trees. Site 42 is way too exposed and right behind the rest room building. Site 43 opens to site 42 and the rest rooms, but it's secluded on the sides and offers views of the bay to balance the view of the rest room. Sites 46 and 45 are rather open, while sites 47, 59, 38 and 60 are another set of wide open field sites.

You're getting closer to the water at sites 55–58. These are open to the road and each other, but they're very sunny and breezy. You'll feel what is practically a constant breeze easing in (and sometimes rushing in) off Frenchman Bay.

The sites that open to the ocean are where you really want to be at Lamoine State Park. Sites 48–54 are set along the campground road facing the open view of the ocean. These are Rockefeller-worthy views of Frenchman Bay and its islands. The view from sites 51–54 is through loose crabapple and maple trees growing in the picnic area. From 50, 49, and 48, you view the bay through a majestic stand of spruce.

All these sites are spacious and open to the road, but they're also open to the view and they're fairly well secluded from each other. Sites 49 and 50 probably feel the most isolated and furthest from their neighbors. Each site is surrounded on three sides by dense undergrowth and shrubs. They open to the bay view through a grove of loosely spaced spruce and pines, trees of hardy stock that stand up to the steady salty breezes. There's a short path down to the water right across from site 49. You can also get to the 1-mile Loop Trail.

Site 48 is oddly placed. It's on the outside corner of where the bayside campground road turns and heads back up into the woods. It's very open to the road, but shares the dramatic bay views filtered through the grove of spruce.

The scent here is that potent Maine blend of the evergreen forest and the salty tang of the ocean, topped off with a bit of wood smoke as the day draws to an end. Take a moment after you've set up your campsite to sit back, draw in a deep breath, and enjoy the sights, sounds, and scents of this oceanside campground.

LILY BAY STATE PARK

Greenville

In northern Maine, nestled on the eastern shores of Moosehead Lake, is Lily Bay State Park. This is true Maine north country. There is a sense of remote wilderness about the entire area that is refreshing and invigorating.

There are two separate camping areas at Lily Bay State Park and a large number of sites. Still, there really isn't a bad site. This campground is also home to some of the most dramatically scenic campsites in New England. Many of the walk-in lakeside tent sites are practically magical. On the first business day in January, when the reservation office opens for the first day of the season, the lakeside sites start filling up. So make plans early if you want to secure one of these world-class campsites.

There are several secluded sites in the Dunn Point Area. Drive up a short road off to the right, and you'll find site 245 tucked way off on its own. Just past the entrance to the site at the end of its "driveway," there's a trailhead for the 1.6-mile hiking trail that leads to Rowell Cove.

The sense of solitude at sites 200 and 201 is priceless. These are moderately spacious and very well isolated walk-in tent sites. Each requires a short (20 to 30 feet) hike to the site. They are set up on a bluff overlooking the lake. The views from these breezy sites are positively epic.

Further along on this same bluff, site 202 is less exposed to the views and the breeze,

CAMPGROUND RATINGS

Beauty:	★★★★★
Site Privacy:	★★★★★
Site Spaciousness:	★★★★
Quiet:	★★★★★
Security:	★★★★★
Cleanliness/upkeep:	★★★★★

Lily Bay State Park is just one facet of the north Maine woods jewel that is Moosehead Lake. Do what you can to score a waterfront site.

MAINE

but still offers sliver views of the lake vista and the hills beyond through the woods. Site 203 is the last site in this cluster on the bluff. It's very spacious, and the breezes and the views are filtered through a wall of conifers. The forest in this part of the campground is a moderately dense mixture of white pines, maples, and birch.

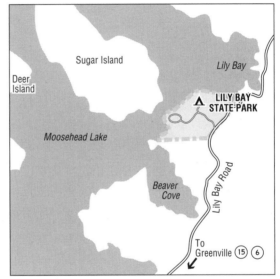

There's a trail leading to the lake's beach right before you get to sites 205 and 206. Site 205 is massive. You could land a helicopter here, but you might end up doing a bit of unwelcome pruning to the dense grove of conifers that encircles the site. Across the campground road, site 206 is much smaller but very well secluded in dense forest. Sites 207–209 are moderately roomy and private.

At site 210, the forest opens up to the lake again. This site is very well isolated on one side by a two-level wall of young and old white pines, along with some other coniferous trees. The forest opens dramatically at the opposite side of the site, allowing for sweeping views of the lake through the loosely-spaced trees that pepper the site down to the water's edge.

Set within a loose grove of conifers, sites 211 and 213 are relatively spacious and overlook the lake. Sites 213–215 require a short walk to the sites, and they are all right on the lake. These lakeside sites are jewels, with a perfect mix of forest and lakeshore. The walk to these sites is short. Each is no more than 40 feet from parking. It's well worth the short haul. Not that you'll be able to take your eyes off the lake for very long, but these sites are also fairly isolated from each other. It's very quiet throughout the campground. All you'll hear is the soft splash of the lake and the cool rush of the wind through the trees.

You might want to avoid sites 216 and 220, as they are a bit close to the bathroom. Site 219 is spacious and secluded by a wall of conifers at the back, but otherwise open to the road. Site 218 is spacious and mildly secluded and has a view of the lake.

The next group of walk in tent sites includes sites 221–224. This group of sites is completely secluded from the rest of the campground and moderately secluded from each other. These sites share the same clear view of the lake as the 213–215 group.

So by now you must think you have to be right on the waters of Moosehead Lake to have one of Lily Bay's primo sites, eh? Well think again. Wait until you see site 231. This site is incredibly spacious, and set up on a small knoll in the middle of the forest. It's absolutely secluded from neighbors on all sides and from the campground road. Its added elevation will help you catch some of the onshore breezes. Just outside the site, there's a trail leading down to the beach.

The forest encircling the site is characteristic of the area's fantastically diverse population of mature spruce, birch, and maple. There's also a small nursery of baby white pine trees to the left of the site as you walk in. Encircled by forest, this spot feels like it's deeper in the Maine wilderness than you might expect.

A shared entryway brings you to sites 235 and 236. These would make a good pair of sites for a larger group or family needing two sites—that is if you can't score two magical lakeside sites! Another option for big families is site 240. This

KEY INFORMATION

Lily Bay State Park
HC 76, Box 425
Greenville, ME 04441

Operated by: Maine Department of Conservation, Bureau of Parks & Lands

Information: Lily Bay State Park, (207) 695-2700 (summer) or (207) 941-4014 (winter)

Open: May 1–September 15

Individual sites: 91

Each site has: Stone hearth or fire ring, picnic table

Site assignment: First come, first served or by reservation

Registration: At ranger station as you enter the campground

Facilities: Pit toilets, water spigots, boat launch

Parking: At sites

Fee: Maine residents, $12; nonresidents, $16

Restrictions:

Pets—On leash only

Fires—In established fire rings only

Alcoholic beverages—At sites only

Vehicles—Parking at sites only

To get there: Follow Route 6 north to Greenville. From Greenville, take the Lily Bay Road off to the right and follow this to the park.

site has a U-shaped driveway you could pull right through. Those two openings though, do leave it fairly exposed to the road.

The Rowell Cove Area also has some dramatic lakeside walk-in tent sites. Sites 33–38 are hike-in tent sites perched along a craggy peninsula that recalls the revered A Peninsula at the eponymous campground on Mount Desert Island. Site 33 is the largest of the group.

There are ample views of the lake through loose trees from sites 20 and 21. They are also nicely secluded by dense spruce just open enough to view slivers of the lake. Site 23 is sizeable, but a bit open for my tastes. Sites 25 and 28 each have a nice sense of solitude, plus a slice of the lake view through the forest.

Several massive conifers frame one side of site 26. The inside loop sites in this part of the campground are all fairly well secluded from each other. However, sites 29 and 30 are both open to the campground loop road. They're also located near the parking for sites 39–41.

The cluster of sites that includes 39–46 is another majestic spot. These sites are all quite spacious, set right on the lake within a small cove and beneath a loosely spaced grove of spruce trees. The site floor is a soft bed of pine needles over a firm, sandy surface. The sites are very open to the lake, so the breezes and views are exceptional. Walks to the sites vary from 50 to 70 feet.

Site 31 opens right to the parking area, so it feels too open for me. Site 32 is huge and very secluded. It's surrounded by a thick wall of forest and further isolated because it's a bit further down the campground road.

The lower-numbered sites here aren't quit as impressive, but they aren't bad. Even though it's set right where the campground loop road rejoins itself, site 8 is spacious and well isolated. Site 7 is similar, with slivers of lake views. Site 5 feels very exposed, being open to the road, but it has a view of the lake.

It may be tiny and exposed to the road, but site 12 is set way off from any neighboring sites. Site 13 has a similar character. It's carved out of fairly dense forest. Site 14 is spacious, secluded, punctuated by three massive spruce trees, and encircled by dense mixed forest.

There are sparkles and slivers of lake view through the forest here near the sites in the upper teens. Site 15 is very open to the road and close to the rest rooms. Site 16 is colossal, and tucked well off the campground loop road for a deep sense of solitude. Site 17 is large and set off from its neighbors, but it's a bit open to the road. It's also very open to the sky, and has a short footpath leading to the lake, which is visible from the site.

Obviously, Moosehead Lake is the centerpiece of Lily Bay State Park, if not the entire town of Greenville, Maine! Do what you can to get a site on the water or at the very least with a view of the lake. You will be richly rewarded.

I thought it was poetically appropriate that, on my last night researching this guidebook, I camped at site 36, a lakeside site on its own pristine peninsula, with a sweeping view of the lake and the distant hillsides. A cool, steady breeze swept through the site all night, reminding me why I was doing all this work in the first place. The evening was spectacular, but then, of course, it rained at two in the morning. I saw this as further poetic justice, reminding me that a little funky weather seems to accompany any camping excursion.

MOUNT BLUE STATE PARK

Weld

Mount Blue State Park is actually a pair of parks. There are two sections to the park, one up on Mount Blue itself and the other down alongside Webb Lake. The trails on and around Mount Blue, Tumbledown, Little Jackson, Blueberry, and Bald Mountains are suitable for hikers of all abilities. There's also a multi-use trail in the Center Hill section of the park for mountain bikers, hikers, equestrians, and ATVs.

The park's campground is located in the Webb Lake section. All of the 136 sites in the campground are within a fairly short walk of the lake. The sites are set within a dense, diverse forest with thick undergrowth. The woods are a mix of deciduous and coniferous trees, with lots of spruce, birch, and maple. There is also a mix of young and old trees.

While the forest is dramatically varied, the sites here have a relatively standard shape and layout, though they differ in size. Surprisingly, it's not the quietest place in the world. As I set up camp at Mount Blue, the density of the forest lent me a pleasant sense of seclusion, but I found that sound traveled through the forest quite freely. After dinner, when night settles in, the campground quiets right down, but during the daytime, you'll hear noise from surrounding campsites.

As you enter the camping area, sites 1–10 are spread out along the main campground road. The remaining sites are grouped in two loops. The first ten sites

CAMPGROUND RATINGS

Beauty:	★★★★
Site Privacy:	★★★★★
Site Spaciousness:	★★★★
Quiet:	★★★
Security:	★★★★
Cleanliness/upkeep:	★★★★★

There's a dense, diverse forest covering the campground at Mount Blue State Park, and the lush quality recalls a rainforest.

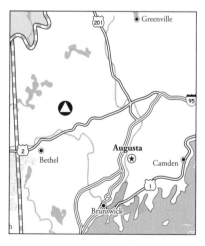

MAINE

are quite spacious, but very open to the road A fair amount of traffic drives by, as everyone going in and out of the campground has to pass these sites. Within this cluster of sites, site 1 is actually the most secluded, thanks to the forest at the site's edge. It's still quite close to the road, however. Sites 4 and 5 have a pretty solid barrier of trees buffering them from the road, but sites 7 and 8 are quite exposed.

The forest enshrouding the loop with sites 11–78 is populated primarily by moderately tall spruce and deciduous trees. The trees aren't huge, but they are numerous and crowded with undergrowth. There is almost a primeval feel to the forest that translates into a wonderful sense of seclusion at most of these sites. The sites are very clean and well kept. Some have a bit more forest buffering them from their neighbors, especially sites 18, 7, and 5. Site 19 and the sites in the lower 20s are more tightly packed than the rest of this loop, but encircled by thick woods.

There's a trail leading down to the lake between sites 26 and 28. Set a good distance from site 30 at a bend in the road, site 31 is tucked into a dense stand of trees, so it offers an additional measure of privacy.

Site 34 is small, but it feels quite isolated within a bucolic grove where spruce tower above a dense blanket of ferns. Surrounded by dense deciduous forest with plenty of room between it and the nearest site, site 35 maintains a marvelously secluded feel.

Sites 38, 40, and 41 are set within a mature forest of tall maples and birch. The loose arrangement of trees in this part of the campground lets more sunlight filter to the floor of the site. Site 44 is colossal. You could land a space shuttle here, if that's how you happened to arrive at the campground.

Though they vary in size, sites 47–78 share a similar layout. They are also uniformly spaced from each other. Site 54, in a loose grove of tall spruce, is large and open to the sky. Another trail heads off to the beach between sites 57 and 58.

Set along the outside of the loop, sites 58–62 are spacious and open. Sites 69 and 71 are particularly secluded, distant from their neighbors and carved out of a dense, deciduous forest with thick undergrowth. Size 69 is only moderately sized, but 71 is huge.

Within the loop containing sites 79–136, the forest is crowded with trees and underbrush. The sites are uniformly distributed along the inside and outside of the loop. The space between most sites is roughly equal to an average site, affording quite a sense of privacy. Sites 128 and up seem to have slightly more forest in between them. There are no hookups in the park, but even if an RV should happen to land near you, the thick forest in this loop will obscure your view.

A trail to the lake leaves this section between sites 109 and 110. There are trails to the centrally located rest rooms spread throughout both site loops. You'll never have to walk very far to find one.

Due to the dense forestation at Mount Blue Campground, not many sites are open to the sky. There are a few exceptions to this, sites 44, 54, 93, and 106 among them. If you like to gaze at the night sky, check out one of these sites.

Otherwise, once dusk settles, you'll feel enshrouded by the deep woods.

> **To get there:** From the town of Weld, follow Route 142 to Weld Corner. Follow the signs for the Webb Lake section of Mount Blue State Park.

KEY INFORMATION

Mount Blue State Park
RR 1, Box 610
Weld, ME 04285

Operated by: Maine Department of Conservation, Bureau of Parks & Lands

Information: Mount Blue State Park, (207) 585-2347 (summer) or (207) 585-2261 (winter)

Open: June 15 –Labor Day

Individual sites: 136

Each site has: Stone hearth, picnic table

Site assignment: First come, first served or by reservation

Registration: At ranger station as you enter the campground

Facilities: Hot showers, flush toilets, pit toilets, water spigots

Parking: At sites

Fee: $17

Restrictions:

Pets—On leash only

Fires—In established fire rings only

Alcoholic beverages—At sites only

Vehicles—Parking at sites only

Other—Quiet hours 10 p.m.– 7 a.m., checkout by 11 a.m.; max. stay is 14 days, 6 people per site max.

MOUNT DESERT CAMPGROUND

Mount Desert

Nestled near the apex of Somes Sound on Mount Desert Island, Mount Desert Campground provides a tent camping experience as close to perfect as any campground outlined in this book. The entire campground is artfully carved out of the rolling woods that reach all the way down to the shoreline. The pristine mixed forest of maple, balsam, cedar, pine, and spruce exudes an aromatic essence to accentuate the spectacular scenery. The campground is also conveniently situated near the main entrance to Acadia National Park and right near the Eagle Lake and Witch Hole Pond Loops, both good spots to start your hiking or biking foray on the massive network of carriage roads that wind throughout the park.

The Mount Desert Campground doesn't have any areas set aside specifically for tent camping, but there really isn't a bad site in the place. The A, B, and C area sites are the best, especially the contiguous sites on the A peninsula, A13–A15 (which actually accounts for four sites, since site A14+ was added). To get to these sites, you have to walk about 50 feet along the peninsula. Once you're there, you feel like you have the place to yourself. If those sites are taken, as is often the case, another piece of prime camping real estate is site A5, located on a small bluff overlooking the water.

I've been to Mount Desert Campground more than any other in New England, and

CAMPGROUND RATINGS

Beauty:	★★★★★
Site privacy:	★★★★
Site spaciousness:	★★★★
Quiet:	★★★★★
Security:	★★★★★
Cleanliness/upkeep:	★★★★★

Perched on the rugged shores at the apex of Somes Sound, the Mount Desert Campground is nestled in an absolutely pristine setting.

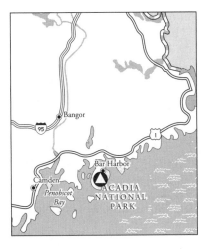

MAINE

only twice have the camping Gods smiled upon me with an open A area site. One time was the last weekend of the season, and my friends and I were the only people out there. It was fabulous. The only sounds we heard all night were the cheerful snap of the fire and the soft, steady breeze rustling through the trees.

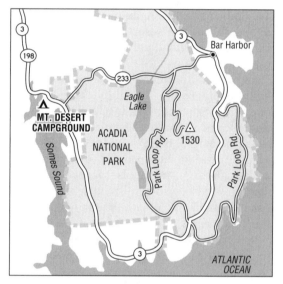

You're in Maine. You're on an island. Do what you can to get a water site. It's well worth it. If you set up somewhere for a night or two, then a water site opens up, it will be worth the effort to move. Just make sure the site is truly vacant, not reserved, and let the owners know you've relocated. By the way, if you do move your site, I do not recommend trying to ride a mountain bike while carrying a fully erected tent. I have no personal experience with this sort of lunacy, of course, but I've been told it can be hazardous.

The waterside sites at Mount Desert follow the undulating terrain as it dives into the headwaters of Somes Sound. The terrain is beautiful, it is dramatic, it is anything but flat. If you saw it from a distance, you'd wonder how you could ever pitch a tent here.

When you check in at the main entrance, they'll ask you if you need some nails. Excuse me, did I somehow volunteer for some campground maintenance? Say yes; you'll need them. Every site at the water's edge or on any uneven terrain has a solid wooden deck on which you can set up your tent, using nails in lieu of stakes If the campground owners hadn't built these tent platforms, they would be lucky to have one or two sites flat enough to pitch a tent.

Each area has its own facilities building with sparkling clean, well-kept rest rooms, and coin-operated showers. Here's another hint: even in the summer, the mornings will be cool. Bring more quarters than you think you'll need. Having the water go stone cold over a head full of shampoo may cause itchiness, headaches, and loud cursing.

There's a charming little camp store on the road leading into the campground that sells bundles of firewood, camping-appropriate groceries like cans of soup and Jiffy Pop popcorn, all sorts of items you may have forgotten like batteries and toothpaste, and guidebooks to the hiking trails and carriage roads that take you to some of the island's magical spots. It's also handy to pick up a quick cup of coffee and a muffin at the store before you get your own breakfast fire going. You can get some fresh-baked goodies for dessert later that night or make a special trip down with the kids (of any age) for an afternoon ice cream.

Just outside the campground, there is so much to do on Mount Desert Island and in Acadia National Park, you could write an entire book about it. In fact, people have! You can hike, bike, paddle, or just find a spot to relax and enjoy the view, which alone can restore your soul. This is classic Maine wilderness, with gentle, rolling forested mountains sloping right down to

To get there: From Ellsworth, follow Route 3 onto Mount Desert Island. Follow Route 3 to Route 102/198 South. Stay on Route 198 when it turns left. The campground will be on the right, about a mile after Route 198 splits from Route 102.

KEY INFORMATION

Mount Desert Campground
Route 198
Mount Desert, ME 04660

Operated by: Owen and Barbara Craighead

Information: (207) 244-3710

Open: May 15–September 25

Individual sites: 150

Each site has: Fire pit with grate, most have tent platforms

Site assignment: Reservations accepted for stays of one week or longer, otherwise first come, first served

Registration: At camp headquarters at main entrance

Facilities: Rest rooms, hot showers, pay phone, camp store

Parking: At or near individual sites

Fee: $20 and up, depending on site

Restrictions:

Pets—Not allowed

Fires—Within established fire pits only, do not leave unattended

Alcoholic beverages—At sites only

Vehicles—One per site

the rocky, craggy coast. The Atlantic obliges and completes the view with an endless supply of crashing surf.

Rent a canoe or kayak and launch out into Somes Sound, the only fjord on the East Coast. Between the rolling mountains, the rocky shoreline, and the water that glistens like a carpet of diamonds, the paddling is perfect. Just off the dock and boat launch at the campground, you'll paddle past a small island as you enter the sound. This is actually a part of Acadia National Park, and atop the tallest pine, in the center of the island, is a bald eagle's nest.

On one brilliant August afternoon, while paddling out into Somes Sound, I was visited by several pods of brown Atlantic dolphins swimming up the sound. I first heard the quick puff of their breath as they surfaced. It didn't take long to determine the source of the noise once I saw the slender dark shapes rising and disappearing into the water in front of me. One of the dolphins actually dove under my kayak and surfaced behind me. I almost tipped over trying to snap a picture of that bold little guy.

Both inside and outside the Mount Desert Campground, you can do as much or as little as you like, but you couldn't ask for a more peaceful setting in which to pitch your tent. One cool foggy evening, while kicking back by the campfire, I heard someone playing the flute. The song was Paul Simon's "Lincoln Duncan." If you know that tune, you know it has a hauntingly beautiful flute melody. Hearing that echoing throughout the trees, smelling the wood fire and watching its glowing embers through increasingly sleepy eyes is a memory I will always cherish.

ORR'S ISLAND CAMPGROUND

Orr's Island

Much of the Orr's Island campground, like many privately owned and operated campgrounds, caters to the RV crowd. As you drive into the campground and see the herds of RVs gathered around their hookups, you may be tempted to silently curse my name and wonder why I've included this campground in a book about excellent tent camping spots. Well drive on, and explore the tent-only areas.

Orr's Island is quite far out into Casco Bay, so the campground is cool and breezy. From Brunswick, you drive out over Great Island before you get to Orr's Island. Just the drive out there will melt away your stress.

The letter-designated sites A through G, perched along the waterfront side of Cove Road, and sites 31–41, situated on the inland side of Cove Road, are the prime sites for tent camping. This row of sites overlooks Reed Cove. The lettered sites in particular are only moderately spacious, but they are extremely secluded from the other sites, as they are carved out of dense undergrowth. Most of the cove-side sites also have short paths leading down to the rocky beach on Reed Cove. These sites overlook the water and are perfectly situated to catch the cool breezes blowing in off the ocean. If you can sit at one of these sites looking across the ocean and still remain stressed out, seek professional help.

CAMPGROUND RATINGS

Beauty:	★★★★★
Site Privacy:	★★★★★
Site Spaciousness:	★★★★
Quiet:	★★★★
Security:	★★★★★
Cleanliness/upkeep:	★★★★★

There may be a flotilla of RVs nearby, but the secluded te sites and the views of Harps Bay make this campground ell worth a look.

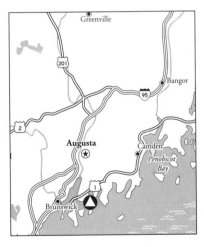

MAINE

The numbered sites are also fairly well isolated from the rest of the campground and from each other. You can just barely see the tops of the more monstrous RVs, but you'll be spending more time looking out over the bay anyway.

Site A is moderately spacious, and the site itself is very open, though it is remarkably secluded by dense undergrowth on all sides. The side of the site facing the cove is open, so you'll have a clear view of Reed Cove. Site B looks out toward the bay but is more shaded, encircled by lots of dense undergrowth and framed by several birch trees.

There's also a very secluded feel to site C, although it's smaller and narrower. Nestled within the dense undergrowth that characterizes this area, the site is encircled by a grove of birch and maple trees. Site D is fairly roomy and has a wide-open view of the water. It's set against a dense wall of deciduous trees and dense undergrowth, so it offers a solid sense of privacy.

Though it is well isolated, there's a spacious and sunny feel at site E, which boasts an open view of the water and a definitive feeling of seclusion. However, it's also nicely shaded on one side by a wall of high trees. The moderately-spacious site F is very shaded and secluded, and it has a clear view of the water.

Site G is the real prize of this campground. This site is incredibly well-isolated, and surrounded on all sides by dense undergrowth. The trees and hedges that fill in the forest are of the short, hardy stock that grows along the craggy coast of Maine. The only opening in the band of undergrowth encircling site G faces the ocean, so you're rewarded with a perfect bay view. This site is open to the sky above as well, so it receives sunlight and moonlight. This is the most spacious of the letter sites on this side of Cove Road.

The Cove Road letter sites are perfectly situated for tents and kayaks—what a stellar combination. After a night spent in one of these sites, you'll have that pleasant ache in your lungs from the fresh salt air. As I said before, it's physically and psychologically impossible to gaze out on the ocean from these sites and remain distracted or stressed out.

The number-designated sites are set along the other side of Cove Road, the side opposite the water. Cove Road is very quiet and the letter sites across the road are set off by a dense wall of undergrowth, so the general sense of openness at the numbered sites does not translate into a lack of privacy. A solid wall of trees blocks the view from Cove Road of the RV row behind the sites. There is also a nice grassy surface at these sites, a good soft base upon which to pitch your tent.

Site 37 is very open. You'll get lots of breezes blowing through the site and it's a good site for sunbathing, but you might crave a little shade on those hot summer afternoons. It may be a bit small, but site 39 is nicely secluded. The site is carved out of the dense deciduous forest and undergrowth. A craggy, sweeping beech tree guards the entrance to the site and gives it a deep wilderness character. Site 41 and the unnumbered site just past it

To get there: From Brunswick, follow Route 24 South onto Orrs Island. Turn right at the sign for the campground.

KEY INFORMATION

Orr's Island Campground
45 Bond Point Road
Orr's Island, ME 04066

Operated by: The Bond Family

Information: Orr's Island Campground, (207) 833-5595

Open: Memorial Day– September 15

Individual sites: 73 sites total, 17 tent-only sites

Each site has: Fire ring and picnic table

Site assignment: First come, first served or by reservation

Registration: At office; call campground for reservations

Facilities: Hot showers, dumping station

Parking: At sites or near camp store

Fee: $21 for tent sites ($25–$32 for hook-up sites)

Restrictions:

Pets—Dogs on leash only

Fires—Only in established fire pits

Alcoholic beverages—At sites only

Vehicles—One per campsite

Other—Two-day min. for reservations (three-day min. for holiday weekends).

on the left are small sites, but very well secluded as they are carved out of the dense undergrowth.

The sites off Cove Road are most conducive to tent camping, but other sites are suitable. Sadly, the open sites up on North Bluff all have hookups for RVs. The view of Harpswell sound might make you forget about the land yachts, though. It's worth checking out this part of the campground, even if you're just walking the trail that circumnavigates the campground. The view, the sun, and the breezes up on North Bluff are invigorating.

Plus, from North and South Bluff, you'll have access to the shore for beach-combing, hanging out on the rocks, or swimming—if you're cast of sturdy Scandinavian stock. Site 51 up on the bluff is quite isolated from the sites on either side, so this would be a good one to sneak into. The South Bluff sites are much more open. Skip these sites or else you'll feel like you're stuck in a land yacht regatta.

There's another secluded cluster of tent-only sites over on the other side of the campground as well. Sites 64, 66, and 68 are set aside from the RV crowd for our tent-bound brethren. These sites are tucked off to the right of Port Road (all the short roads leading through the campground have nautical names).

There is an intense sense of seclusion to site 64. There's no bay view, but it's extremely private and encircled by the dense forest. It's smaller than site 68, but still reasonably spacious. Site 66 is also a bit smaller. It doesn't extend quite as far down from the road as site 68. It is very secluded on the sides though, as it's carved out of the short, dense forest. It's also very open to the sky, and there's a tantalizing slice of sound view through the trees. Site 68 is very spa-cious. It's long, narrow, and covered with a nice grassy surface. There's a beau-tiful, but distant, view of Harpswell Sound through the trees at the end of the site.

Once you've set up your campsite, take a moment to walk around and drink in the views of Muscongus Bay, Harpswell Cove, and Reed Cove. Close your eyes and feel the breeze and the sunlight washing over you. Draw in a deep breath of ocean air. This is the place to be.

PEAKS-KENNY STATE PARK

Dover-Foxcroft

Driving into Peaks-Kenny State Park will remind you why we seek out natural places. The long, winding road to the park travels through a corridor of tall, statuesque pines. Following this entryway inspires a feeling of reverence. I found myself involuntarily driving much slower and gazing in awe at the magnificent forest through which this road was carved, and wishing I was already out of my car and walking through the woods.

Peaks-Kenny is an exceptionally quiet and remote campground, where all you'll hear is the wind rushing over the treetops. The forest is a dense blend of coniferous and deciduous trees, including numerous birches, lots of dense undergrowth, and large boulders scattered throughout the park. This area must have been one of the last stops for a southbound glacier a few million years ago.

The sites here have hard, sandy surfaces that hang onto those tent stakes. They're also impeccably clean. The diverse character of the dense forest and the gently rolling topography, peppered with glacial boulders, makes these woodland campsites very scenic and attractive. There are 56 sites located near the shores of Sebec Lake. Most are nicely secluded from the rest, especially on the outer side of the loops. The other sites are a curious blend of solitude and openness.

CAMPGROUND RATINGS

Beauty:	★★★★★
Site Privacy:	★★★★★
Site Spaciousness:	★★★★
Quiet:	★★★★★
Security:	★★★★★
Cleanliness/upkeep:	★★★★★

The awe-inspiring column of conifers you'll see as you drive into Peaks-Kenny State will put you in the perfect frame of mind for your camping trip.

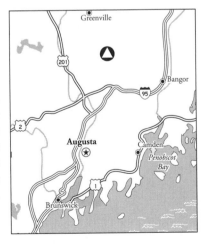

MAINE

Site 1 is redolent of the drive in. The site resembles a natural cathedral or amphitheater. Its location at the start of the campground loop road is unfortunate, since it is consequently exposed to the road. Two massive white pines frame the site, and a large boulder declares its rear border. Its roadside location aside, this is a spectacular site.

There is a nice open feel and no neighbors to site 6, but it is quite open to the road as well. Site 7 feels particularly secluded. It's a huge site set in open woods. Site 9 shares a similar character. Though sites 7 and 9 are somewhat close together, the dense forest surrounding them defies the proximity of your neighbors.

There's a long entryway leading into site 8, which is set further off the campground road. The only drawback to this site is that it's close to the bathroom. Site 11 is a bit too open and close to the bathrooms as well. Site 10, however, is quite spacious and encircled by a brilliant green wall of deciduous forest.

Site 12 is small, but secluded. It's also pitched at a bit of angle, so don't use one of those slippery sleeping pads here or you'll end up in a heap at the bottom of your tent by morning. Likewise, there may not be much space in site 14, but it's way off on its own. The surrounding forest is open, but its location gives it a great sense of solitude.

There's a boulder garden at the back of site 13 that provides solid delineation of the site and adds privacy. It's also fun to climb on, for kids of any age. Sites 15 and 16 are right across the campground road from each other, but they're set off from the sites on either side. These might be a good choice for a family requiring two sites.

Site 17 is too open to the road, plus it's fairly small. There's a trail to the lake right across from site 19, which is rather exposed and quite close to the bathroom. Site 20 is spacious, but feels very open to the road. Site 21 is very well secluded, but backs up against the rest room.

Site 23 is very open and up off the road. It's also quite open to the sky for stargazing. The rest of the sites in the 20s are moderately secluded, but also convenient to the trail to the lake and the bathrooms. The sites on the outside of the loop provide the greatest solitude, particularly site 29, which is on the smaller side, but it's encircled by dense forest and undergrowth.

There's a tall birch marking the entrance to site 30, and a moderately dense forest of hemlock and mixed deciduous trees surrounds the site. Located at the top of a small hill on the campground road, the site feels nicely isolated.

Massive hemlock trees frame site 33. It's good sized but otherwise feels a bit open, and it's perched right at the intersection of the campground loop road. Sites 31 and 32 are close to the bathrooms. Site 37 is exposed to the road, but it's otherwise very well secluded, as it's on a small rise and encircled by dense coniferous forest. There's a cool, dark, sylvan atmosphere to this site.

There is a fantastic sense of seclusion to site 38. This site is set back from the campground road amid a dense grove of mostly hemlocks, with a few deciduous

To get there: Follow Route 153 north from Dover-Foxcroft for about six miles until you see signs for the park.

KEY INFORMATION

Peaks-Kenny State Park
Route 1, Box 10
Dover-Foxcroft, ME 04426

Operated by: Maine Department of Conservation, Bureau of Parks & Lands

Information: Peaks-Kenny State Park, (207) 564-2003

Open: May 15–September 30

Individual sites: 56

Each site has: Fire ring, picnic table

Site assignment: First come, first served or by reservation

Registration: At ranger station as you enter the campground

Facilities: Hot showers, flush toilets, water spigots, canoe rentals

Parking: At sites

Fee: Maine residents, $13; nonresidents, $17

Restrictions:

Pets—On leash only

Fires—In established fire rings only

Alcoholic beverages—At sites only

Vehicles—Parking at sites only

Other—Two-day min. for reservations

trees mixed in. You can barely see this site from the campground road, and vice versa. Site 39 is more open, but it's set way down off the road in its own grove of conifers. Several birch trees frame site 40, which is open to both the campground and the sky.

There's a curiously arranged wall of boulders encircling the back of site 41. One of those boulders has a white pine growing right on top of it. Site 43 has a boulder ledge at the back of the site and sits in a stately stand of hemlocks. Site 46 is way too open for me. It's set well off the road, but still lacks privacy. Site 47 is kind of small, but very well isolated from its neighbors within a moderately dense grove of smaller mixed deciduous and coniferous trees. Sites 48–51, especially 49 and 51, are too exposed to the rest of the campground.

Being set off the road gives site 52 a nice sense of privacy and seclusion. There's a long entryway leading into the site with just enough of an opening to the sky to allow shafts of sunlight to filter down to the site. There's a trail to the lake right near the entrance to site 52 as well.

Site 53 is close to the bathrooms. Site 55 is large and well secluded, encircled within a moderately dense, mostly deciduous forest. There's not much undergrowth in this part of the campground, so there's an open feel on the forest floor.

Several massive boulders block site 56 from view of the road. The site itself is set down off the road as well, and framed on one side by a stand of hemlock and beech trees that further block the site from view of the road. The forest opens up toward the back of the site, giving it a combined sense of solitude and openness.

Most of the activities in which you'll participate while camping here will be on Sebec Lake—the showcase of Peaks-Kenny State Park. Bring your canoe, kayak, and fishing gear, and you won't have any reason to leave the lake or the campground. There are several hiking trails that run through the campground as well, including the Brown's Point Trail and the Birch Mt. Ledge Trail. Neither of these trails are particularly steep or challenging, so they make for a nice, relaxing hike.

RANGELEY LAKE STATE PARK

Rangeley

The campground at Rangeley Lake State Park is exceptionally quiet. You'll occasionally hear the sound of a motorboat cruising by on the lake, but other than that, it's just you, the wind through the trees, and the birds. The sound of loons out on the lake is an essential part of the soundtrack to an evening at Rangeley Lake State Park.

There are 50 sites here spread out around a single large loop. Sites 3, 6, 10, 14, 17, 21, 27, 33, 42, and 48 are first come, first served. The rest can be reserved. The campsites here are set beneath a dense, truly mixed forest of young and old, deciduous and coniferous trees. A nice amount of forest and space between sites provides a solid sense of seclusion for just about all of the sites here. This is a very remote campground with relatively few sites, so there is an excellent sense of solitude and silence.

There is a delightfully secluded atmosphere at site 9. It's surrounded by a dense forest of birch and spruce trees. Just past site 9, there's a footpath leading down to the beach on Rangeley Lake. Just past the footpath is a small open field with a playground area and a volleyball net. The playground is quite scenic itself, overlooking the lake through the trees.

Site 11 is also extraordinarily secluded. This moderately spacious site is carved out of a dense grove of conifers. All the sites numbered in the teens are actually very well screened from each other. Site 13 is a

CAMPGROUND RATINGS

Beauty:	★★★★
Site Privacy:	★★★★
Site Spaciousness:	★★★★
Quiet:	★★★★★
Security:	★★★★★
Cleanliness/upkeep:	★★★★★

Rangeley Lake is the perfect spot to seek out if you just want to unplug for a while in the sylvan solitude of western Maine.

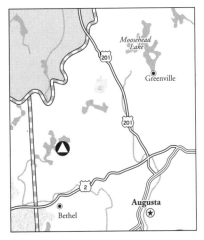

MAINE

bit more open, but you can catch brief glimpses of the lake through the woods. Site 17 is very secluded, carved out of the coniferous forest.

A thick wall of forest encircles site 19, but privacy isn't the best aspect of this site. There's a 50-foot path leading from the site to your own little slice of the lake. This artfully composed lakeside cove has several birch trees growing out over the lake and a short rock jetty leading out from shore. (I suspect some of the other sites on the lake side of the loop also

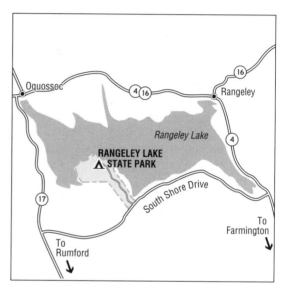

have these little escape routes to the water, but I couldn't intrude on my neighbors' sites to find out.)

There is also a path leading to the lake from site 23. There's a more airy feel to this site. It's open to the sky and set within a loose grove of young trees. As you come to site 25, the campground road starts to head slightly uphill. Site 26 has a very open, sunny feel. The site is encircled by a grove of mostly young deciduous trees that form a solid green wall. Site 30 is similarly bright and green. Sites 27 and 29 are quite close to the rest rooms, so I'd stay away from these.

Sites 30 and up seem to have a bit more forest between them generally. Though site 33 is small, it's tucked into dense forest and relatively distant from its neighbors—even site 34 across the road. Site 34 is back at an angle from the road and screened by a dense stand of trees. The site has a dark, cool feel.

There's a solid sense of seclusion to site 35, but it's also open to the sky, so sunlight makes its way to the site floor. Site 36, like site 34, is nestled in the trees. There's a large hemlock tree growing on the right of the site as you enter. Site 38 is secluded, but very spacious and open to the sky.

The sites on the outside of the loop, including sites 40 and up, have plenty of forest between each other for privacy. Most of these sites are also open to the sky, so stargazers take note. Site 42 has a long entryway, which adds to the considerable sense of seclusion.

Site 44 is open to the road, and thus has less privacy than most of the other sites at Rangeley Lake. Site 47 is right across from the rest room, but it's set back and up from the road in thick mixed forest. Sites 49 and 50 are spacious, but they're situated right where the campground road splits off and consequently receive more traffic noise.

Rangeley Lake is pristine. Its remote location in northwestern Maine means it receives a lot less traffic than Sebago Lake further south in Maine or Lake Winnipesaukee in New Hampshire. The lake is perfect for whatever draws you to water; canoeing, kayaking, swimming, or fishing. If you're of the latter persuasion, you'll appreciate that Rangeley is renowned amongst anglers for its population of landlocked trout and salmon.

There's plenty to do on land here as well. There are hiking trails for all abilities around the park. Try the nearby three-mile trail up Bald Mountain, a 2,443-foot peak with commanding views of the lake and the surrounding forests and hills. Within the park, the Moose Country Corridor Trail is a good choice for a short hike with the little ones. As always, when in this remote, densely forested part of Maine, the bird-watching and wildlife viewing are unparalleled. When passing any wet marshy spots in your travels, keep an eye out for moose.

To get there: Follow Route 4 North from Farmington to Rangeley, and follow the signs to the state park.

KEY INFORMATION

Rangeley Lake State Park
HC 32, Box 5000
Rangeley, ME 04970-5000
Operated by: Maine Department of Conservation, Bureau of Parks & Lands

Information: Rangeley Lake State Park, (207) 864-3858

Open: May 15–September 30

Individual sites: 50

Each site has: Fire ring, picnic table

Site assignment: First come, first served or by reservation

Registration: At ranger station as you enter campground

Facilities: Hot showers, flush toilets, playground, boat launch

Parking: At sites

Fee: Maine residents, $13; non-residents, $17

Restrictions:
  Pets—On leash only
  Fires—In established fire rings only
  Alcoholic beverages—At sites only
  Vehicles—Parking at sites only

SEAWALL CAMPGROUND

Southwest Harbor

The Park Service manages two campgrounds within Acadia National Park: Seawall and Blackwoods. The latter is more popular, and more often crowded, by virtue of its location right along the oceanside Park Loop Road. I've often camped there just for that reason. It is extremely convenient to the Park Loop Road's prime attractions, Sand Beach, Thunder Hole (a hole in the rocks carved out by the surf in which the waves cause a thunderous boom), Otter Cliffs, and some great hiking trails up and over the short, steep cliff known as The Beehive.

I was pleasantly surprised, if not completely converted, the first time I pulled into Seawall Campground. There are three areas to check out at Seawall, the drive-in tent sites in areas A and B and the walk-in tent sites in area D. There are no tents allowed in area C, but that's the RV section, so why would I want to be there anyway?

The A loop is set beneath a dense coniferous forest. The character of the forest and the fact that most of the sites are set well off the road gives them a complete sense of solitude. The campground road runs along two sides and rejoins itself after making a large loop right at site 1, which is a bit open but quite spacious. Site 2 is also a spacious site, and it's set further from the road in a dense grove of mixed conifers. Site 3 is tucked into a grove of slender, young

CAMPGROUND RATINGS

Beauty:	★★★★
Site Privacy:	★★★★
Site Spaciousness:	★★★★
Quiet:	★★★★
Security:	★★★★
Cleanliness/upkeep:	★★★★★

The "village" of walk-in tent sites is reason enough to come camping at Seawall. Its setting on Mount Desert Island and near all of Acadia National Park makes it just that much better.

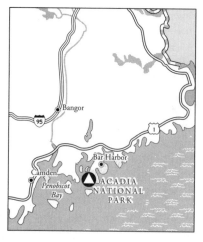

MAINE

conifers and is open to the sky. Site 6 is way back from the road and has a nice sense of isolation. Sites 7 and 8 share an entryway. Site 8 is completely secluded from the road and site 7 is partially secluded. Site 10 is buffered on the sides, but it's a bit close to the road.

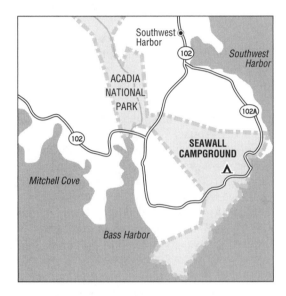

Dense undergrowth surrounds sites 11 and 13, giving them an air of deep woods seclusion. Sites 14 and 15 are open and abut a clearing. They are open to each other, which may appeal to groups and large families, but fairly secluded from the campground road. Site 16 is set far back in this clearing, further from the road but open to the field shared by 14 and 15. A wall of foliage surrounds the field, clearly defining its borders.

Perched at a campground road intersection, site 20 feels too open to the road. Sites 19 and 22 are set within the woods way off the road for an absolute sense of solitude. Sites 23 through 25 also have moderately long entryways. They are screened by greenery but open to the sky. There's a long entryway into site 31, which is very well secluded but a bit close to the rest rooms. Site 33 also has a fairly long "driveway."

Even the sites that feel open here are thoughtfully spaced within the ample, thick forest. The ingenuity of the layout joins the beauty of the setting to complete your experience of sylvan solitude. Another positive element this campground's design, site 27 is intended for disabled access.

Site 35 is a prime example of the smart layout at Seawall, placed so as to be unseen from the road. This site is fantastically secluded and set within dense hemlocks. Sites 36 and 38, however, are a bit open to the road in comparison.

A more loosely spaced forest is predominant along the B loop, at least at the forest floor level. There's much less undergrowth and the forest is populated with older spruce and hemlock that are bare halfway up the trunks, so there's an airy feeling on the ground with a soothing, evergreen canopy overhead. The predominantly coniferous forest here imparts a heady perfume, a lingering spicy, tangy scent.

Site 3 is tucked into the trees off the road. Site 5 is a bit small and open, and sites 6 and 7 are very exposed to the road. Sites 8–11 are moderately secluded from each other. These sites are all quite spacious and set within a stately hemlock grove.

Sites 12 and 13 are very open to each other and somewhat open to the road. However, these sites are huge, so they're perfect for a group needing two contiguous sites. Sites 15 and 16 are another good pair of sites, although they're a bit smaller. Another pair of large sites, 21 and 22 share an entryway and are fairly open to each other.

There's a nice sense of solitude to site 19, as it is set well off the road. Site 26 is a very spacious site also fairly distant from the campground road. Note, however, that sites 23 and 24 are very open to the road and the dumpster, of all things. I don't know of anyone who would want one of these lurking just outside their campsite. Also, site 27 is oddly positioned just outside the B loop and susceptible to passing traffic.

To get there: Follow Route 3 onto Mount Desert Island. Bear right onto Route 102/198 toward Southwest Harbor. Stay on Route 102. Follow Route 102 to Route 102A. Stay on Route 102A and follow the signs to the campground.

KEY INFORMATION

Seawall Campground
Route 102A
Southwest Harbor, ME

Operated by: National Park Service

Information: Acadia National Park
P.O. Box 177
Bar Harbor, ME 04609
(207) 288-3338

Open: Late May–late September

Individual sites: 170 tent sites (plus 5 group sites and 43 sites in the RV loop)

Each site has: Fire ring, picnic table

Site assignment: First come, first served (get there early in the summer!)

Registration: At ranger station as you enter the campground

Facilities: Flush toilets, water spigots

Parking: At sites and central area within D loop

Fee: $13

Restrictions:

Pets—On leash only

Fires—In established fire rings only

Alcoholic beverages—At sites only

Vehicles—Parking at sites only, or parking areas near D sites

Other—Quiet hours 10 p.m.– 7 a.m., 6 people per site max.

Generally, the spaciousness of the forest in the B loop doesn't mean a lack of privacy, though you will see your neighbors. It's more like you're nestled within the deep woods. There's a comforting openness to the forest floor, with moss and fern ground cover that lends a rain forest feel to the woods. The dense, deep, rich greens of the trees contrast dramatically with the lighter greens of the ferns. It's also very quiet here, except for the sounds of the woodland birds and critters. The caws of seagulls remind you that you're not only in the forest, but also right near the ocean.

The D area has the walk-in tent sites. This is the stuff. This "village" of tent sites scattered throughout the forest is sublime. You park along a central loop, then walk into your site. The sites are anywhere from 20 feet to more than 100 feet from the parking area. There are signs along the parking loop that tell you which sites you're parking near.

These tent sites are all relatively uniform in size and character, and they are liberally sprinkled throughout the fairly thick forest of slender coniferous trees. The sites are all moderately spacious. You'll be able to see a few of your neighbors, but there's not an obnoxious lack of privacy so much as a quiet sense of being covered by the forest canopy. There's an airy quality to the "sub-canopy" here similar to that of the B loop. At night, the forest seems to close in around you and your campsite. It is very quiet here. All you'll hear are muffled conversations punctuated by the occasional snap of a campfire.

This community of tent sites is unlike anything I've seen at any other campground. The sense of solitude here is deep and complete. There's a network of walking paths just inside the woods that lead you to all the sites. There are little signposts at the intersections that guide you to specific sites. It could get a bit confusing back here, so you'll definitely want to make sure you have one of the campground site maps handy.

The whole D area is phenomenal. There are a few sites spread further out than the others, but overall the character of the forest, the site spaciousness, and sense of solitude are relatively similar throughout the sites. Anywhere within the D area is a great place to spend a few nights in a tent.

You can tell the veteran D area campers (like the veteran campers at Grout Pond in Vermont), they arrive with some sort of wheeled cart or wagon to haul in their gear. Whether you have wheels or not, it is well worth the extra effort to get yourself to one of these sites within the D area tent village in the woods. You will be rewarded with a deep sense of wilderness solitude.

SEBAGO LAKE STATE PARK

Casco

Every site at the Sebago Lake Campground is just a short walk from either Witch Cove or Naples Beach, both on Sebago Lake. So if you want to camp where you can spend a lot of time in the water, this is a great choice. There are a lot of sites packed into the Sebago Lake Campground, but a dense forest covers most, if not all, of the campground, so there's a nice, woodsy feel.

Sebago Lake State Park is a big campground, and the lake is an extremely popular recreation destination. This means you're not exactly going to get the completely secluded, deep-wilderness experience you'll find in other Maine state parks, but it's still a welcome retreat. Like all Maine state parks, many of the sites are designated as first come, first served. Those non-reservable sites are marked by a triangle on the map. The rest of the sites are available either by reservation or upon arrival when available.

The tent-only area at the Sebago campground should be the first place you check out. Sites 105–119 are set up on a small knoll overlooking the lake. The small cluster of tent-only sites that includes sites 111–119 is a short walk in from the nearest parking area. These sites are quite closely grouped, but they overlook the lake so the view and the breezes are well worth it. The sites are moderately spacious and set beneath a loose forest of mostly deciduous

CAMPGROUND RATINGS

Beauty:	★★★★
Site Privacy:	★★★
Site Spaciousness:	★★★★
Quiet:	★★★
Security:	★★★
Cleanliness/upkeep:	★★★★

Sebago Lake is a popular destination and a large campground, but every site is just a short walk to the beach.

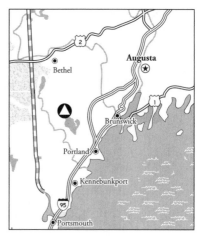

MAINE

trees. There's a light, breezy atmosphere to the forest here that lets a lot of sunlight filter down to the sites and allows breathtaking views of the lake. The only drawback to these sites is that there isn't much in the way of privacy due to their proximity to each other and the loose forest.

There's another group of sites perched on the same knoll, set back from the lake a bit further. Sites 105–110 feel a bit more secluded than the 111–119 group, but they're still set within a fair-

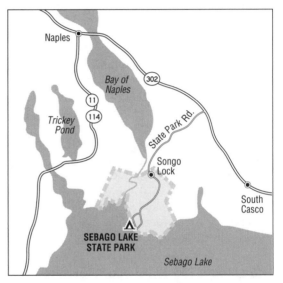

ly loose forest. Site 105 is probably the most secluded of the group. You may be somewhat close to your neighbors up on the tent-only knoll, but you can rest assured they will be neighbors in tents, not RVs!

Considering they are set right along the campground road, sites 120 and 121 are surprisingly secluded. There's a separate parking spot for these sites, then a 20- to 30-foot walk to the sites. The forest is a bit more dense here, which helps isolate the sites from the road and the parking area.

Speaking of the campground road, this is a very popular campground, especially with families. The campground road is paved, so there will be lots of families and kids walking, riding their bikes, and in-line skating. Drive very slowly while you're within the park boundaries.

The Witch Cove area includes sites 122–249. The sites within this area are set beneath a loose forest of tall spruce trees with virtually no undergrowth, so there's a very open, cathedral-like quality to the forest. The open sense cuts down on the privacy a bit, but allows for breezes and views of the lake, even from campsites set a bit further from the water.

The sites here vary in size from quite compact to absolutely enormous, and are marked by size on the campground site map so you'll have a good idea what to look for when searching for a site. There may not be much privacy in the open forest, but I like the comfortable lakeside, wooded-glen feeling to this side of the campground. As the evening starts to settle in, you'll hear a symphony of snaps and cracks as people start to fire up their campfires. In the last light of day, you'll see and smell the smoke wafting through the trees.

The sites are all quite close to Witch Cove beach, so it can be a bit noisy during the day, but you can't beat the easy access to the beach. Given the character of this side of the campground—the level of seclusion and feel of the sites is relatively similar throughout—I'd opt for a site near the lake. Why not? Your view will be clearer and you'll have a super-short walk to the beach. Failing that, I'd opt to be way back in the campground in one of the sites set against the forest for a slightly greater sense of seclusion and privacy and fewer neighboring campsites. Either end of the spectrum works for me.

The configuration and layout of the Witch Cove sites is similar to Blackwoods campground in Acadia National Park. There is a large outer loop intersected by a bunch of shorter roads cutting across the loop, with sites spread along either side of both the intersecting roads and the outer loop.

The sites on the outer side of the far end of the loop, numbered 206 and up,

KEY INFORMATION

Sebago Lake State Park
11 Park Access Road
Casco, ME 04015

Operated by: Maine Department of Conservation, Bureau of Parks & Lands

Information: Sebago Lake State Park, (207) 693-6231

Open: May 1–October 15

Individual sites: 250

Each site has: Fire ring, picnic table

Site assignment: First come, first served or by reservation

Registration: At ranger station as you enter campground

Facilities: Hot showers, flush toilets, water spigots

Parking: At sites or at several general access areas (for walk in sites)

Fee: Maine residents, $13; non-residents, $17

Restrictions:

Pets—Not allowed

Fires—In established fire rings only

Alcoholic beverages—Not allowed

Vehicles—Two per site max.

Other—6 people per site max., visitors allowed 9 a.m.–8 p.m. only, check out by 11 a.m.

To get there: Follow Route 302 east from Naples. Turn left at sign for park. Follow this road for several miles and follow signs to campground.

provide a bit more seclusion than most of the centrally located sites, if for no other reason than because you'll have fewer neighbors. Generally speaking, the sites located on the outside of the main loop tend to be a bit larger and a bit more private. Site 213 is right next to a short trail leading to another little cove around the corner from Witch Cove. This looks like it would be a great spot to drop a hook in the water.

Site 231 is a bit further off the campground road. The site bends around to the left beneath a loose grove of spruce trees. This site has a more secluded feel than the others along this stretch of the campground loop road.

Over on the other side of the campground is the loop near Naples Beach containing sites 1–102. This side of the campground has a similar layout, with a large loop with shorter roads intersecting, but the inside roads are a bit more helter-skelter than the uniform arrangement at Witch Cove. Also, the forest is more dense and there's a lot more undergrowth on this side of the campground, so most of the sites provide a deeper sense of seclusion. Sites 9–13 are set down within a mixed forest right on Naples Beach. These sites are set within loosely spaced woods and they are very close to the lake.

Being situated at the end of a short loop and backed up against a large rock pile gives the small group of sites 29, 42, and 31 a remote and interesting character. The "dead end" feel of this part of the campground road and the rocks add to the sense of seclusion within these sites. This cluster of sites, with the added degree of seclusion and the proximity to the small drumlin of rocks and the lake, are well worth investigating.

Further back from the lake, both the forest and the undergrowth grows more dense, so the inland sites generally provide a better sense of solitude and privacy. There's still a fairly open feel, but not wide open like the other side.

When camping at Sebago, it's all about the lake. All the campsites are close to the lake, one whole side of the campground is mostly lakefront beach, and most (if not all) of the activities from which there are to choose are based on the lake. This is the place to be if you want your summer camping days to be filled with swimming, water-skiing, sailing, canoeing, kayaking, even scuba diving.

Sebago Lake is the primary attraction in southwestern Maine, so it does get a little crazy during the day. If you're camping here, though, once all the boaters and skiers and day crowds have packed up and gone home, you'll still be there by the side of the lake, enjoying the sublime transition from day into night.

WARREN ISLAND STATE PARK

Lincolnville

When you journey to Warren Island, you'll see the truth in the statement "half the fun is getting there." After all, Warren Island is an island! You can't drive there, you can't hike there, and you certainly can't park an RV there. You can get there by kayak or canoe, one placid paddle stroke at a time. You can also get there by motorboat or sailboat, but most of the people you'll see camped out on Warren Island arrive by sea kayak.

While most of the island's ten campsites (and arguably the nicest sites) are spread along the shore, the rest are located toward the center of the island. There are eight primitive tent sites, and two Appalachian Mountain Club–style lean-tos. The day-use picnic sites and the overnight camping sites are available by reservation or, otherwise, on a first come, first served basis. The only sites you can't reserve are 4, 5, and 6.

The island is covered in a verdant, dense spruce forest. Island camping in general, and certainly a night spent on Warren Island, is an olfactory sensation. At any moment, with any breath, you can smell the crisp aroma of the spruce forest and the rich, heady scents of the sea.

It's funny to look down as you're walking along the Island Trail and see bits of shell mixed in with the pine needles and fallen leaves on the forest floor. The Island Trail is a walking trail that essentially circumnavigates the 70-acre island and brings you past most of the sites.

CAMPGROUND RATINGS

Beauty:	★★★★★
Site privacy:	★★★★★
Site spaciousness:	★★★★★
Quiet:	★★★★★
Security:	★★★★★
Cleanliness/upkeep:	★★★★★

Warren Island is a slice of paradise. After an adventurous day of paddling on the ocean, you can relax by your campfire and enjoy the pristine view and the magnificent scent of both sea and forest.

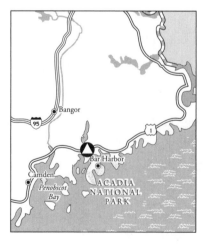

MAINE

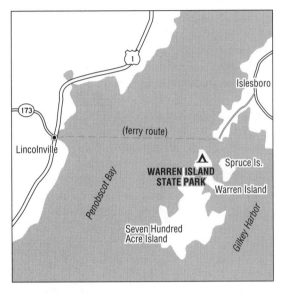

As you start to set up your camping gear, you'll notice a five-gallon white bucket next to every fireplace and grill. It should be full of water. If it's not, be a good citizen and fill it up at the shore. This is Warren Island's volunteer fire department. You're the firefighter. If your fire gets out of control, there's no calling 911. There's no truck on the island waiting to come douse the flames. An out-of-control campfire could be lethal, and that scenario is a major concern for island dwellers and Warren Island State Park's ranger. Be extra cautious with your fire, and make sure that bucket is full and next to the hearth.

There's no camp store on Warren Island, and it is strictly forbidden to cut down or otherwise damage any trees. The rangers leave small caches of firewood here and there for campers. Be frugal and conserve wood. Only build a fire as large as you need to cook, stay warm, and keep the fireside ambiance in your site. You'll save wood, minimize the risk to Warren Island, and still have a fantastically peaceful evening. Okay, end of sermon—I promise!

After reaching the island from whichever direction you approach, you can access the island via the pier on the east side, facing the Islesboro ferry terminal. Just off the end of the pier is the ranger station and the day-use area with grills and picnic tables. If you're just pulling in for the day, the fee is $1, which you pay at the Iron Ranger posted at the head of the pier.

Head out on the Island Trail to the north (or to the right as you look onto the island from the end of the pier) and you'll find the campsites. Site 1 is situated on a grassy area, close to the rest rooms and the pier, on the island's eastern shore. This site is on the inland side of the Island Trail.

Site 2 is the first of the sites situated right on the water. This site is marvelously spacious and very well secluded. You can see the narrow bay that separates Warren Island and Islesboro through the loosely spaced trees that define the site. This site has two picnic tables, as well as a stone hearth.

Deep in the woods on the forest side of the trail, site 3 is very secluded and private. The inland sites at Warren Island are indeed lovely campsites. But this is an island, so you'll probably be tempted to try and secure a waterfront site. It's well worth a little extra effort or wait.

The next oceanfront site is site 3A. This site is very spacious and open, with cool breezes blowing off the ocean through the site. It has dramatic views of the bay. You can pull your kayaks right up to the edge of the site. If you arrive by a larger boat, or don't paddle right up to the campsite, there are wheeled carts available for hauling your gear from the pier.

Keep heading up the trail past sites 3 and 3A and you'll come to the North Shelter, one of the island's lean-tos. The North Shelter is set in an open grove of birch and spruce trees, and it looks out over Penobscot Bay to the north. Its location perfectly blends a woodland setting and proximity to the island's shoreline.

The remaining inland sites are 4, 5, and 6. These sites are set in a grassy field and a loose grove of mixed forest in the center of the island. To reach them, take the short hiking trail that leads straight from the pier (heading west), past the ranger station on the left. There are remnants from the foundation of a historic mansion out

---

To get there: Drop your kayak in the water in Camden Harbor, Lincolnville Beach, or Ducktrap Harbor and paddle east toward Islesboro. Warren Island is just southwest of the Islesboro ferry terminal.

KEY INFORMATION

Warren Island State Park
P.O. Box 105
Lincolnville, ME 04849

Operated by: Maine Department of Conservation, Bureau of Parks & Lands

Information: Contact Camden Hills State Park, (207) 236-3109 or (207) 941-4014 (off season)

Open: Memorial Day–September 15

Individual sites: 8 tent sites, 2 lean-tos

Each site has: Picnic table, stone hearth, fire bucket

Site assignment: By reservation or first come, first served

Registration: At ranger station on island

Facilities: Pit toilets, water spigots, pier and moorings

Parking: Pull your kayak up on the beach!

Fee: Maine residents, $12; non-residents, $15; day use fee, $1

Restrictions:

Pets—On leash only

Fires—In established fire rings only

Alcoholic beverages—Not allowed

Vehicles—No vehicles on the island

Other—Cutting or damaging trees is prohibited; campers must carry out all trash; no dish washing at water spigots

here. There's a water pump located between sites 4 and 5, within the stone piles that belie the fact that a mansion stood here more than 80 years ago.

This mansion must have been quite a sight. Once the property of William Folwell, a woolen manufacturer from Philadelphia who purchased the land in 1899. When it was built at a price of $75,000 (in turn-of-the-century dollars), it was believed to be one of the most expensive log cabins ever built in New England. The elegantly appointed "cabin" had 22 rooms, including a massive living room, dining room, and kitchen. Sadly, the cabin burned to the ground in 1919.

Beyond sites 4 and 5 and the remnants of the Folwell mansion, site 6 is set off in its own little field. The trio of inland sites is quite open and extraordinarily spacious. They offer less privacy than the shoreline sites, and lack ocean views, but they are still beautiful. The breezes, the scent of the ocean, and the melancholy cry of the seagulls will remind you you're on an island.

The West Shelter is set way down on the Penobscot Bay (west) side of the island. Follow a short hiking trail from the open area near sites 4 and 5 and you'll find the shelter, which faces an absolutely priceless view of the bay.

Site 7 is down toward the southern end of the island. You can pull up to the pier on the east side and cart your gear down, or spot the site from the water and paddle right up to the site. Not surprisingly, I prefer the second option.

This site has the most complete and deep sense of seclusion of any campsite in New England. You're at least 100 feet from the nearest site, and all you can see are the woods and the bay. There are two picnic tables at site 7 and makeshift log benches by the fireplace. The site is set within a moderately spaced grove of spruce and other deciduous trees, and it is quite open from above, so plenty of sunlight and moonlight filter downwards.

More often than not, there's a nice breeze blowing through the island, but on those still days, or during the morning and evening lull, the bugs can be ferocious. There is simply no escape. Think ahead, and be prepared. Bring a head net and some of your favorite bug repellent.

Despite my earlier reverie about peaceful paddle strokes, the crossing from Camden or Lincolnville to Warren Island is wide open across more than three miles of Penobscot Bay. I've crossed the bay when it was still as glass. I've also crossed it with clenched teeth, white knuckles, and the bow of my kayak slicing into the oncoming swells like a broadsword. Penobscot Bay is big water. Exercise all sorts of caution. Don't paddle to Warren Island on your first kayak camping trip, or even your second for that matter. Plan your trip carefully with respect to the winds, the tides, and the weather. If you're at all hesitant, either wait for better weather or hire one of the area's registered guides.

If you do go over by yourself and get in a jam so you don't feel comfortable paddling back, paddle over to the ferry terminal on nearby Islesboro and see if you can hop on the ferry, which leaves Islesboro every hour on the half hour. A one-way adult ticket runs $3.25. Bikes are $2 and vehicles less than 20 feet are $10.50. A kayak would be somewhere in between, I'd imagine.

A trip to Warren Island is one you'll remember for a long time to come. The combination of paddling or boating there, exploring the island, falling asleep to the delightful rustling of pines in the sea breeze, and waking up to the panorama of Penobscot Bay completes a mystical experience.

NEW HAMPSHIRE

BEAR BROOK STATE PARK

Allenstown

Bear Brook State Park is a huge place. It is actually the largest state park in New Hampshire. The first time I visited, I drove around for a while before I even found the campground within the park. It's size (the entire park spans 8,008 acres) and the myriad outdoor activities available here make this as much a destination as a place to set up camp.

On the long road leading through the park and to the campground, I was convinced I had missed it and worried I had left the park after passing several private residences. If you get this sensation, keep cruising because you're almost there. You'll come to another Bear Brook State Park sign that points the way into the campground. The last stretch is a beautiful ride through a stately forest of pine and spruce trees that are at least 100 feet tall. Be sure to roll your windows down to get that olfactory blast from the conifers.

Bear Brook State Park has a massive network of trails, some of which pass right through the campground. You'll pass trailheads for the Broken Boulder Trail and the Pitch Pine Trail on the last section of the campground road. Both of these trails eventually lead to Smith Pond.

The first loop within the campground with sites 1 and up is set beneath an open forest with very little undergrowth. These sites don't offer a lot of privacy, but they are quite spacious and centrally located

CAMPGROUND RATINGS

Beauty:	★★★★
Site privacy:	★★★★
Site spaciousness:	★★★★
Quiet:	★★★★★
Security:	★★★★
Cleanliness/upkeep:	★★★★★

Spread out along the shore of Beaver Pond, Bear Brook State Park has some perfectly isolated sites—great spots to camp while you explore the rest of the park on foot, on a bike, or in a canoe.

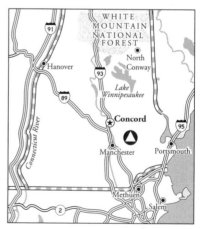

NEW HAMPSHIRE

within the campground. They're also covered by a blanket of pine needles. This loop is near an open field with a baseball diamond. There is even a small playground with a slide and swings, which is nice if you're camping with kids. If you want to be near these parts of the campground, check out sites 35 and 36, which are right near the border of the field.

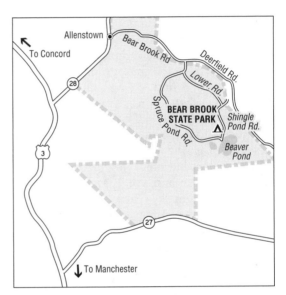

Past the baseball field, there are sites tucked into the woods on the stretch of the campground road leading down to the small beach area on Beaver Pond. Sites 22–24 are nicely secluded and quite close to the pond. Of the other sites near the pond, site 31A is nice, as it's set off on the end of a short road jutting off the main campground road.

The beach at Beaver Pond is a great spot to spend an afternoon. You can paddle, fish, or just sit in the sand. Being out in the deep woods and far from the ocean, there are no seashells on this beach—only pine cones! You don't have to worry about finding anything else in the sand either, as there are no glass bottles, pets, or horses allowed on the beach. The Beaver Pond trailhead is at the far end of the beach. This trail circumnavigates the pond, coming back in through the campground. There's also a small dock toward the end of the beach to help you launch your kayak or canoe adventures.

Heading back toward the main part of the campground, sites 40 and 41 are quite spacious, although they're close to the headquarters and set within the open forest that covers most of the central campground loop. Like the lower numbered sites, these sites are also blanketed with pine needles.

Site 55 is excellent, one of the more secluded sites at Bear Brook. It is set off by a short perimeter of pines, standing around the border as if guarding the site. Its neighbor site 56 is another nicely isolated site.

If you set up camp at site 64, you'll be able to pick up the Beaver Pond trail right next to your campsite. Site 65 is off on its own near the rest room, with a view of the pond through the loosely spaced forest that divides the campsites from the shores of the pond in this section of the campground.

Further back on the campground loop road, away from the campground headquarters, you'll find site 94, another of Bear Brook's better sites. This is a very spacious site set off on a small loop heading away from the pond. There is very open forest on the far side of this site, as well as overhead, so a lot of sunlight reaches the site and you'll have a nice view of the night sky. There's also a self-guided nature trail that heads out right next to site 94.

Site 95, however, is the ultimate site at Bear Brook State Park, in my opinion. This site is truly secluded, set at the end of a short road leading off the main campground road. It has its own little cul-de-sac right in front of the site, so it's extremely spacious as well. It's set up against a small embankment and nestled within a grove of mixed hardwoods and conifers. Sound good? It gets better. Just outside the site to the left, there's a break in the forest that gives you access to the pond. There's no beach, but there's plenty

KEY INFORMATION

Bear Brook State Park
157 Deerfield Road
Allenstown, NH 03275

Operated by: New Hampshire Department of Parks and Recreation

Information: Bear Brook State Park, (603) 485-9869 (campground office) or (603) 485-9874 (park office)

Open: Early May–mid-October

Individual sites: 96

Each site has: Fire ring, picnic table

Site assignment: First come, first served

Registration: At campground headquarters

Facilities: Flush toilets, showers, laundry, camp store, boat rentals

Parking: At sites

Fee: $15

Restrictions:

Pets—Dogs on leash only

Fires—In established fire rings only

Alcoholic beverages—At sites only

Vehicles—Parking at campsites only

To get there: Take Route 93 North through Manchester to the exit for Routes 28 and 3 North. In Suncook, take Route 28 toward Allenstown. Turn right on Bear Brook Road toward park.

of room to launch a canoe or kayak. This site is also right near a trailhead that leads out of the campground.

Site 75 is another nicely secluded site, set at another end of the campground loop road, right on a dirt road leading out of the campground proper. Overall, the sites within the 46–75 area are more secluded. Some are much more spacious, and a few are positively perfect. The shower and laundry facilities are located within this group as well.

If your daytime plans while at Bear Brook include fly-fishing or even just plain old dropping a hook in the water, you're in luck. There's a special pond just for fly-fishermen near the beginning of the road winding in toward the campground. The season runs from the fourth Saturday in April through October 15, and there's a limit of two brook trout per day. There are also two archery ranges within the park, which are apparently the only ones within the New Hampshire state park system.

If hiking, mountain biking, and paddling are more your speed, there's plenty of room for those as well. There are myriad trails winding throughout Bear Brook State Park. There are more than 40 miles of trails here, so you will have to spend a lot of time here before you cross over the same trail twice. The trails lead you to some of the park's most secluded and spectacular spots—wetlands, mountaintops, and remote ponds—good stuff.

BIG ROCK CAMPGROUND

Lincoln

The moment you pull into Big Rock Campground, you'll see the unique geological feature for which the campground was named—a huge rock. Besides being a namesake and a curiosity, this massive chunk of granite (a phrase that proved far too cumbersome for a campground name) gives climbers a good spot for a little spontaneous bouldering. It's a nice way to warm up for or cool down from a day spent climbing the massive walls of Cathedral Ledge in nearby North Conway.

Big Rock is actually quite a small campground, which makes it an excellent place to set up camp. There are only 28 sites, many of which have a decent amount of space and a feeling of moderate solitude. If you've come camping with a group or need several sites, try to secure some of the sites in the 24–29 loop. There's a small parking area that's central to these sites, so you'll have to haul your gear in, but not too far. These sites are atop the small hill around which the campground is situated, so they provide a nice sense of isolation from the rest of the campground, if not from each other. There's also a rest room right down the access road for this group of sites.

Other prime tent spots within Big Rock are sites 7–10 and 13–18. All these sites are actually on the same loop, which is the main loop of the campground. The forest here is a bit thicker than the open woods of nearby Hancock Campground (see page

CAMPGROUND RATINGS

Beauty:	★★★★
Site privacy:	★★★★
Site spaciousness:	★★★★
Quiet:	★★★★★
Security:	★★★★
Cleanliness/upkeep:	★★★★

You'll know how this campground got its name as soon as you pull in.

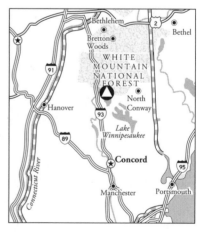

66

NEW HAMPSHIRE

82). It's a mixed forest of coniferous and deciduous trees, so at the height of summer, the dense woods give each site a sense of being off on its own.

I especially like the fact that it's such a small campground. Yes, it fills up quickly as a result, but if you get here early enough during the day and secure a spot, you can rest assured that you'll have peaceful, quiet nights in the woods. Big Rock is only the second campground you'll come across as you travel east on

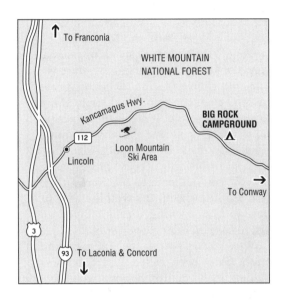

the "Kanc," (as this delightful stretch of road is known to the locals and regulars) so it's still fairly close to Lincoln.

According to the U.S. Forest Service, which operates and maintains Big Rock and the other Kancamagus campgrounds, Big Rock is open year-round. However, on two attempts to enter Big Rock during the winter, I was met with a monstrous snowbank at the entrance, and therefore had no place to park and unload gear. If you plan to come to the Kanc during the chillier months, plan on Hancock or Blackberry Crossing, which are open for winter camping.

Big Rock is a great spot from which to launch your outdoor adventures. It's within a short drive or walk from some prime hikes and sights along the Kanc. Right across the road runs the Hancock Branch of the Pemigewasset. You can stroll over there with a fishing rod or a towel, depending on your preference.

Several hiking trails are just a stone's throw down the Kanc. Turn left out of the campground heading toward Conway and you'll soon come to trailheads for the East Pond Trail and the Hancock Notch Trail. This trail follows the

North Fork of the Pemigewasset for a while, then bears east toward Mount Huntington, Hancock Notch, and the Sawyer Pond Scenic Area. This would be a fairly sturdy hike from the Hancock Notch trailhead all the way to Sawyer Pond, so bring plenty of food and water if you're coming this way.

Across the Kanc from these trailheads is the Greeley Ponds trail that leads to the Greeley Ponds Scenic Area. If you hike in this far and still want to explore, the Mount Osceola Trail leads you up to East Peak, West Peak, and Mount Osceola. You'll also be able to sneak occasional views of Mount Kancamagus to the east.

It can sometimes be a challenge to secure one of the prime tent spots at Big Rock campground. It is one of the first to fill to capacity during the busy summer weekends, but its compact size also makes for a quiet, cozy atmosphere. Even if you've come to the Kanc at the height of the season, it's well worth your time to take a swing through Big Rock just in case there's an open spot.

Who knows what the campground might have been called had a careless glacier not casually dropped that massive boulder near the entrance several million years ago? On the other hand, who cares? Big Rock is small and cozy, and, in my view, that makes it a perfect-sized campground and a great spot to pitch a tent.

To get there: From Lincoln, follow Kancamagus Highway to Big Rock campground on left. From Conway, follow Kancamagus Highway to Big Rock campground on right.

KEY INFORMATION

Big Rock Campground
Kancamagus Highway
Lincoln, NH

Operated by: U.S. Forest Service

Information: Saco Ranger Station
33 Kancamagus Highway
RFD #1, Box 94
Conway, NH 03818
(603) 447-5448

Open: Mid-May–mid-October

Individual sites: 28

Each site has: Fire ring, picnic table

Site assignment: First come, first served

Registration: Select site then pay at self-service fee station

Facilities: Vault toilets

Parking: At sites

Fee: $14

Restrictions:
Pets—Dogs on leash only
Fires—In fire rings only
Alcoholic beverages—At sites only
Vehicles—Two per site max.
Other—8 people per site max., 14-day max. stay

BLACKBERRY CROSSING CAMPGROUND
Albany

There may be just six sites set aside for tent camping at Blackberry Crossing Campground, but its character, history, and location on the Kancamagus Highway make a trip here time well spent. It's another of the area's fairly small campgrounds, about the same size as Big Rock.

The six tent sites are set off in a small field on the eastern edge of the campground. They are tent-only sites by virtue of the fact that you have to lug your gear in a short distance from the parking area for this loop. Sites 21–26 are at the woods' edge around a central clearing about one-quarter the size of a football field. The open space between these tent sites adds a nice, community flavor to this campground. On those crystal clear, jet-black New England nights, you'll be thankful that you're far from any light pollution that might interfere with stargazing. The break in the trees over the field affords magnificent views of the skies. Keep an eye to the sky if you're there in mid-August, and you could catch the dazzling display of the Perseid meteor showers.

During the daylight hours, the field is a great spot for playing a quick game of Frisbee or a group picnic. It's a nice area to let the kids run around and blow off steam while you kick back in the sun, or in the shade of the birch, pine, and mixed deciduous forest. Either way, you'll still have a full view of your gang. It's also just six

CAMPGROUND RATINGS

Beauty: ★★★★
Site privacy: ★★★
Site spaciousness: ★★★★
Quiet: ★★★
Security: ★★★★
Cleanliness/upkeep: ★★★★

Blackberry Crossing is rich in history, with tall stone heart remaining from its days CCC ca p.

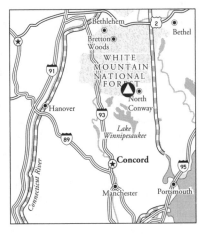

NEW HAMPSHIRE

miles west of Conway if you need anything, from groceries to a hot pizza.

If you've come to pitch your tent at Blackberry Crossing during the winter, the clearing in the middle of the tent loop is especially nice because you'll get the full benefit of the sun, when it's out. The campground isn't plowed in the winter, so you'll have to ski or snowshoe in with your gear, but the campsites are half price. Of course, during the winter, you might not need to hike your gear over to the

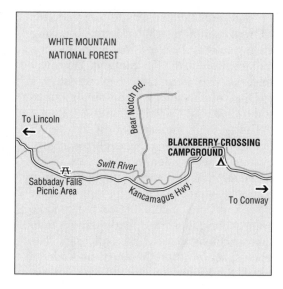

tent loop. Hancock tends to get most of the winter campers, so you might have Blackberry Crossing all to yourself.

Blackberry Crossing looks quite different than it did 60 years ago. Nearly 200 men lived and worked here between 1935 and 1941 as part of President Roosevelt's "Tree Army." Blackberry Crossing was home to Company 1177 of the Civilian Conservation Corps, which cut most of the trails in and around the White Mountains that we still enjoy today.

Besides preserving and providing access to wilderness, the CCC employed men during the depths of The Great Depression. There are still a few remnants from Blackberry Crossing's days as a CCC encampment, most notably two large stone hearths, one right by site 20 and the other in between sites 8 and 9. These are all that remain of the camp's headquarters and recreation hall.

The sites in the tent loop are obviously the best for tent camping, but if you've come with a large group or several families and that loop is already occupied, you could also look into sites 7–10. These are located around the central loop, ahead and off to the left as you enter the campground. You'll be close to one of the beautiful old stone hearths and a historic marker with photos of the camp as it appeared in the late 1930s and early 1940s. These sites are wide open, but they're set amidst a lovely grove of birch trees. Sites 14 and 15, roughly between the central loop and the tent-only loop, are also set off on their own.

Out of the campground, take a left and head over to Rocky Gorge. Whether you've come to Blackberry Crossing to camp for one night or for a whole week, don't miss Rocky Gorge. This series of natural pools and rock baths leads into a fairly steep and wild waterfall. The Swift River gets narrow and speeds through Rocky Gorge. There's a footbridge right over the waterfall, so you can get a spectacular view of the show beneath.

Follow the footbridge to the trail on the opposite side of the river, and a short hike will lead you to Falls Pond, a placid, quiet pond in direct contrast to the thundering water just a few feet away. There's a hiking trail that leads all the way around the pond as well.

Blackberry Crossing campground is directly across the street from Covered Bridge Campground (the following profile), which is kind of amusing. It's your choice. I'd say if you're camping with a large group or have a particular affinity for historic sites, Blackberry Crossing is definitely worth a look. If it's just you and a friend or a couple of friends, check across the street at Covered Bridge—another spot rich in character and wilderness sense.

> **To get there:** From Lincoln, follow Kancamagus Highway to Blackberry Crossing campground on your right. From Conway, follow Kancamagus Highway to Blackberry Crossing campground on your left, right across the street from Covered Bridge Campground.

KEY INFORMATION

Blackberry Crossing Campground
Kancamagus Highway
Albany, NH

Operated by: White Mountain National Forest

Information: Saco Ranger Station
33 Kancamagus Highway
RFD #1, Box 94
Conway, NH 03818
(603) 447-5448

Open: Year-round; not plowed in winter so sites are $7

Individual sites: 26

Each site has: Fire ring and picnic table

Site assignment: First come-first served, no reservations

Registration: Select site then pay at self-service fee station

Facilities: Vault toilets, hand pump for water

Parking: At sites, separate parking area for tent loop

Fee: $14

Restrictions:

Pets—Dogs on leash only

Fires—In fire rings only

Alcoholic beverages—At sites only

Vehicles—Two per site max.

Other—8 people per site max., 14 -day max. stay

COVERED BRIDGE CAMPGROUND

Albany

What do Big Rock and Covered Bridge Campgrounds have in common (besides the fact that they're both located on the Kancamagus Highway)? As soon as you pull in to either, you'll see the campground's namesake. In the case of Covered Bridge Campground, you soon come to a classic New England covered bridge that spans the Swift River. The original bridge was built in the late 1800s by the townsfolk of Albany; it was rebuilt in the 1970s.

On either side of the road leading onto the bridge, there are huge timbers spanning the road at an eight-foot height to ensure that "adventurous" RV or camper owners don't try to drive through the bridge. While effective and admirable as a means of preserving this historic covered bridge, it also helps keep the larger RVs out of Covered Bridge Campground. (You can get into the campground from the Dugway Road, six miles west of Conway, but don't tell anyone, especially in an RV!)

Coming into the campground from the Kancamagus, you'll pass under the RV trap with ease, traverse the covered bridge (keep an eye out for pedestrians, as covered bridges throughout New England always draw camera-toting crowds), and bear right on the Dugway Road. The campground is on the left about half a mile down the road. As soon as you cross the bridge and bear right, you'll see the parking area and trailhead for the Boulder

CAMPGROUND RATINGS

Beauty:	★★★★★
Site privacy:	★★★★
Site spaciousness:	★★★★
Quiet:	★★★★★
Security:	★★★★
Cleanliness/upkeep:	★★★★★

The campground's proximity to massive rock gardens and two trailheads make Covered Bridge a great spot for hikers.

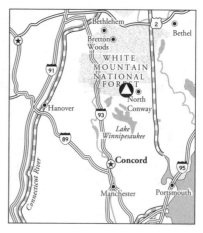

NEW HAMPSHIRE

Loop Trail on the right. Take a mental note and walk back for a quick hike later.

Covered Bridge campground is moderately sized, with 49 sites. There aren't any sites designated as tent-only, but there are some practical landscape considerations that make this a great campground for a night in the nylon. As soon as you pull into the campground, keep bearing left. This will bring you to the small, dead-end loop with sites 25–27. These are great sites, set off on their own

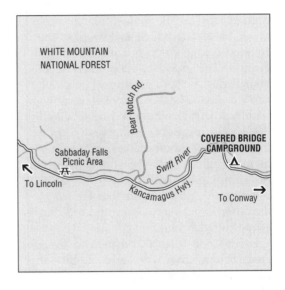

amidst the fairly dense, mostly coniferous forest. Just outside this loop is site 24, which is an interesting site set against a garden of massive boulders, no doubt spilled over from the Boulder Loop Trail.

Generally speaking, the outer loop sites are the best. If you're fortunate enough, you'll be able to score one of the northernmost sites that are set off on their own platforms, which means you have to lug your tent and other gear up a short incline. If you're on the southern end of the loop, you might be somewhere near an RV, but the sites are spacious and distant enough to provide a nice sense of solitude.

The northern loop sites that are the prime tent spots at Covered Bridge are 17, 19, 41, 43, 45, 47, and 49. Additionally, these sites back up to a massive cliff that rises just behind the campground. During the summer, the forest may be too dense for you to fully appreciate this grand formation, which is part of the granite pile left by the glaciers that scraped through here thousands of years ago.

One other way to appreciate the geologic uniqueness of this area is to head down Dugway Road back toward the covered bridge and take a spin around the Boulder Loop Trail. The trail will take you up and around the side of this cliff and through a delightful garden of huge boulders. The beginning of this trail resembles a massive stone staircase. You almost expect it to lead to a giant's castle. The glaciers inadvertently created a hiker's playground here, but watch your step. It's quite easy to twist an ankle when hiking and bounding through the boulders.

Another nice trailhead right near the campground is the Lower Nanamoco-muck Ski Trail, which is just past the covered bridge coming from the campground. This makes a nice, fairly level hike during the spring, summer, and fall, and a dramatic backcountry ski or snow-shoe trek in the winter. While Covered Bridge Campground isn't open during the winter, Blackberry Crossing, which is literally right across the street, is open for camping at half the regular rates since it isn't plowed out like Hancock, the other Kancamagus campground that is open all year long.

There's one historical aspect to Cov-ered Bridge that can add a bit of panache to your ghost stories around the campfire. As soon as you enter the campground, there's a small, fenced-off burial plot. After dinner, take a stroll down to the burial site, make sure no one from the Lane family (the name on the headstone) is up and about, then whip up a couple of ghoulish, ghost sto-ries with a local connection!

To get there: From Lincoln, follow Kan-camagus Highway to Covered Bridge campground on your left. From Conway, follow Kancamagus Highway to Covered Bridge campground on your right, right across the street from Blackberry Crossing campground.

KEY INFORMATION

Covered Bridge Campground
Kancamagus Highway
Albany, NH

Operated by: White Mountain National Forest

Information: Saco Ranger Station
33 Kancamagus Highway
RFD #1, Box 94
Conway, NH 03818
(603) 447-5448

Open: Mid-May–mid-October

Individual sites: 49

Each site has: Fire ring, picnic table

Site assignment: First come, first served, or by reserva-tion, reservable sites include 9–17, 29, 30–37, 39–49

Registration: Select site and pay at self-service fee station or proceed to your reserved site; for reservations, call White Mountain National Forest at (877) 444-6777

Facilities: Vault toilets, near fishing pier on Swift River

Parking: At sites

Fee: $14 per site, per night

Restrictions:

Pets—Dogs on leash only

Fires—In fire rings only

Alcoholic beverages—At sites only

Vehicles—Two per site max.

Other—8 people per site max., 14-day max. stay

DOLLY COPP CAMPGROUND

Gorham

The White Mountain National Forest is a paradise for camping, hiking, biking, fly-fishing, canoeing, and nearly every other outdoor pursuit: "The Land of Many Uses" as the Forest Service signs proclaim. All those sound like pretty good uses to me, and I'm certainly not alone. During all four seasons, a steady flow of fun hogs pours into the Mount Washington Valley. Don't be too dismayed if it seems like everyone else in the free world is heading north with you. Many also come for the indoor activities, like outlet shopping in North Conway.

You can escape some of the crowds that may not head any further north than the outlets by heading further north yourself to Dolly Copp Campground. The campground is just north of Mount Washington and right off Route 16. Don't make the mistake of pulling into the Dolly Copp picnic area. The campground is another mile up the road.

Dolly Copp is a good-sized campground, and it's not crowded with sites. There are 176 sites and four separate areas within the campground, and there is plenty of room between the different areas. There aren't any tent-specific areas within Dolly Copp, but there are a few areas where trailers aren't allowed. These loops are more secluded, densely forested, and perfect for pitching a tent. The only area that you would definitely want to avoid is

CAMPGROUND RATINGS

Beauty:	★★★★
Site privacy:	★★★★
Site spaciousness:	★★★
Quiet:	★★★★
Security:	★★★★
Cleanliness/upkeep:	★★★★

Dolly Copp is like a few small campgrounds rolled into one. The tent camping loops have lots of secluded spots tucked into the dense forest.

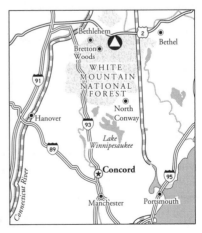

NEW HAMPSHIRE

the Big Meadow area, which includes sites 1–50. This area has most of the open sites where the land yachts come to drop their anchors.

A respectful distance further up the campground access road is where you'll find the prime tent sites. Brook Loop is a great spot for tent campers. No trailers are allowed here. This loop includes sites 75–91. Within Brook Loop, sites 80–84 are in their own little mini-loop that is perfect if you're camping with a large group. Even if some other folks are already camped out in the 80–84 loop, you'll still be able to experience a sense of solitude. From where you park your vehicle, you have to walk up to tent platforms for two of the sites within the loop, and down to a platform for another, so they are a bit more set off and secluded.

Spruce Woods is another great spot for tents. No trailers are allowed here, and the road is narrow and winding, so you're not likely to see any large self-contained campers. The Spruce Woods Loop includes sites 51–72. As soon as you turn off into this loop, you'll feel as if you're driving deeper into the forest. The whole area is densely wooded with fir, pine, and spruce trees, so there's a nice sylvan atmosphere. The forest floor remains cool even on the sultriest summer day, and the sunlight filters down through the trees in fractured columns, adding a mystical air to the woods. Even if you have neighbors on both sides of your site, you may not be able to see them. This is my favorite section of Dolly Copp.

The only drawback to the dense forest is that you won't have a very good view of the night sky for stargazing. On a clear night, you can always take a short walk to an open area or even down to the banks of the Peabody River, which flows by just outside the campground.

There are several campground hosts who stay at the same well-marked sites throughout the season. The hosts are a good source of friendly information on campground regulations, what to do in the area, and a bit of Rockwellian local lore, if you have a moment to chat. The rangers at Dolly Copp also run various visitor programs and interpretive walks during the season. If you've come to the White Mountains for some fly-fishing, you'll be able to find quite a few secluded fishing spots on either the nearby Peabody River or the Moose River, which is just a bit further north.

Then, there's the hiking. It's everywhere. Dolly Copp is a great place to set up your base camp if you have come to the White Mountains to hike Mount Washington, the rest of the Presidential Range, or anywhere within the White Mountain National Forest. Driving along the Kancamagus Highway or up Route 16, there are numerous trailheads. You can find a hike that is long, short, steep, gradual—whatever suits your mood, energy level, or the amount of time you have before heading back to the real world.

If you don't have much time or just want to get someplace to enjoy a world-class view of the sloping eastern flanks

KEY INFORMATION

Dolly Copp Campground
Route 16
Gorham, NH 03581

Operated by: White Mountain National Forest

Information: Saco Ranger Station
33 Kancamagus Highway
RFD #1, Box 94
Conway, NH 03818
(603) 447-5448

Open: Mid-May–mid-October

Individual sites: 176

Each site has: Fire pit

Site assignment: First come, first served or by reservation

Registration: At campground headquarters; for reservations call (877) 444-6777

Facilities: Flush toilets

Parking: At sites

Fee: $15

Restrictions:

Pets—Dogs on leash only

Fires—In fire pits only, do not leave unattended

Alcoholic beverages—At campsites only

Vehicles—One per site, no trailers allowed in Spruce Woods or Brook Loop

To get there: From North Conway, follow Route 16 North past the AMC Pinkham Notch Base Camp and the Mount Washington Auto Road. The campground will be on the left. From Gorham, follow Route 16 South to the campground on your right. If you come to the Mount Washington Auto Road traveling south, you've traveled too far.

of Mount Washington and the precipitous steep pitches of the mighty Huntington and Tuckerman Ravines, take a quick hike up the Square Ledge Trail. The trailhead is right across from the Pinkham Notch Base Camp on Route 16. The well-marked half-mile hike takes you up to Square Ledge over a rocky, root-crossed, and occasionally steep trail. Near the base of Square Ledge, you'll have to do some hand-over-hand scrambling to make it up, but it's well worth the effort once you walk out onto the ledge and drink in the cathedral-like view of the tallest mountain in New England.

As someone who skis Tuckerman Ravine every spring, I always find myself questioning my sanity when I get a good view of the Left Gully and the rest of the ravine without snow. It's almost unthinkable that people hike up there, much less ski down.

If you come to the Mount Washington area for winter activities like mountaineering or ice climbing and you want to camp, you won't be able to camp in Dolly Copp, as it closes in mid-October. However, Barnes Field, which is right off the same access road leading into Dolly Copp, is open year-round for winter camping or for group camping in season by reservation only.

DRY RIVER CAMPGROUND

Twin Mountain

---

on't get confused as you drive up through Crawford Notch. The state park campground where you'll want to land is called the Dry River Campground. There is a Crawford Notch Campground as well, but it lacks the deep wilderness appeal of Dry River.

Dry River is one of those campgrounds where there's not a bad site in the place. It's a small campground set within a moderately dense forest of mixed deciduous trees. There are lots of maple, birch, and ash trees in the forest. All of the campsites are very clean and very spacious. Its setting in Crawford Notch doesn't hurt one bit either. From your campsite, you are minutes from dramatically beautiful and challenging trails, world-class rock climbing at Frankenstein Cliffs, and towering waterfalls. You won't run out of things to do or places to explore when staying here.

Most of the campsites are spread out along a short loop that shoots off to the left as you enter the campground. There are several sites down a short road running straight off to the right, but we'll get to those later. Sites 2 and 3 are quite close to each other and would make a good pair of sites for a larger group. Site 4 is set well off the campground road and is nicely isolated, although it's close to the rest room and shower building. The last time I visited Dry River Campground, the shower building was under construction. The ranger

CAMPGROUND RATINGS

Beauty: ★★★★★
Site privacy: ★★★★★
Site spaciousness: ★★★★★
Quiet: ★★★★
Security: ★★★★★
Cleanliness/upkeep: ★★★★

Dry River Campground is quiet and intimate. It's one of those campgrounds where there's really not a bad site in the whole place.

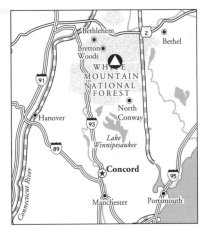

NEW HAMPSHIRE

told me it was scheduled to be completed before 2002, so by the time you read this, you should be able to shower off after a day of hiking in Crawford Notch.

No matter which site you land on here, you'll experience a nice sense of seclusion in a deep wilderness atmosphere. The trees open above most of the sites, which allows lots of light to filter down. Overall, Dry River's sites are thoughtfully laid out, both individually and in relation to one another. The sites aren't too densely packed together, and they fit in well with the forest character.

To Twin Mountain

DRY RIVER CAMPGROUND

Frankenstein Cliffs

302

To Glen →

The campsites situated on the outside of the campground loop road provide the greatest sense of seclusion. They are also a bit larger. In fact, site 12 is huge! This would be a great site if you have the five adult maximum in your camping group. You'll have plenty of room to spread out your tents and the rest of your gear, and still have room to let the kids run around and tire themselves out.

There is simply more room to spread out on the outer side of campground loops, and there's typically more forestation between sites, which deepens the sense of solitude. Sites 9, 11, and 16–21 are located on the outside of the campground loop road, and all provide a pleasant sense of isolation and spaciousness. Just past site 9, there's a trailhead for a short path down to Dry River.

One of the nicest sites here is site 16. This site is set up off the campground loop road, with lots of room between it and the neighboring sites. It's also the site closest to the Dry River. Between sites 18 and 19, there are trails to the Dry River Connection. From the campground, it's 0.2 miles to the Dry River, 2 miles to the Webster Cliff Trail, and 3 miles to the historic Willey House site.

Set way off on its own, site 20 is another epic site. It's incredibly spacious and surrounded by colossal deciduous trees with a few conifers mixed in, which makes for a diverse and interesting character to the forest.

There is still a decent sense of solitude to site 8, even though it's probably the most open site at Dry River. It's situated right where the campground loop reconnects with itself. Sites 4–7 and 22–24 are set up along the campground road leading to the loop, but they are all well off the road for a decent sense of seclusion.

Sites 27–31 are closer to Route 302, but they are among the nicest sites I've seen. Situated along a short spur off the campground road, just off to the right as you enter the campground (even before the ranger station), these sites are very spacious and very spread out.

The only site to which I wouldn't immediately gravitate is site 31, which is set at the very end of this short road. The site opens directly to the road, so anyone driving down the road would look like they're going to just drive right into your site. Still, it's very spacious and otherwise quite isolated, so it's not that bad. The only other drawback—and this is very minor—is that these sites are closer to Route 302. This can make for a bit of daytime road noise, but at night, it's as silent as the rest of the White Mountains.

The character of the Dry River campground mirrors that of its setting within Crawford Notch. There's a pleasant, diverse character to the forest and the campground, and no matter where you end up, you'll be in an excellent spot.

To get there: From North Conway and Bartlett, continue north on Route 302 and look for signs for the campground on the right as you head north.

KEY INFORMATION

Dry River Campground
Crawford Notch State Park
P.O Box 177
Twin Mountain, NH 03595

Operated by: New Hampshire Division of Parks and Recreation

Information: Crawford Notch State Park, (603) 374-2272

Open: Mid-May–mid-December

Individual sites: 31

Each site has: Fire ring and picnic table

Site assignment: First come, first served or by reservation

Registration: At ranger station; for reservations, call (603) 271-3628

Facilities: Hot showers, pit toilets

Parking: At sites

Fee: $13 for 2 adults and children under 18; each additional adult is $6.50, up to a max. of 5 adults

Restrictions:

Pets—On leash only

Fires—In established fire rings only

Alcoholic beverages—At sites only

Vehicles—Parking at campsites only

Other—Quiet hours 10 p.m.–8 a.m., check out by noon

HANCOCK CAMPGROUND

Lincoln

If you start traveling along New Hampshire's fabled Kancamagus Highway heading east, or from the Lincoln side to the Conway side, Hancock Campground is the first of the six Kancamagus campgrounds you'll encounter.

It's also one of two campgrounds along the Kancamagus that is open year-round. The other is Blackberry Crossing, at the other end of the "Kanc," as the locals call it. If you come to the Kanc for cross-country skiing or snowshoeing, or if you come to ski at nearby Loon Mountain and you want to do it on the cheap and with a dash of added adventure, pitching your tent at Hancock is the way to go.

Sites 1–21 are Hancock's tent-only sites. Within this tent zone, the sites that seem the most off on their own are 1, 2, 10, 12, 14, and 15. Check out these sites first to see if they're available and if they fulfill your need for solitude.

There's a central parking area situated near the two loosely spaced loops along which all the tent sites are located. You don't park right at the site as is the case with many campgrounds, so be prepared to lug in your gear a short distance. There are several areas within the Kancamagus campgrounds that have these types of sites, which are perfect for tent camping.

The tent-only sites at Hancock are moderately sized and reasonably spaced apart. This area also has its own bathroom, locat-

CAMPGROUND RATINGS

Beauty:	★★★★
Site privacy:	★★★
Site spaciousness:	★★★
Quiet:	★★★★
Security:	★★★★
Cleanliness/upkeep:	★★★★

Hancock is open year-round for winter camping, and it's close to Lincoln so it's a good spot to camp with kids.

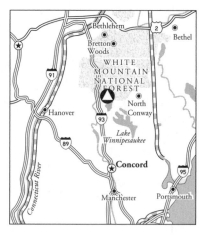

NEW HAMPSHIRE

ed right across from the sites in the parking area, so you don't have far to walk for those times when nature calls in the middle of the night.

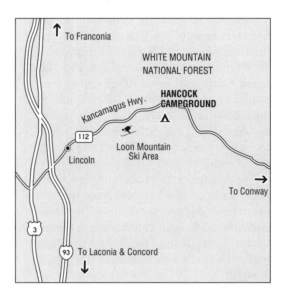

The rest of the campground's 56 sites are located a respectable distance from the tent-only area. You shouldn't discount these sites (22–56), even though you might find an RV or two. The sites are fairly spacious, and since the forest is pretty dense here, they're nicely buffered from each other, especially those on the outer end of the loop (sites 35–40).

These sites are also set within a beautiful birch grove. The first time I visited Hancock campground was on a classic New England fall day. There wasn't a cloud in the sky and the air was cool and dry. The sky took on a crystalline azure color. With the combination of the brilliance of the sun and the reflection of the light off the green and yellow leaves of the birches, the forest seemed to sparkle.

Also within this loop is where you'll find the trailhead for the short path to the East Branch of the Pemigewasset River, which is a perfect spot to drop a hook in the water (the trail departs between sites 43 and 45 on the outer side of the loop). There are also a few spots where you can drop yourself in the water, but be careful. Even late in the summer, that water can be mighty chilly. When you're looking for the path, just look beyond the trees for the looming presence of Black Mountain to the south of Hancock Campground and you'll know you're heading in the right direction.

All of the Kancamagus campgrounds are a stone's throw from a pristine river or any of a number of fabulous hiking trails. It would take you most of the summer to hike them all. Hancock is certainly no different. Right across the street, there's a trail that takes you up and over Potash Knob and Big Coolidge Mountain (and all the way to Mount Flume and Mount Liberty if you're so inclined). For a mellower hike, you can walk along the course of the Pemigewasset River.

Hancock is also the campground on the Kancamagus that is closest to civilization. At five miles east of Lincoln, it's close enough to run over and pick up bread, milk, batteries or anything else you may have forgotten or run out of. You could also have dinner or see a movie if you've been sleeping in a tent for several nights on end and need a little diversion.

The proximity to Lincoln makes Hancock one of the better Kancamagus campgrounds for families with small children. Kids love camping, but sometimes their tastes for dinner might include a pizza or hamburger, and if the weather hasn't been cooperative, an afternoon matinee can be just the antidote for a case of crankiness.

To get there: From Lincoln, follow Kancamagus Highway to Hancock campground on your right. It's the first campground you'll come to. From Conway, follow Kancamagus Highway to Hancock campground on your left. From this side, it will be the last campground you come to.

KEY INFORMATION

Hancock Campground
Kancamagus Highway
Lincoln, NH

Operated by: White Mountain National Forest

Information: Saco Ranger Station
33 Kancamagus Highway
RFD #1, Box 94
Conway, NH 03818
(603) 447-5448

Open: Year-round

Individual sites: 56

Each site has: Fire ring and picnic table

Site assignment: First come, first served

Registration: Select site then pay at self-service fee station

Facilities: Flush and vault toilets, fully plowed in winter

Parking: At sites or within the parking area for tent sites

Fee: $16

Restrictions:

Pets—Dogs on leash only

Fires—In fire rings only

Alcoholic beverages—At sites only

Vehicles—Two per site max.

Other—8 people per site max., 14-day max. stay

JIGGER JOHNSON CAMPGROUND

Albany

Jigger Johnson is the largest campground on the Kancamagus, but with its well-spaced loops, there's plenty of room for some quality tent camping beneath the statuesque conifers of the forest. There's one tent-only loop, which has nine sites reserved for our nylon-bound brethren, but the rest of the campground has plenty of sites where you can experience an air of woodland solitude.

The tent loop is the first loop on the left, containing sites 1–9. These are all nice, spacious sites set amidst the rolling contours of the forest floor. There is also a water spigot and a rest room just for this loop, so you won't have to go far for those essentials. Sites 6, 7, and 8, located at the far end of the loop, are the most spread out within the tent-only area. Whether you're only occupying one site or have come with several sites worth of campers, head to the end of the loop first to see what's available.

If the tent loop is full, don't despair. There are plenty of other great sites throughout Jigger Johnson. Most of the sites along the northeastern end of the campground near the banks of the Swift River are spacious and set amidst fairly dense forest. I especially like sites 47, 48, 50, 51, 53, 54, and 57. These sites have the most insular feel to them, plus they're close to the water spigots and the Swift River.

The sites on the loop off to the right as you enter the campground, while a bit

CAMPGROUND RATINGS

Beauty:	★★★★
Site privacy:	★★★★
Site spaciousness:	★★★★
Quiet:	★★★★
Security:	★★★★
Cleanliness/upkeep:	★★★★

Jigger Johnson is the biggest campground on the Kancamagus, but it still has a cozy feel.

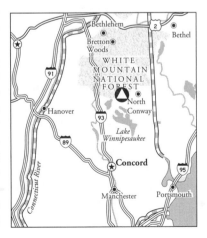

NEW HAMPSHIRE

more out in the open, are also excellent spots. True, you run the risk of an RV lumbering up next to you, but if there are already a number of tents in the area and on either side, which is often the case, you know you'll be in for a nice night. Most of the RVs seem to gravitate toward the sites on the main road heading through the campground.

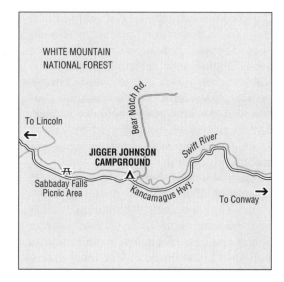

Over on the right side loop, the shorter trees and lower brush are somewhat sparse. This does open up the whole area at the ground level, but that effect combined with the towering pines that form the tall forest canopy engenders a surreal, almost mystical quality to the forest. This is particularly noticeable as dusk draws near. The sky overhead is still light, and the smoke from the campfires wafts through the trees and up to the forest canopy as darkness sneaks in beneath the pines. There's a cathedral-like atmosphere in this part of the campground in the quiet hours after dinner. The stillness is broken only by the occasional crack of a campfire.

Jigger Johnson, like the other campgrounds along the Kancamagus, is a self-serve kind of place. Enter the campground and find your perfect spot, then return to that odd-looking green cylinder, the "Iron Ranger" in Forest Service vernacular. Here's where you fill in your registration envelope, pay your fee, and slip it through the Iron Ranger's drop slot. If you need to speak with a real ranger or buy some firewood, you'll find the rangers down the road that leads off to the right just past the Iron Ranger.

This is also where you'll find the showers. Jigger Johnson is the only campground along the Kanc that has coin-operated hot showers, so don't be surprised if there are a few people waiting to clean up. There's even a little parking loop off to the left as you enter the campground for shower seekers from the other Kanc campgrounds.

There is a series of interpretive programs on Saturday evenings throughout the summer. They focus on a particular aspect of the local flora and fauna and can be quite informative and entertaining. The rangers who present these programs truly know their stuff, and they love to share their knowledge. The programs are usually held in the small, open area off to the left as you're heading down the short road to the showers. Check with the ranger for an update on the week's presentation, or check in at one of the well-marked campground host sites. The hosts are people who spend the entire season at the same site, and besides selling firewood, they are a fabulous source of campground information, suggestions for things to do in the area, and local yarns.

Jigger Johnson is located near the intersection of Bear Notch Road and the Kanc, so you could get there easily from Bartlett or from either side of the Kanc. If you run out of something, it's 9 miles to Bartlett and 13 miles to Conway.

The campground is also very close to some classic White Mountain hiking. Turn left out of the campground to get to trailheads for the Champney Falls Trail (which leads to the Three Sisters and the Middle Sister trail) or the Bolles Trail. Turn right on the Kanc out of Jigger

---

To get there: From Lincoln, follow Kancamagus Highway to Jigger Johnson campground on your left. From Conway, follow Kancamagus Highway to Jigger Johnson campground on your right, shortly after Bear Notch Road, also on the right.

KEY INFORMATION

Jigger Johnson Campground
Kancamagus Highway
Albany, NH

Operated by: White Mountain National Forest

Information: Saco Ranger Station
33 Kancamagus Highway
RFD #1, Box 94
Conway, NH 03818
(603) 447-5448

Open: Late May–mid-October

Individual sites: 76

Each site has: Fire ring, picnic table

Site assignment: First come, first served, no reservations

Registration: Select site then pay at self-service fee station

Facilities: Coin-operated showers, flush toilets, water spigots

Parking: At sites

Fee: $15

Restrictions:

Pets—Dogs on leash only

Fires—In fire rings only

Alcoholic beverages—At sites only

Vehicles—Two per site max.

Other—8 people per site max., 14 -day max. stay

Johnson to get to the Oliverian Brook, Downes Brook, Sabbaday Brook, or Sawyer Pond trails. Pack a few extra energy bars and plenty of water if you embark on a hike up the Champney Falls or Middle Sister trails. These lead to Mount Chocourua and the Three Sisters, a beautiful but energetic hike.

You can enjoy some great hikes leaving right out of the campground as well—no driving required! The trail that leads down to the banks of the Swift River intersects with a trail that runs along the backside of the campground. This mellow trail follows the Swift both upstream and downstream for quite a way, passing some beautiful bends in the river and through delightful aromatic groves of birch and pine. It's a great hike to take with kids, because it's relatively flat and there are all sorts of wonderful things to see and experience. Kids can spend hours poking around the banks of the Swift River, and despite its name, this segment of the river is usually fairly tame.

The last time I visited Jigger Johnson, after I had enjoyed my dinner and completely extinguished my campfire (note the not-so-subtle safety tip there), I grabbed a mug of tea and strolled through the campground. I wandered down the path leading to the Swift River. Down by the sandy riverbanks, I sat on part of an old tree trunk as the moon rose from behind the forest into the night sky. I must have sat there for hours basking in the serene, silvery light.

LAFAYETTE CAMPGRO ...

Franconia

Simply by virtue of its location, Lafayette Campground is worth inclusion in this guidebook. The fact that it's a super campground makes it that much better. Lafayette is nestled in the base of the Franconia Valley. As you drive up the Franconia Notch Parkway toward the campground, your view is framed by Cannon Mountain to the left and Mount Lafayette to the right.

Franconia Notch is a veritable sculpture garden displaying works shaped by the forces of nature. From the glaciers that carved the landscape millions of years ago to the tenacious and incessant wind and water, the lay of the land here is as dramatic as anywhere else in New Hampshire. From the waterfalls of the Flume Gorge and the swirling pools of the Basin to the Old Man of the Mountain and Indian Head formations presiding over the eastern flanks of the Presidential range, you could spend weeks here before crossing your paths.

The notch is also headquarters for just about any outdoor activity. There's fly-fishing at nearby Echo Lake, a bike path that winds along the base of the notch, and some fantastic treks for hikers of any ability. Right from the campground, the Lonesome Lake Trail takes you 1,000 feet above the floor of the notch to Lonesome Lake. The trailhead for the 1.5-mile hike is near the entrance to the campground.

CAMPGROUND RATINGS

Beauty: ★★★★
Site privacy: ★★★
Site spaciousness: ★★★★
Quiet: ★★★
Security: ★★★
Cleanliness/upkeep: ★★★★

Lafayette Place is tucked into the valley of Franconia Notch, home to some of the White Mountain's most spectacular hiking and mountain vistas.

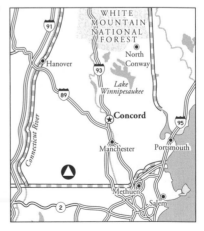

NEW HAMPSHIRE

There's also a trailhead over between sites 67 and 68 that leads to the Basin. From the Basin, you could hike up to Kinsman Falls on Cascade Brook. Follow the half-mile Basin Cascades Trail from the Basin to reach this beautiful and secluded spot.

Lafayette Campground is set beneath a fairly dense forest of conifers and hardwoods. Sites 1–51 are available only by reservation, so if you haven't made a reservation, start your site search at site 52 and work your way up.

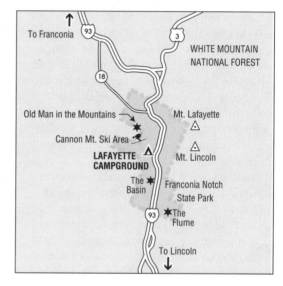

The sites numbered in the upper 40s are very spacious. The forest overhead is open to the sky, which lets a lot of sunlight filter down through to the floor of the campsites. Sites 47 and 49 are too open for me. These sites are also situated right along the campground road. Site 50 is open and set right on the road, but it also has the Pemigewasset River running along behind the site. Site 51, across the campground road from 50, is also very exposed to the road.

Further down the campground road on this side, site 52 is a nicely secluded site. It's set off the road and also has the Pemigewasset running along behind it. The platform where you'd set up your tent and picnic table is down a bit lower than the road, which adds a degree of seclusion.

The Lonesome Lake Trail runs right between sites 53 and 54. Sites 54, 56, and 57 are very open and have little privacy from each other or the neighboring sites. Sites 56 and 58 would be good pair of sites for a larger group needing two contiguous sites. There is a bit of road noise in the background in this part of the campground from the Franconia Notch Parkway. This decreases as you get further back from the road and deeper into the woods.

There's a nice sense of seclusion between sites 61 and 63 and the neighboring sites. These two sites are also quite spacious. Sites 64 and 66 are another good pair of sites well suited for a large group. These sites are also situated right along the banks of the Pemigewasset, which defines the eastern border of the campground.

Both the ground cover and the forest canopy are less dense in this corner of the campground, so there's a very spacious and sunlit character to sites 58–70. Lots of breeze flows through the sites.

A huge maple tree grows up through the center of site 88. This spacious site is set up on the outside of the campground loop. It's fairly well isolated from the neighboring sites on either side, but a bit open to the road.

Set up off the campground road on a small rise and surrounded by a fairly dense grove of young deciduous trees, site 97 provides a nice sense of seclusion. However, it's right across the road from the rest rooms. Sites 92 and 94 are too open for me, and 94 is also next to the rest room building on the same side of the road. The Lonesome Lake Trail runs through the campground between sites 93 and 95 on one side of the road and sites 92 and 94 on the other, so these would be good sites to choose if you wanted to be right on the trail, but expect passers-by.

The area with sites 73–78 is nice. These sites feel a bit more set off than some of

To get there: Follow Route 93 North to the Franconia Notch Parkway. This is a divided highway, so you'll actually drive past the campground and take the next exit off the parkway, then head south. From there, follow the signs for the campground on the right as you head south.

KEY INFORMATION

Lafayette Campground, Franconia Notch State Park Franconia Notch Parkway Franconia, NH

Operated by: New Hampshire Division of Parks and Recreation

Information: Lafayette Campground, (603) 823-9513

Open: Mid-May–Columbus Day

Individual sites: 98 sites

Each site has: Fire ring, picnic table

Site assignment: First come, first served; sites 1–51 are available by reservation only

Registration: At ranger station as you enter campground; for reservations, call (603) 271-3628

Facilities: Hot showers, flush toilets, water

Parking: At sites

Fee: $16

Restrictions: *NO PETS*

Pets—On leash only

*Fires—*In established fire rings only

*Alcoholic beverages—*At sites only

*Vehicles—*Parking at sites only

the sites on the outside of the campground loop. Site 73 is very spacious, open, and sunny. Site 76 is a bit more shaded. Site 75 is also bright and airy, and framed by a wall of maple trees. Alas, site 79 is too close to the rest room buildings.

Now, back to the reservation-only sites. Perched at an odd little intersection of the campground loop roads, site 43 has lots of woods surrounding it with no neighbors on either side. By virtue of its location, this site provides a nice sense of seclusion. Sites 40 and 29 are also at odd angles in this three-way intersection, but consequently they provide a decent sense of seclusion. Site 29 is very open and sunny, with large granite boulders framing the back border of the site.

Sites 36 and 37 are set up for disabled access. These are nice spacious sites set within a grove of fairly dense mixed forest. Site 27 is very spacious, however it's a bit too open for me and it's set right on the campground loop road.

Set in the woods around a small grassy field, there's a nice, open pastoral sense to sites 22–26. They are a bit open and not quite as private as the more densely wooded sites, but very scenic nonetheless. Sites 20 and 21 are also on the outside edge of this open field. Site 21 is a tiny site wedged in between sites 20 and 22, almost as if it were an afterthought.

There's an open, yet secluded sense to site 17, as it's set up on a small rise overlooking the field through a loosely spaced grove of young deciduous trees. Sites 15 and 16 are group sites. Right on the grassy field, these are wide open prairie camping. There's no privacy at all, but you'd have plenty of room for a group, and a clear shot at the sky for stargazing. Sites 18 and 19 are close to the rest room building, but tucked into the woods a bit deeper for a decent sense of seclusion. Within this group, sites 11 and 12 are a bit too close to the rest rooms.

The small loop with sites 1–10 also surrounds a small grassy field. These areas make great spots to let kids run around, throw a Frisbee, or otherwise burn off some steam while you're relaxing at the site. Sites 7–10 are quite nice. They are spacious, open, and fairly well isolated from the neighboring sites. Sites 5 and 6 and sites 1 and 3 would be good pairs of sites for larger groups, as they are very open to each other. If you didn't know your neighbors here before setting up camp, you would shortly thereafter.

There's a small amphitheater and rows of benches at the entrance to the 1–10 loop where the rangers run nature programs. Check with them as you register to find out what's on the sched .

MOUNT MONADNOCK STATE PARK

Jaffrey

Mount Monadnock is renowned as the most frequently climbed mountain in the world, a distinction that used to belong to Mt. Fuji in Japan. On warm, summer weekend days, there is often a veritable conga line of hikers making their way up the fabulous White Dot trail or any of the other classic routes to the bald, treeless summit. Its popularity, however, does nothing to detract from its allure and magnificence.

Why do so many people flock to Monadnock? For one thing, perched as it is in the southwestern corner of New Hampshire, it's fairly accessible from most of southern New Hampshire, northern Massachusetts, and eastern Vermont. It's a moderate hike, certainly when compared to some of the longer or steeper hikes you'll find further north in the New Hampshire's White Mountains or Vermont's Green Mountains. The most predominant attraction has to be the view from the summit of Monadnock. It is absolutely huge. It's expansive. It's a sweeping, panoramic view that extends in every direction as far as you can see, which is pretty far when the air is clear and sun is brilliant.

You see nearby Dublin Lake and the gently rolling and densely forested topography of southern New England. Small towns dotted here and there punctuate the undulating coniferous carpet. The unfettered views from Monadnock's summit

CAMPGROUND RATINGS

Beauty: ★★★★
Site privacy: ★★★
Site spaciousness: ★★★★
Quiet: ★★★★
Security: ★★★★
Cleanliness/upkeep: ★★★★★

Monadnock State Park is the perfect base camp from which to launch your southern New Hampshire hiking adventures. The mountain itself is well traveled, but after the day crowds leave, you'll have it to yourself.

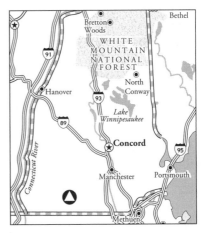

NEW HAMPSHIRE

are a product of Monad-
nock's history. It appears to
poke above the tree line, but
at 3,165 feet, it's really not
quite tall enough. The
mountain owes its treeless
summit to settlers in the
early 1900s who burned off
the forest at the peak in an
effort to control the local
wolf population. Such man-
euvers to direct the forces of
nature rarely work, but it
has resulted in Mount Monadnock going prematurely
bald.

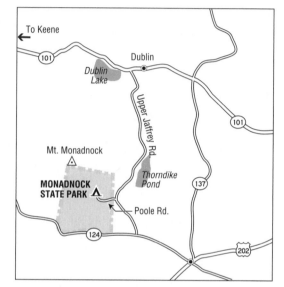

While the day crowds to
the mountain may seem a
bit overwhelming, once they've returned home for the night, you and a
small group of campers will have the park and the campground at the base
of the mountain to yourselves. The campground is fairly small, with 21 individual sites and 7 group sites. As you enter the park, you pass the ranger's
toll station. Here, you instantly discover the park's primary restriction if you
happen to have a four-legged member of the family in your car. There are no
dogs allowed at the campground or anywhere within Monadnock State
Park. Assuming you're not breaking that most sacred of Monadnock State
Park's rules, continue into the park. The campground is just up the road off
to the right.

Most of the sites within this campground are available by reservation only.
The letter-designated sites are the group sites. These sites are available exclu-
sively by reservation. This poses an interesting predicament, as some of the
nicer sites, in my view, are the non-reservable sites. You could wing it and try
your luck getting one of these sites. If fortune smiles upon you, you'll have a
grand camping experience. However, you could also find the campground

full to capacity, which is a very real possibility considering the traffic this state park gets during the summer.

Even though the campground is right off the road leading into the park (near the day parking for hikers, the camp store, and the primary trailhead for getting onto the mountain), you'll still feel as if you've left all that behind when you turn into the campground. Heading right on the campground loop road brings you to sites 6–8. These are tucked off on their own and provide a nice sense of isolation. The forest of mixed conifers, birch, and other hardwoods is fairly dense here so you still feel as if the woods are surrounding you and your campsite. Site 14 is another of the non-reservable sites that's tucked into its own grove of trees. All of these sites on the outer side of the campground seem to have a bit more space in between.

Monadnock State Park is a great spot to come with a group for some weekend hiking. The sites designated for group camping are quite nice, and I'd be thrilled to spend a few nights in one of these group sites with a band of hiking compadres. Site C is one of the nicer group sites. It's set against a gently sloping hill within a grove of loosely spaced, very homogenous pine trees. Site D is another beautiful site that is also set within it's own pine grove. There's a stand of young white pines lining the

To get there: Follow Route 101 to Dublin. If heading west on 101, take the Jaffrey Center Road on the left after going through town. There's a sign for Monadnock State Park. Heading east on 101, take the Jaffrey Center Road on the right, after Dublin Lake and before downtown Dublin. Follow this road for several miles to the campground on the right.

KEY INFORMATION

Monadnock State Park
P.O. Box 181
Jaffrey, NH 03452-0181

Operated by: New Hampshire Division of Parks and Recreation

Information: Monadnock State Park, (603) 532-8862

Open: Year-round, although the campground is not snow-plowed. Sites may be reserved from mid-May–Columbus Day

Individual sites: 21 individual sites, 7 group sites

Each site has: Fire ring, picnic table

Site assignment: First come, first served, or by reservation

Registration: Check in at ranger station; for reservations, call (603) 271-3628 or (877) NH-PARKS (within the state)

Facilities: Coin-operated showers (new showers recently installed), flush toilets, vault toilets, camp store

Parking: At sites, additional parking available

Fee: $12

Restrictions:

Pets—No dogs allowed

Fires—In fire rings only

Alcoholic beverages—At sites only

Vehicles—Parking at sites only

Other— 2-day min. stay at reserved sites, 14-day max. stay

perimeter like a vigilant group of sentries. All of the group sites have two picnic tables (the individual sites have one), which is a thoughtful setup since you'll certainly have more people in these sites needing a place to sit.

There are numerous vault toilet facilities spread throughout the campground, so you'll never have to amble too far when nature calls. If you prefer, there are also flush toilets located just outside the campground. There are several water fountains, but when you need to fill your drinking-water bottles, there's a spring up on the mountain not too far from the campground. Assemble the troops and take a short hike up the White Dot trail to the spring just off to the left, just below the junction where the Spruce Link trail veers off to the left. Treat yourself to some cold, crystal clear, mountain spring water. It's well worth the effort.

Ah yes, the hiking. There is a plethora of hiking trails wending its way throughout Monadnock State Park, all leading up, over, and around the mountain. The White Dot trail is the most popular route up to the summit. The White Cross trail, which forks off the White Dot Trail just past the Spruce Link Trail, is another good option. Both have a few spots where you're doing a little hand over hand scrambling up and over the rocks. Both also pass across a couple of open ledges on the way up where you'll get your first taste of the sweeping vistas.

From the summit, and from several other trails leading off the mountain in all directions, you could hike as far as Mount Sunapee if you're so inclined. That brings up a point about directions. If you're coming into the park from Dublin on the Dublin road, you'll see two places marked as Monadnock State Park. The first is the trailhead for the Birchtoft Trail. Don't turn in here, keep going another half-mile or so to the main part of the state park where you'll find the campground. Keep the location of that trailhead in mind though. If you want to try a longer route to the summit of Monadnock, the Birchtoft Trail is a fantastic hike.

Mount Monadnock does get a lot of hikers, but there's always a bit of the mountain with a good view that you can have all to yourself, just for the moment.

PASSACONAWAY CAMPGROUND

Bartlett

The sites within Passaconaway Campground are all quite spacious. This can be both a blessing and a curse. Of all the campgrounds along the Kancamagus, Passaconaway is probably most conducive to RVs. They are neither catered to (no hookups) nor excluded, but many of the smaller campsites at the other Kancamagus campgrounds naturally preclude land yachts by virtue of their size or shape.

On the other hand, the spaciousness of the Passaconaway sites makes them well suited to larger groups or families that need a little extra breathing room. The relatively central location along the Kancamagus Highway also puts you in a good spot if you're not sure what part of the Kanc you want to explore. You'll be close to Rocky Gorge, Sabbaday Falls, the Swift River picnic area, and the myriad trailheads spread along the length of this superlative stretch of road.

The forest separating the individual sites at Passaconaway is fairly dense, so even if an RV or a larger group plunks down next to you, you won't see all that much of them. There is lots of undergrowth, which provides seclusion and adds to the silence of the woods. Besides spacious sites, quiet is a prevailing attribute of Passaconaway. All you'll hear is an occasional vehicle zipping past on the Kanc and the soft rush of the wind in the evergreens, punctuated by the chatter of the forest birds and animals.

CAMPGROUND RATINGS

Beauty:	★★★★
Site privacy:	★★★★
Site spaciousness:	★★★★
Quiet:	★★★★★
Security:	★★★★
Cleanliness/upkeep:	★★★★

Passaconaway is a relatively small campground with very spacious sites carved out of a dense evergreen forest.

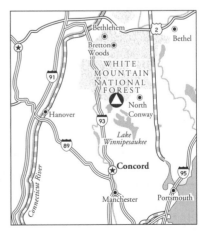

97

NEW HAMPSHIRE

There are two loops in which the sites are situated. Sites 1–11 are in the loop off to the right as you enter the campground. Sites 12–33 are in the loop off to the left. The campsites are carved out of a dense forest of mostly coniferous trees, so there's a cool, dark, shaded feeling to the campground.

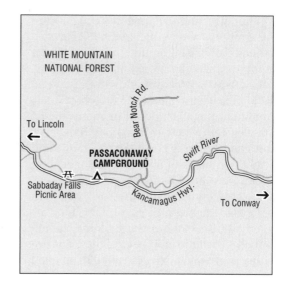

At the beginning of the 1–11 loop, sites 2, 3, and 11 are too open and close to the rest rooms for my taste. Sites 5–11 are set along the outer edge of the loop off to the right. These sites, mostly by virtue of their location on the outside of the loop road, provide the greatest sense of solitude. There's simply more room between the sites.

My favorite site on this loop, and one of the best in the campground, is site 10. This site is set well off on its own, with plenty of space between the neighboring sites on either side. It's also further off the campground loop road for an enhanced sense of isolation.

In the 12–33 loop, the forest is even more dense than in the 1–11 loop. On this side of the campground, the forest is comprised primarily of pines and maples, many towering around 80 feet. A moderately dense understory fills in the forest picture and adds to the sense of seclusion between the individual campsites. In this loop, sites 13, 14, and 15 are close to the rest room.

The sites on this loop are located both along the inside and outside of the campground road. There's a small picnic area near site 13. There are pros and cons to this. It's a nice place to have the kids running around close to the campsite, but it could also tend to be a bit noisier during the day. Like most of life's major decisions, whether or not you choose this site will probably be dictated by the presence of little ones.

There's a trailhead right next to site 18. From the Passaconaway campground, you are near several hiking trails suitable for all ability levels. There are the long, but not too steep Sawyer Pond Trail and the shorter but steeper Downes Brook, Sabbaday Brook, and Oliverian Brook Trails across the Kanc.

The campground host is located at site 19. This is a good place to stop if you need a suggestion on daytime activities, or just to catch a bit of local lore.

The sites numbered in the lower 20s are generally a bit smaller than the rest of Passaconaway's spacious sites and are packed in more tightly. In this group, you're closer to your neighbors and sacrifice a modicum of privacy and quiet, but you're also less likely to have an RV drop anchor nearby. Still, there is a decent amount of forest buffering these sites.

Huge maples frame sites 22 and 23. There are also massive maples growing up within the sites themselves. You feel as if you're camping among magnificent trees, and you truly are.

There's a short hike in to site 24 from where you park. Site 24 is the key site here at Passaconaway. The distance from the campground loop road lends it a deep sense of seclusion.

Site 29 is way too close to the bathroom for me. Sites 31 and 33 are very open to the road.

Considering Passaconaway's central location on the Kanc, it's a fine spot to set up camp, especially if you are able to secure site 10 or site 24.

To get there: Passaconaway Campground is almost in the center of the Kancamagus Highway. From Lincoln, follow the Kancamagus Highway for 16 miles to Passaconaway campground on the left. From Conway, follow Kancamagus Highway for 15 miles to Passaconaway campground on the right.

KEY INFORMATION

Passaconaway Campground
Kancamagus Highway
Bartlett, NH
Operated by: White Mountain National Forest

Information: Saco Ranger Station
33 Kancamagus Highway
RFD #1, Box 94
Conway, NH 03818
(603) 447-5448

Open: Mid-May–mid-October

Individual sites: 33

Each site has: Fire ring, picnic table

Site assignment: First come, first served

Registration: Select site then pay at self-service fee station

Facilities: Vault toilets, hand pumps for water

Parking: At sites

Fee: $14

Restrictions:

Pets—Dogs on leash only

Fires—In fire rings only

Alcoholic beverages—At campsites only

Vehicles—Two per site max.

Other—8 people per site max., 14 -day max. stay

PAWTUCKAWAY STATE PARK
Nottingham

There are campsites at Pawtuckaway State Park that give you the atmosphere of island camping with the ease of car camping. It's a big place, with 193 sites, but the 3 separate camping areas feel like individual campgrounds.

Horse Island has many of the best sites within the campground, that is to say the most sites right on the shores of Pawtuckaway Lake. Big Island has some pristine water view sites, but most of the sites in this area are located inland. Neal's Cove is located near the store, the beach, and the group camping area. These sites, because of their proximity to the beach and playground, are great for families with kids.

Horse Island is home to sites 1–80. The island is covered in a fairly dense forest, which lends a nice woodland feel and sense of privacy to most of these sites. The forest is composed of mixed hardwoods and conifers, although a bit heavier on the conifers, which fill in the forest and provide a cool, dark sense of stillness and seclusion. The sites themselves are clean and spacious, and most have a firm, sandy surface on which to pitch your tent.

I was camped on Horse Island once, and had just finished cleaning up from breakfast when a gray heron walked right through my site as if he owned the place. He may well have, but I was too flustered and spellbound to ask him. At Pawtuckaway State Park, Horse Island is where

CAMPGROUND RATINGS

Beauty: ★★★★
Site privacy: ★★★★
Site spaciousness: ★★★★
Quiet: ★★★
Security: ★★★★
Cleanliness/upkeep: ★★★★

The campground at Pawtuckaway State Park has a lot of sites, but they're split into three different areas so it has a more intimate feel than you might expect. There are also a lot of sites right on the shores of Lake Pawtuckaway.

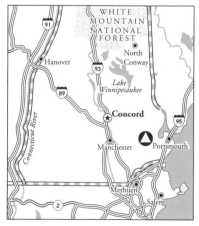

NEW HAMPSHIRE

you want to be. The sites that aren't right on the water at least have a water view.

The top-notch Horse Island waterfront sites include 38, 42, 43, 44, 45, 46, and 47. Swimming is not permitted from campsites because there is a considerable amount of boat traffic in the lake, especially on the weekends. But, you could easily launch a canoe or kayak right from your site. Swimming is allowed in the beach and boat launch areas.

While site 48 is situated near an intersection of the campground road, its lakeside setting more than compensates for any traffic that may pass by. Sites 74, 75, and 77 also have nice lakeside settings.

The cluster of sites 65–70 is grouped at one end of Horse Island. These sites have dramatic, lakeside settings. Sites 67–69 are perched on their own peninsula jutting out from the southeastern end of the island. If your group is large enough to need three sites and you secure these, you will indeed be set.

There is a boat launch and lake access right near sites 58, 60, 62, and 63. These are perfect sites if you like to begin or end your day with a blissful paddle on the still waters of the sleepy lake. Sites 53, 54, and 55 are also primo lakeside spots. These sites are set within loosely spaced forest right on the shores of Pawtuckaway Lake, which allows for dramatic views, cool breezes, and shafts of sunlight. I have no scientific evidence to support this, but these lakeside sites seemed less buggy than the inland sites to me.

Sites 1, 2, and 25 are right off the campground road leading onto Horse Island, but they have a decent sense of seclusion as they are all tucked down off the road amidst a dense grove of spruce. Sites 4 and 7 are nicely isolated and set down off the campground loop road facing a small cove. These sites are in a dense spruce grove, where the forest floor gently rolls down to the lakeside. The main body of the lake is around the corner, so it's quieter here as you're removed from the primary thoroughfare through Pawtuckaway Lake. The lake can get pretty heavily populated with ski boats, Jet Skis, and other vessels making more noise than the rhythmic splash of a kayak or canoe paddle.

The sites numbered in the teens are set beneath a loose forest and within view of a small cove. The water is often peaceful and quiet here, but does get stirred up during the day. Site 21 is on the water and has a perfectly flat, easy access for launching a canoe or kayak. This site is a paddler's dream. Sites 26 and 27 are nicely isolated from both the road and from other sites, but they are close to each other. They would make a nice pair of sites for a larger family or group.

The Big Island (sounds like Hawaii) section of Pawtuckaway State Park is home to sites 81–169. Sites 96–169 are available by reservation only. The first come, first served sites are spacious and set within fairly dense forest. A couple of the sites on the left as you enter the Big Island area have steep driveways.

Overall, Big Island is more hilly than the rest of the campground. There are many sites with steep entries up or down from the road. Just keep that in mind as you select a site so you're not surprised. This is especially true of sites 164–169.

RVs and trailers are not expressly prohibited from the sites on Horse Island or

To get there: Follow Route 101 to 156 in Raymond. Follow Route 156 to Mountain Road, and then follow the signs for the park.

KEY INFORMATION

Pawtuckaway State Park
128 Mountain Road
Nottingham, NH 03290
Operated by: New Hampshire Division of Parks and Recreation

Information: Pawtuckaway State Park, (603) 895-3031

Open: Mid-May–Columbus Day

Individual sites: 193

Each site has: Fire ring, picnic table

Site assignment: First come, first served or by reservation

Registration: At campground headquarters

Facilities: Flush toilets, hot showers, water spigots, boat launch, canoe and paddle boat rentals

Parking: At sites

Fee: $16–$22 (The premium water sites are the more expensive ones. C'mon, go for it. It's worth it!)

Restrictions:

Pets—On leash only

Fires—In established fire rings only

Alcoholic beverages—At sites only

Vehicles—Parking at sites only

Other—2-day min. stay for reservations (3-day min. for holiday weekends), 14-day max. stay

Big Island, but those steep, twisty, or narrow entries leading into the sites would preclude one of these behemoths plunking down next to you. There are some sites that are more open than others, but for the most part, access (or lack thereof) is your best friend.

The Big Island sites are also fairly well isolated from each other, especially sites 162 and 163. These two are situated at the end of a short spur off the campground road, and set within a dense forest of mixed hardwoods and evergreens.

Sites 90–93 are set within a deep, dark spruce forest. After site 93, the forest population shifts to more deciduous trees. Walking through the campground road past these sites, it can feel like someone just turned on the lights. You move from the dense, dark spruce forest to the more open and brilliant green deciduous forest.

Big Island doesn't have as many water view sites, but it does have some. Site 108 gets you back on the water. Sites 113–118, in their own little loop, all have an unfettered view of the lake and access to launch a canoe or kayak.

The most desirable site within this section is site 122. Feel free to request this site, unless, of course, I happen to be traveling to Pawtuckaway that day. Well, in that case you can still request it. We'll just have to share the site, which shouldn't be a problem since site 122 is absolutely huge.

Site 122 booked already? Not to worry. There are plenty of other great sites in this part of the campground and the 123–133 loop. Sites 130 and 133 are very well isolated at the end of this loop. Site 131, on the other hand, is too open. It looks like you could drive right through the site if you didn't know it was there. The sites in this corner of the campground are set beneath an open deciduous forest, so there's a light and open feel to these sites.

At the end of the 134–146 loop, sites 141–143 are quite secluded in their own little cluster. Sites 141 and 142 are actually quite close together, but very well situated for a group needing two contiguous sites. Sites 150–152 are set up off the road for a solid sense of seclusion. Site 96 is perched down off an intersection of the road where the 150–154 road heads off, but the site is well isolated by the dense forest and quite large.

Neals Cove is actually the first camping area you come to on the 2-mile access road leading into Pawtuckaway State Park. Most of these sites are smaller, but carved out of dense forest, so what they lack in spaciousness they make up for in seclusion. There's a dense, inland feel as you enter this part of the campground, even though you're still quite close to the lake. The beach, camp store, reservation-only group camping areas, picnic area, playground, and baseball field are also near Neals Cove.

Within this part of the campground, sites 206 and up are set along the water within a loosely spaced forest for dramatic water views and some nice breezes cooling down your campsite. Site 221 is somewhat open to the road, but set beneath a dense and statuesque spruce grove. The towering spruce trees populating the forest at Neals Cove give the woods a majestic feel. There's a footbridge right next to site 218 leading onto another small island. This island doesn't have any campsites, but it's a perfect spot to hike out with a lunch or to just sit and watch the lake in the early morning or at dusk.

PILLSBURY STATE PARK

Washington

The woods and the water are a powerful combination. Pillsbury State Park
has both and in just the right propor-
tions—a series of crystalline ponds cast
against a dense blanket of forest like scattered jewels. Although it's part of the New
Hampshire State Park system, Pillsbury is
a little known gem. It rests quietly in the
deep forest just south of the far more popular and more frequently visited Sunapee
State Park, and that's just fine.

When I first entered this campground, I
was immediately struck with a moral and
ethical dilemma. "Do I really want to tell
anyone else about this place?" I honestly
didn't ruminate on this thought for long
though. After considering the proclivities
and desires of a reader who sought out this
book and would naturally seek out magical spots like this, I had to include Pillsbury State Park. There is not a bad site in
the whole place, and many of the sites are
elevated to paradise status, especially
those at the water's edge.

As soon as you pull into the lengthy
access road, which winds along the shores
of Butterfield Pond first and then May
Pond, you'll know you've found someplace special. If you've come to fully
immerse yourself in the solitude of the
deep wilderness, you have most definitely
come to the right place. The campsites are
spread out along this road, either alone or
in clusters. Most are right on or very close
to the shores of May Pond. Several are

CAMPGROUND RATINGS

Beauty:	★★★★★
Site privacy:	★★★★★
Site spaciousness:	★★★★★
Quiet:	★★★★★
Security:	★★★★★
Cleanliness/upkeep:	★★★★★

*Many of Pillsbury State Park's
campsites are so spread out from
each other that you'll feel as if you
have the campground to yourself.*

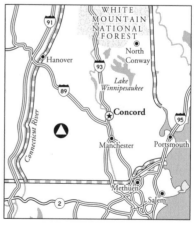

NEW HAMPSHIRE

inland, tucked into the dense forest that surrounds the ponds and marshy areas in the park.

The first sites you'll come to are 1 and 1A, off the main access road to the left at the end of a short drive. You can park at site 1, but 1A is a walk-in site. These are the only two sites on the shores of Vickery Pond, one of the smaller ponds in the park. Want to be off by yourself? Bring a small group, even just two couples, you'll have this pond to yourself.

Next along the main road

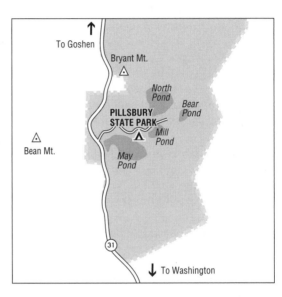

is site 2. Although this site is right off the access road, it is also completely on it's own. This is another great site to choose if you want to enjoy waterfront camping in relative solitude. Site 2 is perched on the shore of Butterfield Pond. The only other site on this pond is site 39, which is on the other side of the pond and is accessible only by canoe or kayak.

Sites 3–7 are grouped together in a small cluster further up the road on the right. These are set on a small peninsula that helps define the border between Butterfield Pond and May Pond. There is also a pair of pit toilets here. Further along the road, also waterside, is the small loop with sites 9–19. These sites are within the largest and most densely packed cluster of sites in the park, but even these are quite nice. Within this loop, go for sites 11, 12, and 14, as they are right on the shores of May Pond. Site 15 is pretty darn close to the pond as well.

Toward the end of the campground road are sites 23, 24, 26, and 40. At site 40, you park across from a footbridge over a small stream. Cross the bridge and turn right on the footpath that leads down to site 40, nestled right on the shoreline of the pond. It is well worth every trip to the car. You'll have your own slice of forest right on your own corner of the pond.

If you're a paddler, do what you can to reserve either site 38 or 39. These are the canoe- or kayak-accessible sites. It's just a short paddle across May Pond to site 38 or Butterfield Pond to site 39. Then you'll feel as if you're camping on an island, and you'll have your canoe or kayak right there to explore both of the interconnected Butterfield and May ponds. Some of the same considerations of island camping apply here, besides the pack-in, pack-out ethic. Be sure you have brought everything you need. A trip back to your vehicle will take some effort.

Besides the paddling, wildlife viewing, and relaxing by the shores of the pond, there is a massive network of hiking trails winding through Pillsbury State Park. The park itself and its trails are part of the Monadnock-Sunapee Greenway, a 51-mile route that connects the two peaks. It's sort of like a mini (very mini) Appalachian Trail.

The Monadnock-Sunapee Trail is the main thoroughfare here. You could get quite far along the trail, so set a predetermined turnaround time to leave yourself enough light to make it back to camp. The peaks of Kittredge Mountain and Lovewell Mountain, both within Pillsbury State Park, are good day hikes from the campground on this trail. The Ayers Pond Trail is a nice, long route that ultimately leads out to Ayers Pond.

Back at camp, the mirror-like surface of a pond will reflect the last light of the day. You may be treated to the sight of a great blue heron swooping down for a final landing, or you might spot a moose wandering about the wetlands. Pillsbury State Park is a true wilderness getaway.

To get there: Follow Route 31 from Hillsborough and Washington. The park is on the right, about 15 miles past the center of Washington.

KEY INFORMATION

Pillsbury State Park
Route 31
Washington, NH

Operated by: New Hampshire Division of Parks and Recreation

Information: Pillsbury State Park (603) 863-2860

Open: Early May–Columbus Day

Individual sites: 40 sites, including two canoe sites

Each site has: Fire ring

Site assignment: By reservation or first come, first served; all but 8 sites can be reserved

Registration: Check in at ranger station; for reservations, call (603) 271-3628 or (877) NHPARKS (within the state)

Facilities: Pit toilet, water spigots, playground, canoe rentals

Parking: At sites or in small parking areas for lug-in or canoe sites

Fee: $13

Restrictions:

Pets—Dog on leash only

Fires—In fire rings only

Alcoholic beverages—At sites only

Vehicles—Park at or near campsites

Other—14-day max. stay, 5 adults per site max.

VERMONT

ALLIS STATE PARK

Randolph

Allis State Park is one place you won't find by accident, but it's definitely worth the trip. It's not too far from Route 89, which cuts through the middle of Vermont, but it's a circuitous route to the park from the highway. You'll turn down a state road that looks like someone's driveway and then it promptly turns to a dirt road. At that point, you're almost there! When you do get there, you'll be glad you found it, as it is a phenomenally peaceful campground. Its isolation is part of its charm.

While there are a few sites set along the edge of an open field in the center of the campground, most are fantastically nestled into the dense forest. Allis State Park has 18 tent sites. Sites 15–18 are set along the border of the forest and the field. This makes for a nice pastoral setting, but not quite as much privacy. You'll also get some delightful breezes blowing across the field and through your site, and you'll be in a perfect spot to relax in the sun or spend some time stargazing at night.

There's a combined sense of isolation and pastoral openness to site 13. It's carved out of the dense forest and set down from the edge of the field. Although sites 17 and 18 are visible across the field, the site is still quite isolated from the rest of the campground.

The next site along the campground loop road is one of the most profoundly secluded sites in Vermont. Site 14 is set along a

CAMPGROUND RATINGS

Beauty:	★★★★★
Site privacy:	★★★★★
Site spaciousness:	★★★★★
Quiet:	★★★★★
Security:	★★★
Cleanliness/upkeep:	★★★★

If silence and solitude are what you seek, Allis State Park is a fantastic choice.

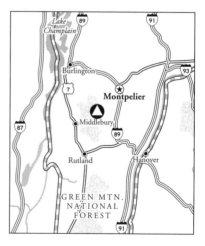

VERMONT

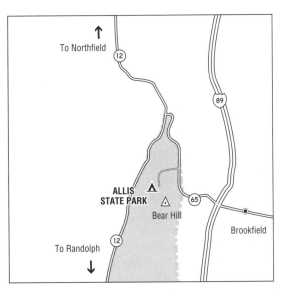

road leading off the main campground loop to the right. This road eventually rejoins the main road leading into Allis State Park, but site 14 is the only campsite on this road, off completely on its own. You couldn't ask for a deeper sense of solitude and wilderness isolation.

The moderately spacious site is set within a fairly dense forest. The undergrowth about the site is thick with lush ferns. The road leading up to and past the site becomes increasingly less maintained, and would make a perfect short hike or mountain bike ride, as its connection with the entrance road allows for a loop route. The beautiful, diverse character of the surrounding forest and its absolute isolation make site 14 at Allis State Park one of the top sites you'll find anywhere in New England.

There's a solid sense of seclusion to site 12 as well, even when compared to the magical solitude of site 14. For site 12, you park right on the campground loop road and hike in about 50 feet. You can see through the forest to neighboring site 13, but it's still very quiet and secluded, set beneath a moderately dense grove of mixed spruce and maple trees.

Site 11 bears off to the left, which adds to the sense of privacy from the road. There's also a lot of woodland between this site and its neighbors. The site is open to the sky, moderately spacious, and set within a grove of mixed birch and maple trees.

The juxtaposition of sites 9 and 10 and the fact that they form a mirror image of each other makes for an unusual situation. Site 10 is set off the road at an angle to the left within a dense grove of spruce. Site 9 mirrors its shape and character to the right. Despite their proximity, each site provides decent privacy, but this would make a good pair of sites for a larger group needing two sites as well.

Site 8 is long and narrow. It's a very open site, but also very spacious. It is quite exposed to the road, which makes it a bit less appealing than some of Allis State Park's other sites, but if you need or want a lot of room, this is a great site to choose. Set beneath a dense grove of spruce, maple, and birch trees, the spacious site 7 bends back to the left from the road, so the trees surrounding the site provide further isolation from the road. The only other site you'll probably be able to see from here is the Elm lean-to (more on the lean-tos momentarily).

There's a charmingly diverse character to site 6. This one is set up off the road on a hill with separate levels for parking your car and setting up your tent. It's mostly covered with grass, punctuated by baby and adult spruce and maple trees. An extraordinarily varied forest of young and old deciduous and coniferous trees frames the site. It faces the road, but is very secluded otherwise.

The drive up into site 5 is actually a short loop. This extremely spacious and secluded site is set beneath a varied forest of young and old birch and spruce trees. From site 5, you can see site 4, but no others. Site 4 is moderately spacious and set in a spruce grove. It has a nice, moss- and grass-covered surface. Between sites 4

To get there: From Route 89, take Exit 4. Head west on Route 66 to the intersection with Route 12. Turn right on Route 12 north. Follow this for 12 miles to Route 65. Turn right here and follow road to park entrance on right.

KEY INFORMATION

Allis State Park
RD2 Box 192
Randolph, VT 05060

Operated by: Vermont Agency of Natural Resources, Department of Forests, Parks, and Recreation

Information: Allis State Park (802) 276-3175 (summer) or (800) 299-3071 (January–May)

Open: Mid-May–Labor Day

Individual sites: 18 tent sites and 8 lean-to sites

Each site has: Stone hearth and picnic table

Site assignment: First come, first served or by reservation

Registration: At ranger station at entrance to park; for reservations, call the park

Facilities: Coin-operated hot showers, flush toilets, water spigots

Parking: At sites

Fee: $12

Restrictions:

Pets—On leash only

Fires—In established fireplaces only

Alcoholic beverages—At sites only

Vehicles—Parking at sites only

Other—Check in after 2 p.m., check out by 11 a.m., quiet hours 10 p.m.–7 a.m.; 8 person max. per site, 2-day min. for reservations

and 5 is a trailhead for the Tower Trail. These two sites would be great for a large group.

To get to site 3, you have to drive down off the campground loop road. Once you're down in the site, you can't even see the road. The towering spruce as you enter the short driveway separates the site from view of the road, but the back side of the site opens to the grassy field in the center of the park so there is at once an open, yet secluded feel. The site itself is also dotted with several birch trees.

Even though it's tucked back off the road, site 2 is still very exposed to the road. It's quite spacious, narrow, long, and grass covered, so it would make a comfortable surface for your tent. Site 1 is huge and grassy, but it's wide open to the road. The water spigot is also located very near site 1, so you'll have thirsty campers tramping past your site.

The lean-tos at Allis State Park are grouped together in a small neighborhood at the far end of the campground loop road. They look like true wilderness cabins with their own yards and lawns.

The Elm, Oak, Hemlock, and Spruce lean-tos are all set on grassy lawns buffered from one another by dense forest. The Apple lean-to is set up for handicap access, so it's also close to the rest room. The Pine lean-to is on the outside of the campground loop road.

The Poplar lean-to is set way off on its own, mixed in with a grove of spruce and birch. This is the one to go for if you want a lean-to and you want seclusion.

The Bear Hill Nature Trail, the nearest and most prominent hiking attraction within Allis State Park, is a self-guided nature trail that highlights the varied stages of forest growth and features a stand of red spruce, butternut trees, and a view to North and South Pond that just opened following the great ice storm of 1998. Eventually though, this view will be reclaimed by the steady and undeniable persistence of the forest.

VERMONT

BRANBURY STATE PARK

Salisbury

There are two separate camping areas at Branbury State Park. In a way, this is poetically appropriate, since the name Branbury State Park originally came from the two neighboring town names: Brandon and Salisbury. One of the camping areas is pretty nice, but the other one is positively spectacular. Branbury State Park is located on the eastern shore of Lake Dunmore, so there's plenty to do on this beautiful central Vermont lake: paddling, fishing, sailing, swimming, or just sitting on a beach chair burrowing your feet into the sand.

The camping area near the lake is set on an open field back from the beach. For the Lake Dunmore side of the campground, the privacy rating is one, since it's an open field. There are a few trees spread out within the field, but for the most part, the only thing between you and the neighboring sites is air. The campsites across the street rate a four on the privacy scale, and some a solid five.

Sites 1–17 are the open sites near the lake. These are nice as they're close to the lake and you'll get some nice cool breezes, but they are all quite similar and all very open. As purely a matter of personal preference, I tend to toward campsites that make me feel as if I'm off in the woods on my own. If you share my proclivity, the campsites across the street, sites 18–41, are where you want to be. The best of these sites are highlighted below.

CAMPGROUND RATINGS

Beauty:	★★★★
Site Privacy (West):	★
Site Privacy (East):	★★★★
Site Spaciousness:	★★★★
Quiet:	★★★★
Security:	★★★★
Cleanliness/upkeep:	★★★★

Branbury State Park is like two campgrounds in one. Choose between campsites on a grassy field near the lake or nestled deep in the woods.

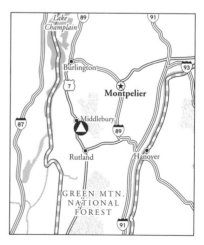

VERMONT

This portion of the campground is set within a beautiful mixed forest of old and young trees. This loop has some scenic and secluded sites, as well as a few lean-tos. In Vermont State Park style, the lean-tos are all named for tree varieties: Elm, Spruce, Oak, and so on. These are unobtrusively mixed in with the tent sites.

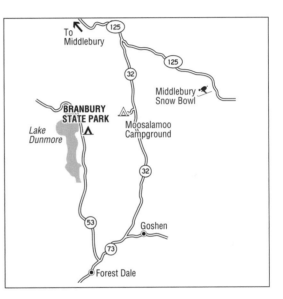

Site 25 isn't bad. It's slightly elevated from the road but right at the entrance to this side of the campground, so it lacks privacy and quiet. The site is right where other campers drive in to this side of the campground. Sites 27 and 28 are probably the least private of the sites on this side, as they have the main road (Vermont Route 53) on one side and the campground loop road on the other. Travel just a bit further up this loop, though, and the sites become increasingly spectacular.

Site 32 is nicely isolated, situated on the inside of the campground loop near the Birch lean-to. Sites 29 and 31 are even further up on the spectacular scale. These well-isolated sites are set up on a small rise from the campground road and are surrounded by thick forest. Site 30 sits right in the middle of these two sites, so it's more open, but it's still a fine site. Sites 29 and 31 on either side are set back enough in the woods that you won't be too close to your neighbors.

Further up the loop, there are several sites set against some small granite cliff walls. These are part of the "subcliffs" surrounding Rattlesnake Cliffs, one of the many hikes you shouldn't miss while you're here. Sites 36 and 37 are tucked right up against these ledges. The whole side of the loop here is quite dramatic in its scenery thanks to the cliff walls, the moderately spaced forest, and gently rolling forest floor.

There are three sites on this side of the Branbury State Park campground that are set at the end of cul-de-sacs within the campground: sites 34, 41, and 21. Site 34 is perfectly situated for a deep, wilderness sense of isolation. It's nestled into a dense grove of conifers, so it feels like a campsite from some deep mystical woods out of Tolkien's Middle Earth.

Site 41 might as well be the companion site to site 34, set off on its own in a pine grove right up against the cliffs. This site is next to the Spruce lean-to. Sites 39–41 are interspersed with the shelters against and amongst the cliffs. Site 39 is a nice, isolated site, even though it sits right next to the Oak Shelter.

Then, we come to site 21 (elated cinematic music should be resounding in your head right now). Site 21 couldn't possibly be a more perfect place to spend a few days camping. There's a short distance to lug in your gear. Make sure to drop your stuff and just look around as you walk into the site. You'll feel like you've entered a cathedral. The site is majestically framed by statuesque spruce trees, set against a steep cliff wall, and Sucker Brook softly splashes by right behind the site. You'll fall asleep to the sounds of the stream as it runs down from the Falls of Lana toward Lake Dunmore.

When I was chatting with the Vermont Youth Conservation Corps members working in the ranger station in early

To get there: From Middlebury, Vermont, travel south on U.S. Route 7, then south on Highway 53 until you see signs for the park.

KEY INFORMATION

Branbury State Park
3570 Lake Dunmore Road, Route 53
Salisbury, VT 05733

Operated by: Vermont Agency of Natural Resources, Department of Forests, Parks, and Recreation

Information: Branbury State Park, (802) 247-5925 (summer) or (800) 658-1622 (January–May)

Open: Mid-May–Columbus Day

Individual sites: 41 individual sites, 6 lean-tos

Each site has: Fire ring, picnic table

Site assignment: First come, first served or by reservation

Registration: At ranger station; for reservations, call the park

Facilities: Flush toilets, water, hot showers, sandy beach on Lake Dunmore, boat rentals

Parking: At sites

Fee: $15

Restrictions:

Pets—Dogs on leash only

Fires—In established fire rings only

Alcoholic beverages—At sites only

Vehicles—Parking at sites only

Other— Check in after 2 p.m., check out by 11 a.m., quiet hours 10 p.m.–7 a.m.; 8 person max. per site, 4-day min. stay for reservations

spring, the coveted site 21 was already reserved for most of the summer. Plan years in advance, do a sun dance, and try to get yourself some time in site 21. You'll be glad you did!

While most Vermont State Parks have a two-night minimum for reservations, there's a four-night minimum at Branbury State Park. That should be fine though, especially if you get yourself into site 21. Otherwise, consider sites 20, 22, 29, 31, 34, and 41 for the most secluded wilderness experience. Once you land there, you won't want to leave for at least four nights!

Besides being able to fish, paddle, and lay in the sun on the shores of Lake Dunmore, the hiking in and around Branbury State Park is as dramatically beautiful as site 21. There's a nature trail that loops around up and over the small cliffs at the backside of the wooded side of the campground. There are two hikes in particular that you won't want to miss if you're spending at least a couple of days here: the one-and-a-half mile, occasionally strenuous hike up to Rattlesnake Point, a rock promontory overlooking the forest and Lake Dunmore, and the relatively easy one-mile hike up to the Falls of Lana, over which Sucker Brook flows on its way toward site 21 and Lake Dunmore.

CHITTENDEN BROOK RECREATION AREA

Chittenden

The Chittenden Brook Recreation Area, like many campgrounds perched along the spine of the Green Mountains in Vermont, offers a deep woods atmosphere and easy access to some of the world class hiking trails that wind through the state.

The 2.5-mile access road (Road #45) into the Chittenden Brook campground is quite a trip in and of itself. It leads up and over a ridge with Chittenden Brook running down on either side along the way. Further up, as you near the campground, the road falls off steeply to the right. Even though the forest is dramatically beautiful here, keep your eyes on the road.

Chittenden Brook is one of those campgrounds (and there are certainly plenty in New England) where there isn't a bad site in the place. It's an intimate campground with only 17 sites, which means it can fill up quickly. Once you're there, it's nice and quiet and has a delightful sense of solitude.

The whole campground is situated near the ridgeline of the Green Mountains, the course followed by the nearby Long and Appalachian Trails. You are at a moderate elevation in the Green Mountains, so the forest isn't quite as towering here. Consequently, lots of light filters down into the sites. There's also the ever-present rush of Chittenden Brook, punctuated by the staccato chirping of the forest birds. It's a profoundly peaceful combination.

CAMPGROUND RATINGS

Beauty:	★★★★★
Site privacy:	★★★★★
Site spaciousness:	★★★★★
Quiet:	★★★★★
Security:	★★★★
Cleanliness/upkeep:	★★★★

Chittenden Brook is a spectacularly scenic and isolated campground deep within the woods of the Green Mountain National Forest.

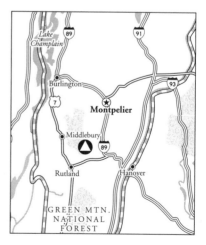

VERMONT

Site 1 is down off the road, near the bathrooms but set off on its own enough to be fairly well isolated. It's also close to the hand water pump. Continuing along the campground loop road, sites 2–5 are fairly close together, but each one has plenty of room. These sites have a more open feel, and they are probably the least isolated sites in the campground. Still, even these offer a reasonable sense of seclusion.

While it doesn't have a lot of dense forest surrounding it, site 6 is nicely isolated, as it is set off from the other campsites. It's also situated right next to a trailhead between sites 6 and 7 that leads to the Chittenden Brook Trail, the Beaver Pond Trail, and the Campground Loop Trail. You can hike right out of your campsite. Site 7 is larger, so it would be perfect for a slightly larger group or large family. It's also next to the rest room.

The tent platform for site 8 is set up off the campground loop and back in the woods, so this site scores higher on the solitude and isolation scale. Between its location and the trees around the site, you probably won't even be able to see your neighbors. Sites 9 and 10 are right across the campground loop road from each other, but both are nice, spacious sites surrounded by trees that lend a sense of isolation on either side, although not directly in front of the campsites.

Sites 11 and 12 are right next to each other and have a loosely spaced, fairly open forest in between, so these would be good sites if you're with a group large enough to need or want two sites. There's another hand pump for water located across from site 13 and next to site 14.

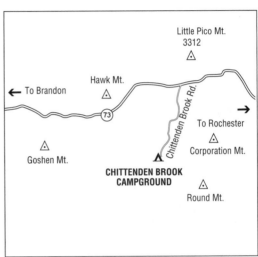

Sites 13 and 15 are set off from the campground loop road, with a short path leading to the tent platform. These sites not only provide a sense of wilderness and isolation, but are also extra scenic since they are set within groves of young deciduous trees, loaded with brilliant green leaves bouncing around in the sunlight that filters through the loosely spaced upper forest.

Sites 16 and 17 are my favorites here at Chittenden Brook Recreation Area. In site 16, the tent platform is set down off the road, and then from there, the space with the picnic table and fire ring is set down further still, so both your sleeping spot and hanging-out spot are off on their own. There's also a buffer of woods between sites 16 and 17 themselves, as well as the sites on either side. Site 17 is a bit more level, but still marvelously isolated, quite spacious, and surrounded by a cloak of young trees. It's located near the end of the campground loop road, and fairly close to the recycling station. These recycling stations are very much in evidence within the Green Mountain National Forest campgrounds and recreation areas. Bravo to that!

This is the place to make base camp if you're planning on exploring portions of the Long Trail or Appalachian Trail. There are trailheads leading right out of the campground. As you drive in on the access road, you'll pass other trailheads also leading off toward the Long Trail.

To get there: Follow Route 73 to Road #45 and the sign for Chittenden Brook Recreation Area, which will be on the left if you're heading west on Route 73, on the right if you're heading east. Follow Road #45 about 2.5 miles to the campground.

KEY INFORMATION

Chittenden Brook Recreation Area
Road #45, Route 73
Chittenden, Vermont 05737

Operated by: Green Mountain National Forest

Information: Green Mountain National Forest Rochester Ranger District 99 Ranger Road Rochester, VT 05767-9431 (802) 767-4261

Open: May 25–September 4

Individual sites: 17

Each site has: Fire ring, picnic table

Site assignment: First come, first served

Registration: Pay at self-serve fee station

Facilities: Pit toilets, hand water pumps

Parking: At sites

Fee: $5

Restrictions:

Pets—On leash only

Fires—In established fire rings only

Alcoholic beverages—At sites only

Vehicles—Two per site max., the national forest is closed to ATV's

Other—14-day max. stay, 8 people per site max.; quiet hours start at 10 p.m., check out by 2 p.m.; pack out your trash

COOLIDGE STATE PARK

Plymouth

When you're hiking through the gentle trails of Coolidge State Park (so named for the nearby birthplace of Calvin Coolidge, 30th president of the United States), you'll come across lots of old stone walls and what's left of old foundations. Close your eyes for a moment and imagine what this area was like when the homes of farmers stood here. The land upon which you're hiking and camping looked a lot different just 100 years ago. What was once agricultural land has been thoroughly reclaimed by the steady persistence of the forest.

The campground at Coolidge State Park is set within a dense, mixed forest of mostly deciduous trees. There's a stately character to the forest, as most of the trees tower 75 to 100 feet overhead. The trees are mostly maples, birch, and pine. The tent sites are generally very spacious, with a lot of space and a lot of forest in between most of the sites, so the sense of seclusion is supreme. The campground is very quiet. The only sounds you'll hear are the woodland birds and the breezes rustling through the trees.

Unlike most other Vermont state parks, there are two distinct areas for most of the lean-tos and the tent sites. The White Birch, Alder, and Poplar lean-tos are the only three mixed within the tent sites. The White Birch lean-to is located at the head

CAMPGROUND RATINGS

Beauty:	★★★★
Site Privacy:	★★★★★
Site Spaciousness:	★★★★
Quiet:	★★★★★
Security:	★★★★★
Cleanliness/upkeep:	★★★★

The character of the forest and the views of the surrounding hillside make this park a gem. If you're in the mood for some scenic, relatively gentle hiking, Coolidge State Park is a good spot to make camp.

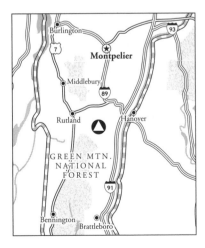

VERMONT

of the tent loop, the Alder across from site 4, and the Poplar off the main campground road.

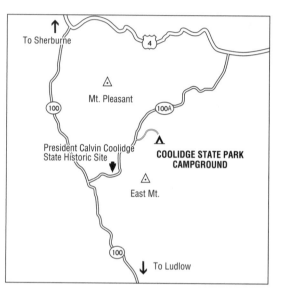

It may be a bit smaller than the other low numbered sites, but site 1 is well isolated. The main campground road runs behind the site, but you won't notice it once the sun sinks beneath the trees. It's also directly across the campground loop road from site 2, which is framed by a grove of spruce and young deciduous trees. A huge, grand old pine tree guards the entrance to site 2, with branches hanging down redolent of a weeping willow.

There's a fairly well isolated air about site 3, although it's close to site 2. A decent amount of forest separates the two, and both are very spacious. Site 4 is also very spacious, and is right across the road from the Alder lean-to. The site is framed by a grove of young deciduous trees and a few older spruce. Site 5 is another well-isolated site. It's at least 100 feet from neighboring sites on either side, but it is open to the back and you can see the bathroom building behind the site. Site 6 is set down off the campground road. It's quite spacious and pretty well isolated. There are no sites close on either side, but it is right across the road from another footpath to the bathrooms.

The trailhead for the CCC Trail (Civilian Conservation Corps) is right across from site 7. This is a convenient site for easy access to the hiking trails that wind throughout the park, but expect passing foot traffic. Sites 7 and 8 are somewhat close together, and set up off the campground loop road. Site 9 is very open and has a small grassy area within the site. It's right next to site 10, so unlike most of the campground, there isn't much privacy between these two sites. These two pairs of sites would suit large groups or families needing two sites.

Site 11 is another open and spacious site. Site 12 is smaller and has a more secluded feel. It's surrounded by a dense grove of young deciduous trees. Site 13 is tucked far off the campground road, so it provides a nice sense of isolation, even though it's right next to a short footpath that leads up to the bathrooms.

There's a shared entranceway to sites 14 and 15, but there's enough space and forest between the two to afford sufficient privacy. Both sites are very spacious and set well off the road. Site 15 is set way back, and offers a fabulous sense of solitude. This site boasts a nice grassy area, plus a brook flowing by beside the site.

There isn't much privacy between sites 16 and 17. However, there's plenty of room on either side of both sites, so they're well isolated from the rest of the campground, if not from each other— another possibility for groups. Site 17 is set up off the road a bit, and has a nice grassy surface in the center of the site. There are also several maples growing up through the site. The site is framed by shorter deciduous trees, mostly maple and birch, and by ferns at the ground level for an added sense of seclusion. The ferns give the site a primeval feel, and fill in the forest with their brilliant green leaves. When the sunlight filters down on a clear day, the forest looks as if it's glowing green.

Site 18 is a bit smaller than 17, but also has a nice grassy surface within the site.

To get there: Follow Route 100 (the skier's highway) to Route 100A in Plymouth. Follow Route 100A for about two miles to the sign for the park on the right.

KEY INFORMATION

Coolidge State Park
855 Coolidge State Park Road
Plymouth, VT 05056

Operated by: Vermont Agency of Natural Resources, Department of Forests, Parks, and Recreation

Information: Coolidge State Park, (802) 672-3612 (summer) or (800) 299-3071 (January–May)

Open: Mid-May–October 15

Individual sites: 25 tent sites, 35 lean-to sites

Each site has: Fire ring, picnic table

Site assignment: First come, first served or by reservation

Registration: At ranger stations; for reservations, call the park

Facilities: Hot showers, flush toilets, playground

Parking: At sites

Fee: $12

Restrictions:

Pets—On leash only

Fires—In established fire rings only

Alcoholic beverages—At sites only

Vehicles—Parking at sites only

Other—Check in after 2 p.m., check out by 11 a.m., quiet hours 10 p.m.–7 a.m.; 8 person max. per site

Site 19 is very spacious and there's plenty of forest on either side of the site, but not too much privacy from the road. I'm always willing to sacrifice a bit of site spaciousness for more forest surrounding the site and a deeper sense of seclusion.

There's a similar character to sites 20–23. Site 20 is up off the road. This is a moderately spacious site, also with a grassy surface within the site. Sites 22 and 23 are right across the road from each other. Site 23A is a lug-in site set up off the road. It's almost a part of site 23, so if you don't know your neighbors in site 23 before your trip, you will afterward. Site 23A isn't a huge site, but it's set way off from the road and the rest of the campground. The site is surrounded by a dense, low wall of ferns and a grove of slender, young spruce trees. It has a deep sense of seclusion on all sides, save where it abuts site 23. In fact, it looks like you have to park at site 23.

One of the last sites on this part of the campground loop road is site 24. This is by far the most isolated site within the loop. It's perfectly situated for a deep sense of wilderness isolation, as it's surrounded by dense forest and it's a good distance from its neighbors. It's not the most spacious site, but it's marvelously well isolated.

There's a dichotomy to site 25. It sits way off on its own, but it's located near the point where the campground loop road rejoins the main state park road. It's moderately spacious and very well isolated from the other sites, but it is right at that intersection.

Between the tent loop and the lean-to loop, there's a little playground near the ranger station as you enter the park. This is a good thing to keep in mind if you're camping with some little ones. The lean-to loop has very dense forest coverage as well. Most of the lean-tos are quite well isolated from each other, although some are positioned in pairs, like Cherry and Larch, or groups, like Beech, Basswood, and Apple. Between the dense forest and the loose spacing, the individual lean-to sites have a nice sense of isolation, especially the Sumac, Willow, and Butternut lean-tos. It also bears mentioning that the Cedar lean-to is disabled accessible.

The Ash lean-to has an outrageously scenic view of the opposing hillsides and valley. It's perfectly situated on that side of the ridge, with a clear, sweeping view. This alone makes it worth keeping the tent packed and hopping in one of these lean-tos. The Aspen, Boxelder, Beech, Basswood, Elm, and Hawthorn lean-tos also share this dramatic hillside view. All these lean-tos face out toward the hills, which would be the first thing you see in the morning. I couldn't imagine a nicer way to greet the day.

Once you're up and about, whether you've spent the night in your tent or in a lean-to, there's plenty of great hiking right within the park. Try the three-quarter mile CCC Trail that connects the tent area and the lean-to area for a mellow first hike—a breakfast hike. Then try the mile-and-a-half trail to the summit of the 2,174 foot Slack Hill and treat yourself to lunch with a commanding view of the surrounding hills.

GIFFORD WOODS STATE PARK

Killington

Gifford Woods is a perfectly situated spot from which to launch your adventures into the Green Mountains and the Killington area. Whether you're here for late season skiing or mountain biking at Killington or hiking along the spine of Vermont, especially portions of the Appalachian Trail or Vermont's Long Trail, this is a good centrally located base camp.

The Appalachian Trail passes right through the park, and it forms the right border for site 12 within the campground. I happened to stay there one night, and found it fascinating to be perched right on that fabled footpath. Turn left from my site and head for Katahdin or turn right for Amicalola Falls, Georgia.

Like other Vermont state parks, the site arrangement at Gifford Woods State Park is a loosely spaced combination of tent sites and lean-tos named for tree varieties. There are two distinct areas within the campground, the Upper Loop and the Lower Loop. The whole upper area of the campground is set beneath a truly mixed woods with deciduous and coniferous trees as well as old and new forest. Sites 1 and 2 are tucked in together right across from the playground, which is also off the Upper Loop's campground road. These are great if you need a pair of contiguous sites for a larger group. Conversely, you will definitely meet your neighbors if you arrive previously unacquainted.

CAMPGROUND RATINGS

Beauty:	★★★★★
Site Privacy:	★★★★
Site Spaciousness:	★★★★
Quiet:	★★★★
Security:	★★★★
Cleanliness/upkeep:	★★★★

Gifford Woods State Park is exceptional both as a relaxing destination and a base camp for Green Mountain hiking adventures. There are myriad hiking trails very close to the park.

VERMONT

Site 3 is spacious, but it's right next to the playground so it's not quite as private and could potentially be noisy if there are a lot of kids on the swings and slide. This would be a great site to secure if you are camping with small kids and plan on spending time at the playground. Besides the playground, kids will like the footpath and self-guided nature tour that winds through the woods behind the playground and picnic area.

Sites 4 and 5 are well isolated sites with a good sense of privacy. Site 4 is a nice, isolated site, even though it's set right at the intersection where the one-way upper campground loop road rejoins itself. Site 5 is tucked off on its own in the woods, set back from the campground loop road.

Sites 6 and 7 are set off the campground loop road a good distance, but they're quite close to each other. Sites 9 and 10 are right across the campground road from each other. They're more open, so they aren't quite as private. Like sites 1 and 2, this pair would be fine for a group needing two sites.

Site 8 is fairly well isolated. It's located next to the Ash lean-to. Site 11 isn't bad, but it's also a bit more open than some of the other sites in the Upper Loop. Site 11 is right across from the Appalachian Trail.

Besides being right on the Appalachian Trail, site 12 is otherwise another of Gifford Woods' top-notch tent spots. It has plenty of space and is fairly well-isolated. Site 13 is a spacious, fairly set back site, but it has a water spigot located right outside the site, so you'll get lots of visitors. If you want to meet a bunch of your campground neighbors, this is the site for that.

The lean-tos are interspersed among the individual tent sites. The Birch lean-to is in a nice isolated spot. This one would be worth getting just for the privacy of the site. Apple is similarly off on its own. Maple and Beech are set right next to each other, and would be a good pair of shelters for larger groups.

Spruce is fairly well isolated on the inside of the loop. Hemlock is across from the frequently visited water spigot at site 13, but it's in the woods a ways, so it's more private than site 13. The Elm lean-to also has a nice distance between the site and the road.

Overall, the upper campground sites are quieter than the lower sites. The surrounding forest is thicker, and you're that much further from Route 100. Still, there are some nice spots on the lower loop as well. The lower loop includes sites 14–27.

Site 27, the first site you come to, is open and quite spacious, but consequently not very private. The same could be said about the first three lean-to sites within this loop: Oak, Walnut, and Poplar. The Willow, Aspen, and Cherry lean-tos are grouped closely together as well. There aren't many trees in between these sites. If you're having a camping family reunion or some other confluence of friends and family, securing either troika of lean-tos would give you the perfect venue.

The Fir lean-to is set off a bit more on its own, and it's right across from the rest rooms. Site 26 is also conveniently located near the facilities, but isn't very private. The Alder lean-to is set up for disabled access.

To get there: Gifford Woods State Park is located right off Route 100, just north of the access road for Killington Ski Area.

KEY INFORMATION

Gifford Woods State Park
34 Gifford Woods
Killington, VT 05761

Operated by: Vermont Agency of Natural Resources, Department of Forests, Parks, and Recreation

Information: Gifford Woods State Park, (802) 775-5354 (in season) or (800) 299-3071 (January–May)

Open: Mid-May–Columbus Day

Individual sites: 27 individual sites, 21 shelters

Each site has: Fire ring or brick hearth, picnic table

Site assignment: First come, first served or by reservation

Registration: At ranger station; for reservations, call the park

Facilities: Coin-operated showers, flush toilets, playground, and picnic area

Parking: At sites

Fee: $13

Restrictions:

Pets—Dogs on leash only

Fires—In established fire rings only

Alcoholic beverages—At sites only

Vehicles—Parking at sites only

Other— Check in after 2 p.m., check out by 11 a.m., quiet hours 10 p.m.–7 a.m.; 8 person max. per site, 2-day min. stay for reservations

Moving further along the loop and back into the tent sites, site 25 is smaller but nicely isolated, a worthwhile trade-off in my book (so to speak). Actually, sites 21–25 are all moderately spaced and well isolated. Next to site 21, there's a short road leading up to another trio of lean-tos—Cedar, Locust, and Larch (Larch? I had never heard of that kind of tree before!). If you have a very large group that wants to bunk out in a trio of lean-tos, Gifford Woods State Park is clearly where you want to be, specifically the Lower Loop, where most of the lean-tos are situated. It sometimes makes you wonder about the naming conventions of these lean-tos. What happens if they start running out of tree varieties? I can see it: if they built another loop full of lean-tos in one of the larger Vermont State Park campgrounds, we might end up with Mangrove, Eucalyptus, and Joshua!

Site 20 is open and spacious, but not as private or set off in the woods as some of the others. Sites 15–19 are larger sites, but you run the risk of having an RV drop anchor nearby. The woods here are moderately dense, but you'll still have one in view if it moors next door. Similarly, site 14 is very open and has plenty of room to spread your wings (or your tarp and your tent's rainfly), but you'll give up a little privacy.

Perhaps the nicest aspect of Gifford Woods State Park is that you don't have to travel far outside the park, or even inside the park , before you run across some hiking trails. The Appalachian Trail runs right through the park, and reconnects with the Long Trail approximately one-and-a-half miles north of the park. Another spectacular sight to see is the seven-acre stand of old growth hardwoods, located right across Route 100 from the campground. This pristine slice of wilderness has some massive sugar maple, beech, birch, and ash trees. Tread lightly, and enjoy this grand old forest.

GROUT POND RECREATION AREA

Arlington

This is no sanitized, drive-in drive-out campground. The campsites at Grout Pond are spread out along a hiking trail that winds around the western shores of the pond. You have to hike your gear in to your tent site. This extra effort will give you a huge payoff, though, when you set up your tent along the shore of the pond and watch the sun set over the hills.

You hike in to any of the 12 tent and lean-to sites via the Pond Loop Trail. This trail cuts through a dense forest, through which you can catch tantalizing glimpses of the pond as you start out. As its name implies, the Pond Loop Trail brings you all the way around Grout Pond. The campsites are liberally spread along the first mile of the trail. No camping is permitted beyond site 12, the last "developed" tent site. Since you hike into the sites, parking is in the small lot past the campground host cabin.

Don't expect to happen upon the campsites as soon as you set out from the parking area. The first site is just under a half-mile hike in. Carry a manageable amount of gear, or better yet, have a wagon or some sort of wheeled cart to transport your stuff. If you're hauling your gear without wheeled assistance, just bring your tent to stake your claim on your site. These sites are completely first come, first served. You can't make reservations, so it's a good idea to have a backup plan if the sites are full.

CAMPGROUND RATINGS

Beauty:	★★★★★
Site Privacy:	★★★★★
Site Spaciousness:	★★★★
Quiet:	★★★★★
Security:	★★★★★
Cleanliness/upkeep:	★★★★

The campsites at Grout Pond are as remote as it gets. These hike-in campsites give you the sense of wilderness isolation typically reserved for extended backpacking trips.

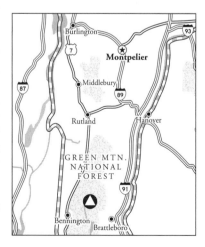

VERMONT

This is very rustic, primitive camping. Pack light for your night at Grout Pond. Even if you get one of the first sites, you still have to lug your gear quite a ways. There's a true wilderness feel to these sites that is usually reserved for backcountry backpacking trips.

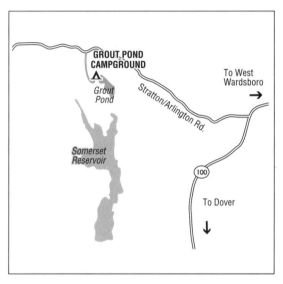

At one-tenth of a mile down the Pond Loop Trail, you'll come to a trailhead for the 3.2-mile East Trail, the one-mile hike to the Kelley Stand parking area, and the two-mile hike to the Somerset Reservoir. Shortly after passing this trailhead, you'll come to another trailhead for the Camp Trail, which follows a shorter loop out from the pond than the winding East Trail. Stay on the Pond Loop Trail to get to the campsites.

As you walk along the Pond Loop Trail, be sure to walk slowly, fully absorb the sights and sounds of the forest, and draw in a deep breath. The air is rich with a balsam scent of unspoiled, remote forest.

Site 1 is set down off the trail on the shore of Grout Pond. It's an incredibly spacious site where you'll get breezes blowing in off the pond and a decent amount of sunlight filtering down through the moderately dense forest. The site is hidden in a very subtle way from the Pond Loop trail by a stand of trees and a short stone wall. Down in the site, you'll have a completely clear view of the pond, as well as access to the pond for your canoe or kayak.

That brings up another point about getting to your site. Once you've marked your site with your tent, you could go back to your car and haul your gear in, taking four or five or however many trips. Or, you could load up your canoe or kayak and paddle to the site. Then you've got your vessel right there at your campsite and can explore the crystalline waters of Grout Pond after you've set up camp. You could also haul your gear inside your canoe or kayak atop of those wheeled carts—just another option.

The next site on the Pond Loop Trail is very isolated from the trail. Standing on the Pond Loop Trail, you can barely see site 2. There's a twisting 50-foot path down to the site. The site itself is a bit smaller than site 1, but just as open to the pond and extremely secluded.

If privacy is more important to you than being right on the pond, site 3 is a perfect choice. This site is set up in the woods away from the pond. You'll cross over a series of short footbridges put there to minimize trail erosion. Please use the bridges. Don't step off or around them. It's set within a very dense forest of mostly deciduous trees, with a lot of maple and beech. It's moderately spacious, but site 1 is clearly the largest at Grout Pond if that's an important factor.

Right across the trail on the pond side is site 4. Like site 2, it's extremely secluded from the trail. Follow a 50-foot path down toward the pond to the site. It's smaller than site 1 or 2, but very sunny and open to the pond.

Just past sites 3 and 4, there's a picnic area located down on the pond. If you're waiting for someone to finish packing up before you occupy a site, this is a great spot to rest and have a bite. When I first walked the Pond Loop Trail, I mistook this for a campsite, but it's clearly marked as a no camping/no fires site.

Another superbly secluded site is site 5. This is set up in the woods, on the

---

To get there: From Vermont Route 100, take the Stratton/Arlington road in Wardsboro, just north of Mount Snow. Follow this to the brown Forest Service sign for Grout Pond on the left (heading north).

KEY INFORMATION

Grout Pond Recreation Area
FR 262
Arlington, VT

Operated by: Green Mountain National Forest

Information: Green Mountain National Forest Manchester Ranger District 2538 Depot Street Manchester Center, VT 05255 (802) 362-2307

Open: Year-round

Individual sites: 12 hike in tent and lean-to sites

Each site has: Fire ring with grate, picnic table

Site assignment: First come, first served

Registration: Register by occupying the site.

Facilities: Pit toilets

Parking: At trailhead to campsites

Fee: Donations accepted

Restrictions:

Pets—Dogs on leash only

Fires—In established fire rings only

Alcoholic beverages—At sites only

Vehicles—In main parking area only

opposite side of the trail from the pond. The spur trail to the site is about 70 feet long. It gets dark early at this site, as very little evening sunlight penetrates the extremely dense, mostly deciduous forest around it. Between the distance from the Pond Loop Trail and the woods encircling site 5, you will feel a complete sense of solitude.

It may be fairly small, but site 6 is also well isolated from the Pond Loop Trail and the neighboring campsites. It's set about 25 feet off the trail. It's a fairly small site, but it has a tent platform, it's very open to the sun, and it's encircled by a dense grove of young maple trees.

If you would rather be way off in the woods, check out site 8. This is a lean-to site accessed via a 150-foot spur trail. The site is set within a grove of moderately spaced beech and ash trees with dense undergrowth.

Site 7 is actually past site 8, and it's located on the pond side of the trail. This is another small site, but it's buffered by dense undergrowth for a good sense of seclusion. It's also very sunny and open to the pond. Site 9 is a lean-to set up in the woods away from the pond in a fairly open part of the forest.

If ever there were a near-perfect site, it would have to be site 10. This site is very isolated by virtue of its remote location on the Pond Loop Trail and the distance from its nearest neighbors. It's a moderately sized site set beneath a loose stand of maples and spruce. There's a nice, flat grass and moss covered area for your tent carved out of the dense undergrowth. There's also a tree hanging out over the pond, which adds a curious character to this site.

There is a complete sense of isolation to site 11. It's on the pond side, about 70 feet from the Pond Loop Trail and quite distant from any neighbor. This is a moderately spacious site, set within a relatively dense forest of mostly deciduous trees. It's also encircled by dense undergrowth.

The last of the crown jewel sites set right on the shores of Grout Pond is site 12, also about a 70-foot hike in from the Pond Loop Trail. This site is set in a grove of mixed deciduous and coniferous trees. It's on the smaller side, but its seclusion more than compensates for that. The dense undergrowth and surrounding forest, the distance from the Pond Loop Trail, and the distance from the nearest site make for a complete wilderness camping experience.

These last few sites along the Pond Loop Trail, sites 10, 11, and 12, are as secluded and wild as just about any you will find in New England. The layout and character of site 10 probably makes it my favorite. It has a Japanese garden feel to it, with the moss cover, the artful spacing of the trees, the one tree growing out over the pond, and the open sense to the site. From site 10, you have a full view of the pond and the openness to enjoy the breezes and the sunlight, or the moonlight once dusk has fallen.

When you arrive at Grout Pond, you'll see some sites up near the campground host cabin, near the day use area. However, these are likely spots for RVs. Pitch your tent here only to wait for one of the pondside sites to open up.

Grout Pond is a body of water of decent size. It's well suited for paddling and fishing, and the water is absolutely crystal clear. The pond and the campsites themselves are extremely quiet. There's no road noise, no chatter from noisy neighbors, no nothing. All you will hear is the wind rushing through the treetops and the occasional soft splash of a paddle on the pond.

HALF MOON STATE PARK

Fair Haven

If you're looking for a campground to make you feel like you've really escaped civilization, Half Moon State Park definitely fits the bill. The absolute stillness and remote location are a huge part of the allure of this campground. It's an exceptional spot for some relaxed paddling, fishing, and swimming in the pristine waters of Half Moon Pond.

The contiguous Bomoseen and Half Moon State Parks are essentially a string of ponds, marshlands, and abandoned quarry sites, all interconnected by several hiking trails ranging in length from one-third of a mile to four-and-one-half miles. From the sheltered enclave of Half Moon Pond, you could hike the Half Moon Pond Trail to the Glen Lake Trail, follow this through Beaver Meadow and past Moscow Pond to Glen Lake. From Glen Lake, the Slate History Trail will bring you to Lake Bomoseen.

The campground at Half Moon State Park is divided into two areas along either side of the pond. The loop with sites 1–35 is off to the left as you enter the camping area, and the rest of the sites, 36–60, are off to the right. Both sides of the campground have sites perched right on the shore of Half Moon Pond. These are the best sites.

As you enter the 1–35 loop, sites 1 and 2 are immediately on your left. They are spacious and set within a loose grove of maples and other deciduous trees. Located right where the campground road splits, site 2 is very open.

CAMPGROUND RATINGS

Beauty:	★★★★★
Site Privacy:	★★★★★
Site Spaciousness:	★★★★★
Quiet:	★★★★★
Security:	★★★★
Cleanliness/upkeep:	★★★★

Half Moon Pond is pristine, and the campground that wraps around either side provides some spectacular pondside camping.

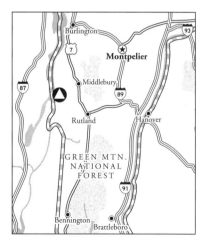

VERMONT

If you drove straight down the campground road, and through site 4, you could drive right into the pond, but that would be ill-advised… unless you had your car modified by James Bond's mechanic.

Sites 4 and 6 are both situated on the shore of Half Moon Pond. Site 4 is quite spacious, and has a partially grass-covered surface upon which to pitch your tent. It's a bit close to site 6, which is on the left as you look at the pond. Still, this is a key spot if you've brought along a canoe or kayak. You could launch your boat right from your campsite. Site 6 is smaller than site 4, but it's also shadier. Paddlers and anglers should reserve sites 4 and 6, as they're perfectly suited for either activity.

There is a deeper sense of seclusion to site 3. It's set up in the woods off the campground road, opposite but overlooking the pond. Site 5 is too open. The back side of the site faces the rest rooms, and the front opens to site 6.

The sites on the forest side of the campground loop road, sites 7, 10, and 11, are very spacious and open, but still offer a mild sense of seclusion because they are surrounded by moderately dense deciduous forest. Sites 8, 9, 12, 13, and 14 are right on the pond, but are bunched in close together. They are all super sites, separated by small stands of deciduous trees, however they're smaller, more closely packed, and less private.

Site 15 is large and well isolated on the sides and back of the site, but it's open to the road. Sites 14 and 16 are right on the pond. Site 16, however, feels jammed in between the other sites. These open sites may not provide as much privacy, but then again, they are on the water. Site 17 is also right on the pond, but it's slightly larger, more private, and right next to the small beach area.

Sites 20 and 21 are well secluded on the sides, if not from the front. Site 19, however, is very open. It's also right next to the rest rooms. There's a similar, exposed character to sites 23 and 24. These spacious sites are nestled within a grove of mixed hardwoods.

The 25–35 section of the loop generally gives you a choice between smaller pondside sites or larger, open wooded sites. There's a nice cool, dark feel to the forest here, as the canopy is high and dense, but at the ground level, the campsites in the low 30s are very open. One plus in this section is a trailhead for the Nature Trail between sites 30 and 31.

Heading off to the right as you enter the campground brings you to its more secluded section with sites 36–60. The boat rental facility is also on this side of the pond. There are several fabulous pondside sites in this area. If you can, try to land in either sites 48, 50, 58, or 60. It will be well worth any effort. More on those sites in a moment.

The location of site 36 provides a complete sense of isolation on all sides. It's tucked into the contours of a small hill to the left of the campground road as you head in. There's no pond view, but it's quite spacious, scenic, and private. The hill on which site 36 is perched is in the center of a small loop where most of the lean-to sites are located, but you can't see them from the site. The seclusion of this site is marvelous.

There's a beautiful open grove of pine trees across from site 38. The dark, slender

To get there: From Route 4 in Castleton Corners, take Exit 4 for Route 30 north. Follow this to Hubbardton. Turn left on Hortonville Road. Follow this to Black Pond Road. Turn left and follow this to the park.

KEY INFORMATION

Half Moon State Park
1621 Black Pond Road
Fair Haven, VT 05743
Operated by: Vermont Agency of Natural Resources, Department of Forests, Parks and Recreation

Information: Half Moon State Park, (802) 273-2848 (summer) or (800) 658-1622 (January–May)

Open: Mid-May–Columbus Day

Individual sites: 60 tent sites and 10 lean-to sites

Each site has: Stone hearth, picnic table

Site assignment: First come, first served or by reservation

Registration: At ranger station as you enter the campground; for reservations, call the park

Facilities: Hot showers, flush toilets, water spigots

Parking: At sites

Fee: $15 per site per night

Restrictions:

Pets—On leash only

Fires—In established fire rings only

Alcoholic beverages—At sites only

Vehicles—Parking at sites only

Other—8 people max. per site; check out by 11 a.m., check in after 2 p.m., quiet hours 10 p.m.–7 a.m.

pines poke up through the rich brown carpet of pine needles. There's a silent, sylvan feel to this site. It's small, but very well isolated. Site 37 shares a similar character, although it's a bit larger. It's also right across from the Hazel lean-to. Site 39 is small, but secluded and right across from the Ilex lean-to.

Just outside site 40 across the road, there's a short footpath that leads to the pond, so it's the next best thing to being on the water. Site 40 is also isolated and shady, as it's set within a grove of young mixed deciduous trees. Site 41 is narrow and on the small side, but it's carved out of a grove of young deciduous trees whose brilliant green leaves brighten the whole site.

Sites 42 and 43 are opposite each other across the campground road. Site 42 is smaller and set in young mixed forest. Site 43 is very spacious and secluded on all sides, but open to the road and site 42. There's a similar layout and arrangement to sites 44 and 45. Site 44 is smaller than 45 and set within a grove of conifers and hardwoods. Site 45 is a little bigger and more secluded in a dense coniferous grove.

Site 46 is very spacious and secluded, set up off the road in a dense mixed forest. Sites 47 and 49 are moderately spacious, but very open. These two are on either side of an open grassy area surrounding the water spigot.

The trade-off of spaciousness and seclusion for a waterside setting is one I am usually quite willing to make. Site 48, for example, is small but right on the pond. There aren't many trees filling in the forest canopy directly overhead, so it has an open view to the sky and easy access to the water.

Site 50 is very spacious and provides a nice sense of seclusion. It's set among towering spruce trees right on the pond. While it's not on the pond and doesn't offer a clear pond view, site 51 does offer an excellent sense of seclusion, with dense forest on all sides. It's also set up off the campground road.

Just before the boat launch area is site 52, which is set within a spruce grove and is relatively roomy and private. Site 53 is a bit smaller than 52, and it's very open to the road. Site 55 is of decent size, but it's also very open to the road. It's right next to the rest rooms and a trailhead for the Glen Lake Trail. It's also right across the road from the boat rental facility. You can rent a canoe for $5 an hour, $15 for a half day, or $30 for a full day.

Dense undergrowth and a stand of trees isolate site 56 from the campground road. Site 57 is also quite private, and moderately spacious. It's set within a grove of mixed deciduous and coniferous trees. Site 58 is very spacious and fairly well secluded, but the best aspect is it's location right on the pond. Site 59 is also quite large and near the pond, but not right on the shore. It's very well secluded on the loop at the very end of the campground road.

Site 60 is also set on this short loop. This site is very spacious, and set in a loose grove of spruce overlooking the pond. It's next to the Tall Timbers Cottage, which is also part of the campground and available for rent, but there's enough forest between the site and the cottage that it's not much of a bother.

While staying at site 60 one night, I could see the silvery shape of a half moon rising up through the trees after dusk had settled. I couldn't help but think how poetically appropriate it was to see that from one of the finest sites on Half Moon Pond.

JAMAICA STATE PARK

Jamaica

Don't even think of coming here without a reservation on one of the river release weekends. When the West River swells to its banks, the campground at Jamaica State Park swells with whitewater kayakers. If you want to score a site for one of those biannual weekends (one in the spring and one in the fall), you'll have to plan way ahead. When I visited the park in the summer of 2001, a ranger told me they had sold out for the fall release weekend (that year September 22 and 23) on the first business day of January—sounds like trying to get tickets to some hot concert tour.

Even for the rest of the year, Jamaica State Park is a heavily reserved park. They do take first come, first served campers, but open sites can sometimes be hard to come by. Do yourself a favor and plan ahead for this one.

There are 43 tent sites and 18 lean-tos. There are several lean-tos arranged in a small loop at one end of the campground, but most sit in a line facing the West River. I can only imagine the scene during river release weekends: These lean-tos packed with camping and paddling gear and the river surging by, dotted with brilliantly colored kayaks and thrilled paddlers.

Generally, the campground and the surrounding park are very quiet. There are no major highways nearby, so there isn't much in the way of road noise. The campsites are situated beneath a moderately spaced for-

CAMPGROUND RATINGS

Beauty:	★★★★
Site Privacy:	★★★★
Site Spaciousness:	★★★★
Quiet:	★★★★★
Security:	★★★★
Cleanliness/upkeep:	★★★★

The atmosphere at Jamaica State Park mirrors that of the river, calm and serene most of the time, but wild when the whitewater is up on release weekends.

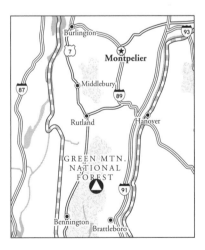

VERMONT

est of towering spruce and shorter, younger hardwoods. The dense undergrowth provides a nice sense of seclusion between most of the individual sites. The sites themselves are quite spacious, and have a hard sandy surface that's perfect for holding down tent stakes.

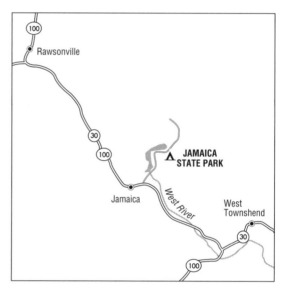

The loop heading off to the right as you enter the camping area brings you to sites 1–11. There's a cathedralesque feel to the forest on this side of the campground, with the towering spruce trees presiding over the woodland. Sunlight and breezes flow easily through the forest to the sites.

Sites 1 and 2 are set back in the woods amongst the loosely spaced forest. Site 1 is open and fairly spacious. Site 2 is larger and set up off the campground loop road. It has a very open feel without sacrificing a sense of privacy.

The added elevation of sites 3 and 4 gives them a better sense of seclusion. These sites, roomy and clean, are set on a small rise, up off the campground loop road. Site 3 is opposite the volleyball net in the day use area, which you can see through the woods. It's cool to be close to the action, but this might be a bit noisy during the day. Site 4 is located next to the rest rooms. Site 5 is a bit smaller than most of the other sites in this loop, but it's set up off the campground loop road, which adds privacy.

Nearby, the Briar lean-to is set up for handicap access. The rest of the lean-tos within this part of the loop are positioned facing out from or perpendicular to the loop road, which adds to their sense of privacy.

The lean-tos are spread out beneath the loosely spaced forest and against a good-sized hill that is liberally peppered with loosely spaced pine and spruce and coated in a soft blanket of pine needles. The effect is captivating. The Hackberry and Ironwood lean-tos are set at the base of the hill. (That wasn't a typo. Though, I must confess, I've never heard of a Hackberry tree before.) The forest is open enough here so that there's plenty of room to pitch tents at the lean-to sites.

A spruce grove and a small embankment give site 6 a nice sense of privacy from the lean-tos behind the site. However, site 6 is open to the Ironwood and Hackberry sites facing the hill. Site 7 is very spacious and airy, but also secluded by a deep spruce grove and young deciduous trees on one side. This is helpful because it's right next to the rest rooms as well.

The added elevation of site 8 enhances its privacy. This spacious site is set up on a platform off the campground road and surrounded by loosely spaced spruce and dense young deciduous trees and undergrowth. Site 9 is set at the base of the hill behind the Hackberry and Ironwood lean-tos. This site is very isolated on both sides, but open to site 8 across the road. Site 9 is large, and there's a handsome, open character to the forest here. Site 11 is roomy and very secluded on all sides, framed by towering spruce trees. Site 10 is also very spacious and private.

The campground loop is split by a short road, on which sites 12 and 13 are located. These sites are spacious, but very open and close to the road. Site 12 is open to the sky so the site itself receives lots of sunlight filtered through the forest. The sites don't offer much in the way of privacy, though.

To get there: Follow Route 30 into Jamaica. Head East on Depot Street for a half mile to the park.

KEY INFORMATION

Jamaica State Park
Box 45
Jamaica, VT 05343

Operated by: Vermont Agency of Natural Resources Department of Forests, Parks, and Recreation

Information: Jamaica State Park (802) 874-4600 (summer) (800) 299-3071 (January–mid-April)

Open: Late April–October 15

Individual sites: 43 tent sites, 18 lean-to sites

Each site has: Fire ring, picnic table

Site assignment: First come, first served or by reservation (recommended)

Registration: At ranger station as you enter park; for reservations, call the park

Facilities: Hot showers, flush toilets, water spigots, playground

Parking: At sites

Fee: $14

Restrictions:

Pets—On leash only

Fires—In established fire rings only

Alcoholic beverages—At sites only

Vehicles—Parking at sites only

Other—8 people max. per site; check out by 11 a.m., check in after 2 p.m., quiet hours 10 p.m.–7 a.m.

The forest is dense along the larger loop to the left as you enter the campground, which has sites 14 and up. The character of the forest adds a sense of seclusion and privacy to the sites. Most of these sites are moderately to very spacious. Site 14 is huge, but doesn't provide much privacy, as it's very open on the sides. Sites 15 and 16 are similar in size and shape. They are both moderate in size and fairly well isolated.

Even though it's right across from the rest rooms, site 17 does have dense undergrowth on all sides. The site is also set up on a small rise, so it strikes a good balance of moderate privacy and convenience to the facilities. Site 18 is spacious and open, but not too private. Site 19 is a bit smaller and secluded on both sides, but open to the road.

There's a deep sense of seclusion to site 20 because it's set down off the campground road. There's also a big rock in the center of the site that you could use as a small table. This site is framed by spruce and dense undergrowth. Sites 21, 22, and 23 are all similar in size, shape, and spaciousness. Site 22 is set up off the campground road and site 23 is set down off the road. These sites are all fairly well secluded and moderately spacious.

Sites 24 and 25 are close together and a bit smaller than sites 21–23. Site 24 is set up off the road a bit. Site 27 is huge, but very open to the road. This site would be good for a larger group. It's framed on the sides by dense undergrowth and spruce trees.

It abuts the back of site 26, but site 29 is set down off the road and otherwise nicely secluded. It's very spacious and surrounded by dense, young undergrowth broken by towering spruce. Sites 28, 30, and 31 are similar in character in that they are moderately spacious and well isolated on the sides. Site 32 is set up off the road in the dense undergrowth. It's smaller, but nicely secluded.

If you're camping with kids, site 33 is a good choice, as it's right near the playground. It's also a good site if you plan to do a lot of hiking. There's a trailhead behind the playground that leads you to the gentle 2.5-mile Railroad Bed Trail that follows the West River to the Ball Mountain Dam, the 2-mile Overlook Trail that takes you up and over the summit of Little Ball Mountain, and 3-mile Hamilton Falls Trail that brings you to the dramatic 125-foot cascade of Hamilton Falls.

At sites 38 and up, the forest opens quite suddenly. These sites are separated by narrow stands of spruce and white pine. They are very spacious, but very open sites. It's up to you how you feel about a site with this character, but I prefer sites that are more densely wooded.

There's a mixed sandy and grassy surface below site 39. The site is framed by loose pines and spruce. This site is also right along the day use parking area, separated by a relatively dense stand of trees.

Sites 39, 40, and 41 are all increasingly spacious. These sites would be good for larger groups needing two or three contiguous sites. They're also great for stargazing or sunbathing, as they are wide open to the sky, and there's plenty of room to pile up paddling gear for those wild river release weekends.

VERMONT

LAKE ST. CATHERINE STATE PARK
Poultney

Visitors to Lake St. Catherine find another good example of the powerful combination of woods and water. While the campground is indeed an attraction in and of itself, the day use area and the beachfront on the lake draw a lot of people on those hot summer days.

There are four distinct loops of campsites within the park; one with sites 1 through 22, another with sites 23 through 28A and most of the lean-tos, another with sites 29 through 42, and the fourth—and most remote—with sites 43 through 50. Many of the tent sites are set within a loose forest, allowing sunlight and breezes to flow through the campground, but reducing the solitude factor. Sites 1 and 2 are right across from one of the bathroom buildings. They are very spacious, but a bit too open.

Apparently, the rangers at Lake St. Catherine needed to find a spot for another lean-to. What used to be site 4 is now the Pine lean-to. Site 5 is now site 4, and it's located right across from the Pine lean-to. Sites 4 and 6–10 are all set beneath a towering, loosely spaced forest of mixed deciduous and coniferous trees without much undergrowth. The sites are quite spacious and clean, but don't provide much of a sense of privacy.

The sites in the 11–14 mini-loop are a bit more set off, but there's still a very open feel to the forest and the campsites here. If

CAMPGROUND RATINGS

Beauty:	★★★★
Site Privacy:	★★★
Site Spaciousness:	★★★★
Quiet:	★★★
Security:	★★★★
Cleanliness/upkeep:	★★★★

Lake St. Catherine can get pretty busy in the summer, but once the day crowd leaves, the place is all yours.

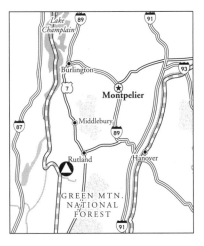

VERMONT

any RVs come here to roost, you may have an unfortunately clear view of them if you camp on this side of the campground. Sites 14 and 15 face each other at the end of this loop. They're open to each other, but they would be a good pair of sites for a group wanting two sites near each other.

You're likely to hear a bit of road noise from Route 30 nearer the campground entrance, but that fades as you get to the campsites located deeper within the park at the higher num-

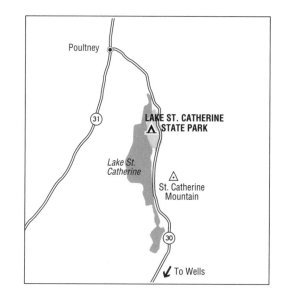

bered sites. Site 16 is moderately spacious, but way too exposed to the campground road for my tastes. Site 17 is huge and feels very open. That same openness characterizes sites 18 and 20. Site 19 is a bit more secluded and set within more dense forest. Site 21 is very open to the sky, but this site abuts the road leading into the campground. Site 22 is a bit more set off from the rest of the loop. It's still very open and doesn't have much forest cover, but it's surrounded by fairly dense undergrowth.

Heading up a short, steep hill on the campground loop road brings you to sites 23–27 and most of the lean-tos. While many Vermont State Parks have lean-to sites in discrete "neighborhoods" or within loops, here at Lake St. Catherine, the tent sites mingle freely with the lean-to sites.

Site 23 is quite spacious. This is the first site you'll come to atop the aforementioned hill. The forest grows a bit thicker at this point, which provides a deeper sense of seclusion. There are also more deciduous trees in the mix, which fills in the forest. There's a shared driveway to site 24 and the Cherry lean-to. The site is nicely isolated from the road, but you'll know the folks in the Cherry lean-to pretty well after a couple of nights in site 24. Site 25 is quite spacious and secluded, set within a towering grove of white pines and maples. There's a very dark, cool character to the forest surrounding this site.

There's a similar sylvan feel to site 26, although it's a bit more open to the road. There's a massive white pine standing sentinel over the site, which provides an interesting character. The layout of the site bends around to the right, so it seems nestled in the woods.

The forest continues to grow more dense and diverse as you move up the road. Groves of young balsams, white pines, and a few hardwoods are interspersed within the woods. The dense forest gives site 27 a solid air of seclusion on the sides from its neighbors, but the site is open at the front facing the road. The Ivy lean-to is just across the road.

Set well off on its own within dense forest, site 28 is fairly spacious and well isolated. Site 28A (which I bet was added after they turned site 4 into the Pine lean-to) is moderately spacious, long and narrow in shape, and open to the campground road on the side.

The sites within the third loop, 29–42, are set beneath a dense, mostly coniferous forest. Many of these sites are also situated along the side of an open field at the border of the forest. The sites here are spacious and there's plenty of woods between each of the sites, but the sites themselves are quite open to the road.

Among the more secluded sites within this loop are 34–36, especially 35; the loop is carved out of a dense grove of conifers. The proximity to the open field

To get there: Follow Route 30 south from Poultney to the park, which will be on the right.

KEY INFORMATION

Lake St. Catherine State Park
RD 2
Poultney, VT 05764

Operated by: Vermont Agency of Natural Resources, Department of Forests, Parks, and Recreation

Information: Lake St. Catherine State Park, (802) 287-9158 (summer) or (802) 483-2001 (January-May)

Open: Mid-May–Columbus Day

Individual sites: 51 tent sites and 10 lean-to sites

Each site has: Stone hearth and picnic table

Site assignment: First come, first served or by reservation

Registration: At ranger station as you enter campground; for reservations, call the park

Facilities: Hot showers, flush toilets, boat launch, snack bar and boat rentals in day-use area

Parking: At sites

Fee: $15

Restrictions:

Pets—On leash only

Fires—In established fire hearths only

Alcoholic beverages—At sites only

Vehicles—Parking at sites only

Other—Check in after 2 p.m., check out by 11 a.m., quiet hours 10 p.m.–7 a.m.; 8 person max. per site, 4-day min. stay for reservations

makes these sites desirable for families who want some open space in which to run around. There's also a playground on the field, so the kids will love it (when they're not splashing around in Lake St. Catherine).

As you move further down this part of the campground road, you get closer to the lake. Sites 36 and 37 are both huge, but otherwise quite different in character. Site 36 is a bit more wooded, and site 37 is open to the road. Sites 37 and 40 are set right against the shores of the lake.

There is an open grassy area leading in to sites 38 and 39. I once saw a truck with a boat trailer parked here, someone making the most of the extra space the campsite offered. These sites are also good for larger groups.

At the end of this section of campground road, sites 41 and 42 are set in their own little cul de sac. These sites are quite nicely secluded and moderately spacious. Site 41 is on the lakeside, and site 42 is on the field side. They are very open to each other, but otherwise secluded from the neighboring sites. I like site 41 a bit better because it opens to the lake, but both are quite nice.

The sites within the 43 to 50 loop are generally the quietest and most secluded at Lake St. Catherine. Site 43 is situated atop a small hill on the right as you enter this loop. It's a huge site, but it's very open and has power lines running over the site. I must say I've never seen that in a campsite before, but it doesn't really detract too much from the site's fairly secluded setting.

There's a delightful isolation to site 44. This site is set up off the campground loop road in a dense, dark grove of conifers. On the other side of the road, site 46 is also set back a bit, so it provides a deeper wilderness air. Site 45 is a bit open to the road, but very well buffered on the sides. It's also quite a large site.

Site 47 is a huge site. It's set along the side of another small grassy area that would make a perfect spot for a volleyball net, which is exactly what I found there the first time I saw this site. The very open character to this site wouldn't make it my first choice of a campsite within this loop, however.

There is a moderately isolated feel to site 48. It's set within a loose grove of conifers near the back of the campground. Site 49 is at the center of the loop on this end of the campground road. It's moderately spacious and offers a fairly decent sense of seclusion. The forest is also very open above, so there's lots of sunlight shining down on the campsite. Site 50 is right against the back border of the campground. It's very secluded from the rest of the campsites, but there's a fence defining the rear boundary of the site.

Lake St. Catherine is a decent sized state park. All the sites are relatively close to the lake; easily walkable and certainly an easy bike ride. A lot of people converge on the shores of the lake in the heat of summer, but if you have a campsite set aside for the night, the park will again be yours at the end of the day.

MOUNT ASCUTNEY STATE PARK

Windsor

Different people associate Mount Ascutney with different things. For some, it's the ski area they first think of (although the ski area is not officially part of Ascutney State Park). For others, it may be the hiking. For a select group of people, hang gliding comes to mind. Mount Ascutney is one of the premier spots in New England from which to launch a hang glider. For those activities (well, at least the hiking and hang gliding), spending the night camped out in the state park at the base of Mount Ascutney is a great way to start.

There are two distinct camping areas within Mount Ascutney State Park. Sites 1–18 are off to the right as you enter the park. Sites 19–39 are in the loop off to the left. The auto road to the summit is directly ahead of you when you enter the park here.

I particularly like the sites in the 1–18 loop off to the right. The sites here are quite spread out, so most provide an excellent sense of solitude and seclusion. The forest here is a dense mix of primarily coniferous trees. The fullness of the woods adds to the air of seclusion. The only caveat is that this side of the campground is fairly close to Route 44, so you will hear a bit of road noise during the day, but not too much at night.

The first cluster of sites includes sites 1–5. The road on this side of the campground is a straight in-and-out, two-way road. The other side has a one-way loop.

CAMPGROUND RATINGS

Beauty:	★★★★
Site Privacy:	★★★★
Site Spaciousness:	★★★★
Quiet:	★★★
Security:	★★★★
Cleanliness/upkeep:	★★★★

Mount Ascutney has an elaborate network of hiking trails, easily accessible from the southern end of the campground.

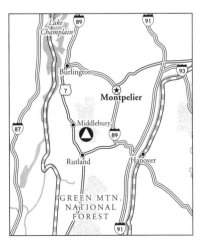

VERMONT

Site 1 is fairly small, and is located right off the campground road. Site 2 is set up off the road, so this site is more isolated. Sites 3, 4, and 5 are grouped together, but site 5 has a long driveway leading into the site that adds to its privacy. Sites 3 and 4 would be good for a large group, as they are quite close together. The mixed forest gives the individual sites a nice air of shaded solitude.

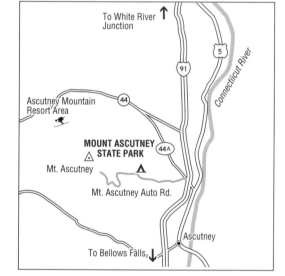

Site 10 is quite spacious, but it's open to the road and right across from the bathroom. Sites 9, 11, and 12 are set in a small group, much like sites 3–5. Site 9 is a bit too open and close to the road for my tastes. Sites 11 and 12 are tucked around a corner off the campground road, so they share a deeper sense of isolation. Again, all these sites are a stone's throw from Route 44 through the woods, so at times there will be some road noise.

The next group of sites you'll encounter as you move down the campground road are sites 6–8. These three sites are also set in a cluster. Site 8 is quite close to the bathroom, which is a good thing for some people and not so good for others. Site 7 is set up on a short spur off the campground road. It's added elevation gives it a bit more privacy. These sites are all moderately spacious.

As you walk up to site 7, you'll see the short footpath leading to site 6 just to the right of the entrance to site 7. Site 6 is very well isolated. There's about a 50-foot hike into the site, so the sense of seclusion is absolute and wonderful. Site 6 has a fire ring instead of a hearth, which I generally prefer. Although the stone hearths are aesthetically pleasing, the iron fire rings seem to be a bit safer, as they can contain fire, ashes, and coals on all sides.

The forest surrounding site 6 is relatively dense, but opens directly above the site to let in lots of sunlight during the day and give you a clear view of the sky at night. There are dark, shadowy spruce trees spread throughout on all sides of the site, giving it a pleasant, dark, cool feel, even on the warmest of summer days. There's still a bit of road noise from time to time, which is my only complaint about this otherwise excellent site.

There's a dense spruce grove with lots of fern ground cover surrounding site 13, so there's a considerable sense of isolation from all sides, but it's a bit open to the road. Site 14 is small, but set down off the road, which gives this site a nice sense of seclusion.

There's a small loop at the end of the campground road where sites 15–18 are set up. There's a stand of towering spruce trees growing out of the center of the circle. Sites 15 and 16 are spacious, but wide open to the road. Site 17 is set up on a small rise from the campground road. This site is moderately spacious and fairly secluded. The best site within this loop is site 18. There's about a 25-foot path leading up to the site from its parking space. The site is set within a relatively dense grove of mixed deciduous and coniferous trees, but it's distance from the road gives this site its exquisite air of seclusion.

Now on to the other side of the campground, where the loop contains sites 19–39 and the lean-tos. Site 22 is located near the trailhead for the Futures Trail. From here, you'll have access to a one-

To get there: Take Route 91 to Exit 8. From there, follow Route 5 almost two miles to Vermont Route 44A. Follow Route 44A about one mile until you see signs for the park.

KEY INFORMATION

Mount Ascutney State Park
1826 Back Mountain Road
Windsor, VT 05089
Operated by: Vermont Agency of Natural Resources, Department of Forests, Parks, and Recreation

Information: Mount Ascutney State Park, (802) 674-2060 (summer) or (800) 299-3071 (January–May)

Open: Mid-May–October 15

Individual sites: 39 tent sites and 10 lean-to sites

Each site has: Stone hearth or fire ring, picnic table

Site assignment: First come, first served or by reservation

Registration: At ranger station as you enter the park; for reservations, call the park

Facilities: Hot showers, flush toilets, water spigots

Parking: At sites

Fee: $14

Restrictions:

  Pets—On leash only

  Fires—In established fire rings only

  Alcoholic beverages—At sites only

  Vehicles—Parking at sites only

  Other—8 people max. per site, check out by 11 a.m., check in at 2 p.m., quiet hours 10 p.m.–7 a.m.

mile hike to Bare Rock Vista, a 3.4-mile hike to the Steam Donkey overlook, a 4.1-mile hike to the junction with the Windsor Trail, and a 4.5-mile hike to the summit of Mount Ascutney.

There's a nice sense of isolation to site 22. It's roomy and buffered on all sides by woods. I like site 22 the best on this side of the campground. Site 21 is also very spacious, but the side of site 21 is the back of site 19. You can see right through one site to the other. Site 20 is spacious and a bit more open than these two, and it's set within fairly dense forest.

The arrangement of sites 19 and 21 makes them a good pair for a group. Site 19 is open and spacious, but again, the site backs up against site 21. You will certainly meet your neighbors if you don't know them already.

A low canopy of spruce trees gives site 23 an added sense of solitude. It's a bit on the small side, though. Site 24 is tucked off to the left, and is also isolated on the sides, but the back of the site opens to the sites behind it and the lean-tos that are set around an open area. Most of the lean-tos at Mount Ascutney State Park are set within an open field and a loose grove of spruce and maple. The Oak and Beech lean-tos are the most open, therefore they are also the least private. The Maple lean-to is set up for disabled access, and is right across from the bathroom and the campground host site. The Pine lean-to is nicely isolated, and set within a tall grove of spruce.

Sites 25 and 26 are both moderately spacious, and set within a loosely spaced grove of spruce with dense undergrowth. These two sites are well secluded on the side, but somewhat open to each other. The White Birch and Cherry lean-tos are set up at the end of a short spur off the campground road. They are close to each other, but great for a larger group.

A grove of maples and other mixed deciduous varieties surround the spacious and open site 27. This site is very open to the sky. It's also set up off the campground road a bit, which adds to its sense of seclusion. Sites 29 and 31 are spacious, but open to the road. You'll still hear occasional road noise from Route 44 on this side of the campground, especially in this part of the loop.

Set up off the campground road, sites 28 and 30 feel well isolated. Site 30 is exceptionally spacious. Site 33 is open to the road, but is nicely separated from neighboring sites. A loose grove of spruce borders the back of the site, and a wall of deciduous trees and dense undergrowth defines the sides. There's a short footpath right next to this site that leads up to the playground area and the bathroom.

There is a slightly longer entryway leading into site 35, buffering it from the campground road. Sites 34 and 37 are right across the road from each other, but well buffered on either side. Site 34 is moderately spacious, but site 37 is absolutely huge and very open to the sky.

Site 36 is just like site 34 in size and shape. Site 38 is also similar, but it's a bit more spacious and very open to the sky. Site 39 is set down off the campground road, so it's very well isolated. It's also set within a dense grove of mixed conifers and hardwoods with lots of underbrush.

Whether it's the hiking or the hang gliding that brings you to Mount Ascutney State Park, a night in one of the campground's secluded sites will be a night well spent.

MOUNT MOOSALAMOO CAMPGROUND

Ripton

Want to feel like you're really out there? Mount Moosalamoo offers an incredibly remote wilderness atmosphere. To get to the campground, you turn off the paved road (actually Vermont Route 7), and start heading down a long and winding dirt road. This is called the Goshen Road, as it will eventually lead you to the town of Goshen. Several miles down on the right, you'll come to the road leading into Mount Moosalamoo Campground. If the campground ratings judged seclusion, this campground would easily get a 6.

Moosalamoo is the Abenaki Indian word thought to mean "the moose departs" or "he trails the moose." The Abenakis traveled through and stayed in this region frequently, and their history and legacy lingers.

The entire campground and all of the campsites within are shaded by a mixed forest of mostly hardwoods, with lots of maple and birch. The brilliant green leaves at the height of spring and summer almost cast a glow over the campground. The forest is young and loosely spaced enough to let generous amounts of light down to the campsites.

There are a total of 19 sites at Moosalamoo. They're set on both sides of the short campground loop road. The sites are spaced apart nicely and very large. There's plenty of room at each site to accommodate the group limit of eight campers per

CAMPGROUND RATINGS

Beauty:	★★★★★
Site Privacy:	★★★★★
Site Spaciousness:	★★★★★
Quiet:	★★★★★
Security:	★★★★
Cleanliness/upkeep:	★★★★

When you're camping at the Mount Moosalamoo Campground, you'll feel as if you are truly out in the wilderness.

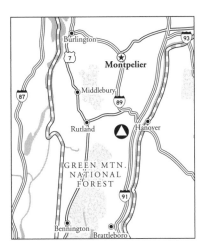

VERMONT

site. Mount Moosalamoo campground would also score a 6 for site spaciousness if the scale went that high!

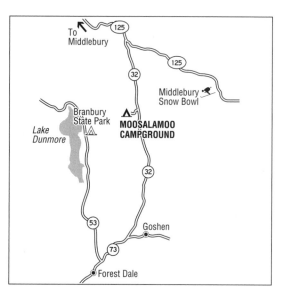

The campground host is in site 1, which is off to the left as you come into the campground loop. Behind site 1, you'll catch your first glimpse of the big open field in the center of the campground. There's also a little arboretum out there with a variety of deciduous and coniferous trees. The sign in front of the arboretum calls it a Backyard Wildlife Habitat. The evergreens within were planted in memory of former campground hostess Sarah Foster.

As you get further into the campground loop, past site 4, the forest becomes a bit more dense and the sites have an even greater wilderness sense and isolated feel. Sites 7, 9, 11, and most of the other odd numbered sites on the inner side of the campground loop abut the open field in the center. If you camp on one of the inner loop sites, you'll be able to walk out the back of your site into this field, which is perfect for a game of Frisbee, laying in the sun, or stargazing.

Most of the sites are fairly uniform in size, but sites 10 and 14 are extra large sites. They even have two picnic tables each. Site 16 and 17 are pretty big sites as well, but only equipped with one table apiece. Any of these sites would be well worth investigating if you're camping with a larger group or family.

Site 19 is right next to the arboretum, so it doesn't feel quite as secluded, but having the arboretum in full view is a nice aspect of this site. It's also quite close to the recycling station.

Mount Moosalamoo Campground is small, intimate, and has a wonderful sense of remoteness. I can think of only one caveat, although it certainly isn't unique to this campground alone: Bring whatever bug spray works best for you. You'll be deep in the woods here, and the insects can be ravenous.

There are plenty of hiking trails within easy access of Mount Moosalamoo Campground. You'll see trailheads for the Mount Moosalamoo and North Branch trails as you enter the campground. The blue-blazed trails are the local hiking trails. The white-blazed trails, the Appalachian Trail and the Long Trail, which overlap through the Moosalamoo region. There's also a trailhead right outside the campground for the Voter Brook Overlook.

Any of these trails intersect with other trail networks that wind throughout the forest in this part of Vermont. Try to get your hand on a trail map, because the trail network is extensive and it wouldn't be too difficult to wander off a bit further than you intended.

To get there: Follow Vermont Route 7 West, past the Middlebury College Snow Bowl and Breadloaf campus. Turn left on Road #32 (Goshen Road). Follow this dirt road for 4 miles and look for the campground signs on the right.

KEY INFORMATION

Mount Moosalamoo Campground
Vermont Route 32
Ripton, Vermont 05766

Operated by: Green Mountain National Forest

Information: Green Mountain National Forest Middlebury Ranger District 1007 Route 7 South Middlebury, VT 05753-8999 (802) 388-4362

Open: May 25–September 4

Individual sites: 19

Each site has: Fire ring, picnic table

Site assignment: First come, first served

Registration: Pay at self-serve fee station

Facilities: Pit toilets and hand water pumps

Parking: At sites

Fee: $5

Restrictions:

Pets—On leash only

Fires—In established fire rings only

Alcoholic beverages—At sites only

Vehicles—Two vehicles per site max.

Other—Check out by 2 p.m.; 14-day stay max., 8 people per site max.; Green Mountain National Forest is closed to ATVs (yeah!)

VERMONT

QUECHEE GORGE STATE PARK

Quechee

In a state full of incredible natural spectacles, Quechee Gorge has got to be one of Vermont's most amazing and unique sights. Plunging 165 feet down to the Ottauquechee River (whew, I'm glad they shortened that to name the gorge), Quechee Gorge looks like the scene in *Butch Cassidy and the Sundance Kid* where Robert Redford and Paul Newman, when cornered by the "good" guys, jump off their perch on a sheer cliff into a raging river. Seen from the Route 4 bridge that passes over it, the depth of the gorge looks almost surreal. You'll be able to tell when you're there, even if you miss the signs for the gorge and the state park. There are always a bunch of people who have stopped to look over the bridge.

Just before you get to the gorge (if you're heading north on Route 4), you'll come to Quechee Gorge State Park Campground, quietly tucked off on the left amidst the tourist shops selling T-shirts and maple syrup lining the other side of the road. For the most part, the campground is set beneath a loosely spaced forest of mostly conifers. There isn't much undergrowth. That factor, combined with the spacing and height of trees, gives the forest a statuesque presence. Visitors feel protected and secluded beneath the forest canopy. The spicy scent of the coniferous forest, mixed in with the musty aroma of wood smoke instantly brings you into

CAMPGROUND RATINGS

Beauty: ★★★★★
Site privacy: ★★★★
Site spaciousness: ★★★★
Quiet: ★★★
Security: ★★★★
Cleanliness/upkeep: ★★★★

The Quechee Gorge campground is in a perfect spot. There are numerous short hikes in and around Quechee Gorge, and you could spend countless hours gazing up into the dramatic formations of the gorge.

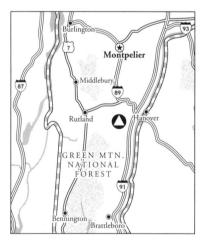

VERMONT

the deep wilderness. These olfactory delights abound in the campground.

Overall, the sites are very spacious and somewhat open. You could land a space shuttle in site 2, yet it still feels fairly isolated from the neighboring sites by the forest and a bit of under-growth. You'll hear some road noise from nearby Route 4, but it's not too bad. At night, it's guaranteed to lessen. Also, the road noise is reduced the further back you get in the campground. While most of the more

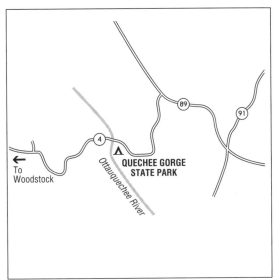

spacious sites would be suitable for handicap access, site 3 is specifically con-figured that way. Site 6 is right across from the rest room and shower building. There's a small playground behind the rest room building. Whether or not you want to be close to these is your call.

There's a steep embankment that falls away from the campground behind sites 7–14. This is not part of Quechee Gorge per se, but perhaps the river once flowed this way many moons ago. This feature of the landscape makes for dramatic scenery, but you'll need to be extra cautious if you have small kids running around. A slip and tumble down this embankment would be grim.

The Birch lean-to is also located along the steep dropoff by sites 7–14. Addi-tionally, you'll find a horseshoe pit near the Birch lean-to. Didn't bring your own horseshoes? No problem—visit the host site (to the right of the shower building) to check out a set of horseshoes.

There isn't much of a sense of privacy at site 8 and it's a bit too open for my tastes. Site 9 is huge. It's covered overhead by the forest canopy, although it's very open at the ground level. You find the same character at sites 12 and 10.

These two sites are also close to each other, which is particularly appealing for a larger group that might want two adjoining sites. Site 16 is another site that is a bit too open for my tastes.

The Walnut and Ash lean-tos are located right next to each other, also a good pair for a group large enough to need two lean-tos. The Hickory and Hackberry lean-tos are also adjacent. With the lean-tos in the Vermont state park campgrounds named for tree varieties, a new species is just one more thing you might learn while camping here.

Another good pair of sites for a larger group would be sites 18 and 19. These two are very open and close together. What these sites lack in privacy, they make up for in spaciousness. Quite close to a large, open field in the center of the campground, these are good sites to consider if you're camping with a tribe of kids and need a place for them to run around and burn off some of their seemingly boundless energy. The swing set and slides are located in this field. There also is a trailhead for the Quechee Gorge Trail located at the nearby intersection of the campground roads. This short trail is perfect for a quick walk after dinner.

Set against the woods bordering the central field, sites 20–22 are moderately spacious and have easy access to the field. The Pine lean-to is also located on the field. It is very open and not too private, but it is configured for disabled access. The campground also winds around a bit closer to Route 4 here, so between the proximity to the road and the field, it can get a bit noisy.

To get there: From Route 89 in Vermont, follow Route 4 north toward the town of Quechee. The signs for the campground are right before Quechee Gorge itself.

KEY INFORMATION

Quechee Gorge State Park
764 Dewey Mills Road
White River Junction, VT 05001
Operated by: Vermont Agency of Natural Resources, Department of Forests, Parks, and Recreation

Information: Quechee Gorge State Park (802) 295-2990 (summer) or (800) 299-3071 (January–May)

Open: Mid-May–October 15

Individual sites: 47 tent sites and 7 lean-to sites

Each site has: Fire ring, picnic table

Site assignment: First come, first served or by reservation

Registration: At ranger station; for reservations, call the park

Facilities: Hot showers, flush toilets, playground

Parking: At sites

Fee: $13 for tent sites, $20 for lean-to sites. Visitor fees: $2 for ages 14 and up, $1.50 for ages 4–13

Restrictions:

Pets—On leash only

Fires—In established fire rings only

Alcoholic beverages—At sites only

Vehicles—Parking at sites only

Other—Check in after 2 p.m., check out by 11 a.m., quiet hours 10 p.m.–7 a.m.; 8 person max. per site; campground host is at site 4

There will be a bit of road noise at sites 23–28. Site 23 is very open and lacks privacy. Site 24 is quite close to the road. In fact, you can see the store on the other side of Route 4 through the woods. However, site 24 does have a nice amount of dense forest separating it on either side of the site.

Site 26 is huge, but wide open. This site is also right next to part of the Quechee Gorge Trail, which is a mere 0.21 miles. Site 27 is open, spacious, and set within a spruce grove. Site 29 is spacious and open, but the back of the site opens to the field and rest room. Site 30 is set within a grove of mixed deciduous and coniferous trees. This site also faces the gorge, so through openings in the forest, there's a view as the gorge drops away below. Site 31 is very spacious, and set beneath a coniferous grove, so the site floor is covered with a blanket of pine needles and leaves upon which you can pitch your tent.

There's a steep dropoff facing sites 31–37. The scenery is nothing short of dramatic, but in these sites there are numerous additional reasons to keep a close eye (or a short leash) on the kids. Sites 32 and 34 are quite open and spacious, but not quiet as private as the rest. Site 35 is very open. The back of the site opens to the back of the lean-to sites.

At the end of this spur off the campground loop road, site 37 is set in a quiet grove of conifers and offers a nice sense of isolation. Site 37 is an incredible campsite. It's very spacious, framed by conifers, and open to the sky to get lots of sunlight. Site 37 is also right next to the Quechee Gorge Trail, which is a short hike down to the gorge from the campground

Site 38 is located between the Walnut and Ash lean-tos. It's framed by dense woods, but very open in front. Within the 42–47 loop, site 47 is huge and somewhat open in front and above, but dense forest isolates the site on the sides. Site 45 is also huge and has an open feel. It's set within a pine grove. Sites 44 and 46 are a bit smaller, but still have a nice isolated feel. Site 43 is huge and open. This site is also set within a grove of pines. This site is a bit closer to the road and the recycling station, however.

It's a bit smaller than some of its neighbors, but site 39 is still quite spacious. This site is carved out of a grove of loosely spaced white pines. Site 40 is open, spacious and set within a loosely spaced pine grove. It's a beautiful site, but it's also on the Route 4 side of the campground, so you'll hear some road noise. Sites 42 and 43 are a bit more open and also closer to the campground loop road, so they're not as quiet as the more secluded sites.

SMUGGLERS NOTCH STATE PARK

Stowe

Ever wonder where the "smugglers" in Smugglers Notch comes from? I always have. Apparently, when President Thomas Jefferson passed an embargo forbidding trade with Great Britain and Canada in 1807, it was especially hard on the folks living in northern Vermont. Most of those industrious, independent Vermonters kept right on trading with Montreal, moving cattle and other goods up through the narrow passage between the towering, 1,000 foot cliffs. They established a grand tradition of smuggling that continued with abolitionists helping slaves head north to seek liberation in Canada and rumrunners bringing liquor south into the country from Canada during prohibition.

These days, things are a bit quieter in the notch. The campground at Smugglers Notch State Park is across the street from part of Stowe Mountain Resort ski area, so you get glimpses of the towering mountain through the trees. You're also surrounded by Mount Mansfield State Forest, so the hiking opportunities are virtually limitless. The campground is set beneath a mixed, mostly deciduous forest, with an open field in the center. It is very quiet, especially at night, and even during the warmest periods of summer, the air is crisp and cool this high up in the Green Mountains.

There's a dense grove of mixed deciduous trees and lots of undergrowth surrounding the moderately spacious site 1.

CAMPGROUND RATINGS

Beauty:	★★★★★
Site privacy:	★★★★★
Site spaciousness:	★★★★
Quiet:	★★★★
Security:	★★★★
Cleanliness/upkeep:	★★★★

Settled high in the Green Mountains, Smugglers Notch Campground has a quiet secluded feel and easy access to some of the best hiking in Vermont.

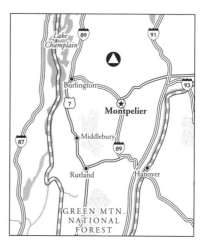

VERMONT

That solid wall of forest gives the site a solid sense of seclusion. The sites here have either a brick or cobblestone hearth for a fireplace. Site 1 has a charming stone hearth. The site abuts site 2 to the back, but it still has a nice feeling of isolation.

A small stand of trees with a spruce and two maples guards the entrance to site 2. A mixed forest with dense undergrowth surrounds this fairly spacious site, which is otherwise relatively open to the campground road. It has a nicely isolated feel, as do most of the sites in the small, intimate campground at Smugglers Notch.

There's a trailhead for a nature trail leading to Mountain Brook right next to site 3. Sites 3 and 4 are very spacious and open. They are situated right across the campground loop road from each other, but both encircled by dense forest.

Site 5 is moderately spacious and isolated on the sides by the dense forest. There's also a huge stump in the middle of the site, which is suitable for an alternate table or a chopping block. It may be a huge site, but site 6 is right next to the rest room buildings. It's set within a loosely spaced deciduous grove.

A dense forest pleasantly surrounds site 7. It's open to the sky above, and near the grassy field at the center of the campground. Site 8 is set up for disabled access. This site is moderately spacious and has an open feel to it. The rest room building is right behind the site for easy access to the facilities.

Site 9 is huge, but open to the road. This site would be perfect for a larger group or a family with small children, since the site is also right next to the open field. About two-thirds of the surface of site 9 is covered with grass, and it has a wooden, split rail fence with a flower box separating the site from the campground road. There's also a huge maple growing on the right side of the site, so what this site may lack in woodland sense of seclusion, it more than makes up for with its pastoral feel.

There's a decent amount of spaciousness and seclusion at site 10, but it is close to the rest room buildings. There's a small stand of deciduous trees at the entrance to the site, which gives it a nice, closed-off feel.

A spur off the campground road to the right brings you to sites 17 through 11 in descending order. Site 17 is quite spacious and set within a dense deciduous forest. It's also open to the sky, so lots of sunlight filters down to the site. This is a pleasant combination of solitude and openness. Site 16 is small, but secluded by a dense wall of deciduous trees, which is good since it's also right across from the rest room building. The site is open to the sky above, which provides a shimmering green glow when the sun reflects off the leaves of the maples, birch, and beech trees framing the site.

You can see Stowe Mountain Resort ski area through the forest surrounding site 15. The site is very spacious, but the forest is less dense. The site is also marked by a small stump at the entrance. A quiet little brook flows by to the right of the site as you see it from the campground road.

A mixed grove of deciduous and coniferous trees encircles site 14. It's very spacious and has a grassy surface on which to pitch your tent. The back of the site is a bit open and you can see some buildings outside the campground. This site is also right next to the Cherry lean-to site.

> To get there: Follow Route 100 North to Route 108. Follow Route 108 past Stowe Mountain Resort to the state park on the right, across the road from the northeastern part of the ski area.

KEY INFORMATION

Smuggglers Notch State Park
7248 Smugglers Notch Road
Stowe, VT 05672

Operated by: Vermont Agenc of Natural Resources, Department of Forests, Parks, and Recreation

Information: Smugglers Notch State Park, (802) 253-4014 (summer) or (800) 658-6934 (January–May)

Open: Mid-May–October 15

Individual sites: 21 tent sites and 14 lean-to sites

Each site has: Stone hearth and picnic table

Site assignment: First come, first served or by reservation

Registration: At ranger station as you enter the park; for reservations, call the park

Facilities: Hot showers, flush toilets

Parking: At sites

Fee: $13

Restrictions:

Pets—On leash only

Fires—In established fireplaces only

Alcoholic beverages—At sites only

Vehicles—Parking at sites only

Other—8 people max. per site; check out by 11 a.m., check in after 2 p.m., quiet hours 10 p.m.–7 a.m.

This would be a perfect site if the forest right behind the site were a bit more dense and grown in, as it's buffered on the sides and open to the sky.

There's a combined sense of seclusion and spaciousness to site 13. It's nicely secluded by the dense forest on the sides and to the back, but feels very open in the center. There's a huge Hemlock right at the entrance to the site. The canopy from that tree and a couple of others give the site a "roof," which adds to the quiet and sense of seclusion.

There's a very open sense both within and above site 12. There are grassy areas to the right and left within the site, and mixed deciduous trees surround it, lending a decent sense of seclusion. Site 11 is very spacious and set off at the end of the campground road across from the Larch lean-to. It's nicely secluded on all sides and open in the front facing the lean-to. It's also open to the sky, the sort of site that allows a nice sunlit feel during the day and brilliant moonlight and stargazing at night.

A stately pair of maples guards site 18 on the left, and one tall, narrow maple on the right. The site winds around to the right and is set within a dense deciduous grove. It's huge and nicely secluded. It's not as open to the sky as some of the other sites on this side of the campground along the 11–17 loop, but the configuration of the site and the dramatic view of the ski area through the trees earn this site high marks. Also, the forest floor drops off and the woods open up as you look into the site, which gives you a deeper view into the forest and a more secluded, wilderness feel. There will be some sporadic road noise from Route 108, but practically none at night.

The back of site 19 is isolated by thick deciduous forest. It's a moderately spacious site, but open and fairly close to the Elm lean-to. It feels open to the campground road along the front of the site, although there is a sparse, narrow stand of young deciduous trees along the road.

There is a similar open feel to site 20. This site abuts the open field in the center of the campground. It's a U-shaped site, so you could probably drive right through the site. The proximity to the field and open view of most of the field is perfect if you have some younger campers who need to run around and burn off some excess energy before you zip them into the tent at night. Like site 19, a narrow stand of maples separates the site from the road, but it still has a very open feel. I love the cobblestone hearths you'll find in most of the sites here.

Site 21 is a bit smaller and has a similar open feel to that of sites 19 and 20. The back of the site is wide open to the field, but again, that's great for kids to have space to play and for you to bundle up, lay on your back, and gaze at the stars at night.

Camping at Smuggler's Notch puts you right across the road from Mount Mansfield. This is Vermont's highest peak and home to some of the world-class hiking for which Vermont is renowned. There are 35 miles of hiking trails winding up and over Mount Mansfield, so plan your hike and pay attention. It wouldn't do to inadvertently come down on the other side of the mountain.

Test yourself on classics like the aptly named Profanity Trail and Subway, or you can opt for any of a variety of routes that connect to the Long Trail. Even below the summit, this ridgeline hike passes by overlooks with stunning views of the Green Mountains.

THETFORD HILL STATE PARK
Thetford

Thetford Hill State Park is a small, quiet campground with a peaceful, pastoral feel. Set atop a small hillside with a gentle trail system well-suited for short walks and trail running, it's near several popular spots like Quechee Gorge, Lake Fairlee, and Hanover, New Hampshire, but far enough away to be blissfully quiet. If you really want to escape and have a peaceful, quiet camping experience, Thetford Hill State Park is a good spot.

There are 14 tent sites at Thetford Hill State Park, carved out of the dense forest of mixed conifers and deciduous trees. All sites are very spacious and clean. There's even a small playground located near the lean-to sites on the way into the camping area.

Like most Vermont state park campsites, each site has a sizeable and sturdy stone or brick hearth for a fireplace. The sites are framed by the dense, mixed forest of birch, maple, and conifers with lots of dense undergrowth, which adds to the sense of seclusion for most of the sites.

As you enter the camping area, sites 1 and 2 are off to the right. Both of these sites are spacious and very well isolated. On sunny days, these sites get a lot of light filtering down through the trees. There's a fair sense of isolation to site 3. This site is tucked off to the left, across the campground road from site 4. It's surrounded on all sides by dense forest, but open to

CAMPGROUND RATINGS

Beauty:	★★★★
Site privacy:	★★★★
Site spaciousness:	★★★★
Quiet:	★★★★★
Security:	★★★★
Cleanliness/upkeep:	★★★★

If you're looking for some peace and quiet, the intimate campground at Thetford Hill State Park should fit the bill.

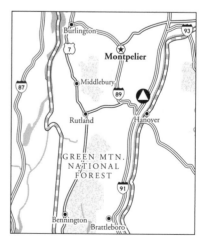

VERMONT

site 4 right across the road. Consequently, site 4 also feels a bit more open, but it's really only exposed to the road. Site 4 is also surrounded by forest, but the forest on this side of the campground road is more deciduous and a bit more loosely spaced.

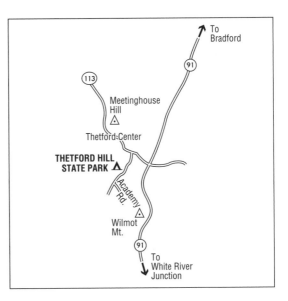

Site 5 has a grassy surface on which to pitch your tent. The loosely spaced forest behind this huge and scenic site is punctuated by a huge spruce tree growing out of a dense ground cover of ferns. The combination of shapes and sizes in the forest behind site 5 makes for dramatic contrasts.

There is also a grassy surface for your tent in site 6, but the site itself is a bit smaller and feels more open to the road. Huge maple, birch, and pine trees frame the site. Site 7 is nicely secluded on the sides and back of the site, but it's right across from the rest room building and the campground host site. Site 8 has a very open atmosphere, but a nice grassy surface for your tent. Site 8 feels a bit too airy for my tastes, but the trio of pines growing out of the middle of the site is a nice addition.

There is a dramatic contrast within the forest beginning at site 9, owing to the blending of tall spruce and younger deciduous trees. This moderately spacious site is nestled within a spruce grove, and smaller trees intermingle toward the back of the site.

A looser, but similarly mixed grove enshrouds site 11. This site feels a bit more open and less private. Site 10 is right across the road, but feels pretty well isolated on the sides and back of the site. Sites 9 and 11 would be a good pair of sites for a larger family or group needing two sites.

A small cluster at the end of the campground road contains sites 12–14. These sites offer the greatest sense of seclusion. Site 12 is fairly small, carved out of a spruce grove and filled in on all sides with young maples. Site 13 is set in a loosely spaced forest, but still provides a decent sense of seclusion by virtue of its location near the end of the campground road.

Site 14 probably has the deepest sense of seclusion of any at Thetford Hill. This site bears off to the left from the end of the campground road. It's a kidney-shaped site, tucked into a grove of fairly young maples, whose lush leaves provide a wall of green around the site. There are towering spruce trees, reaching up to 100 feet or so, growing out of the younger maples on all sides of the site.

The site is also very spacious, and elongated in shape. You could park your car at the entrance to the site, and set up your tent and table so that you wouldn't even see your car from your tent, and you'd still have plenty of room within the site. Site 14 provides a pleasantly reassuring sense of seclusion at the end of the road. This is the prime site at Thetford Hills State Park.

To get there: Follow Route 91 to Exit 14 and Route 113. Follow Route 113 West toward Thetford. Turn left on Academy Road. Follow this for approximately one mile until you see the sign for the park.

KEY INFORMATION

Thetford Hill State Park
Box 132
Thetford, VT 05074

Operated by: Vermont Agency of Natural Resources, Department of Forests, Parks, and Recreation

Information: Thetford Hill State Park, (802) 785-2266 (summer) or (800) 299-3071 (January–May)

Open: Mid-May–Labor Day

Individual sites: 14 tent sites and 2 lean-to sites

Each site has: Fire hearth, picnic table

Site assignment: First come, first served or by reservation

Registration: At ranger station; for reservations, call the park

Facilities: Hot showers, flush toilets, playground, picnic area

Parking: At sites

Fee: $12

Restrictions:

Pets—On leash only

Fires—In established fire rings only

Alcoholic beverages—At sites only

Vehicles—Parking at sites only

Other— Check in after 2 p.m., check out by 11 a.m., quiet hours 10 p.m.–7 a.m.; 8 person max. per site; 2-day min. stay for reservations

UNDERHILL STATE PARK

Underhill Center

The air is clear and cool as you approach Underhill State Park. Perched on the western flanks of Mount Mansfield, Vermont's highest peak, this is the spot to choose for launching your hiking adventures on and around this renowned peak. You can literally begin a hike up Mount Mansfield from your campsite.

Underhill State Park itself feels remarkably isolated. At night, the silence and solitude is complete, the darkness absolute. Most of the sites are hike-in sites, which adds to the sense of seclusion.

Sites 8–11 are spread the furthest from the rest of the campground. These hike-in sites are located up past the park shelter, an open log cabin-type structure in the day use and picnic area. Sites 8–11 all require a hike of between 50 and 70 feet, so they are very well secluded. The only other people you'll see from within one of these sites are your immediate neighbors, and at night, all you'll see are glimmers of their campfire through the forest.

This cluster of sites is set within a moderately dense forest of mostly young deciduous trees, with lots of beech and maples. They are not especially huge sites, especially since much of the center of the site is occupied by the large stone hearth. However, the sense of solitude more than makes up for the modest size of these sites.

There is a separate parking area for these hike-in sites, so you won't have to lug your

CAMPGROUND RATINGS

Beauty:	★★★★★
Site Privacy:	★★★★★
Site Spaciousness:	★★★★
Quiet:	★★★★★
Security:	★★★★★
Cleanliness/upkeep:	★★★★★

Underhill State Park's campsites are mostly hike-in sites. This design and its remote mountainside location add to the campground's wilderness sense.

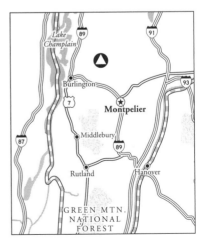

VERMONT

gear quite as far as if you parked down by the ranger station. This parking area is also used by day hikers going up Mount Mansfield, so if it's full when you first arrive, be patient and try again later.

Across the campground road from this small parking area is the Pine lean-to, which is also accessed via a short hike. It would be worth getting this site just for the sense of seclusion. You won't see anyone or anything but the surrounding deciduous forest.

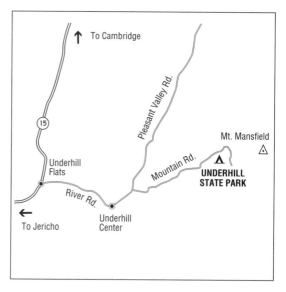

You can also get to sites 8–11 by hiking up past the park shelter. On the way up to site 9, you'll pass a water spigot. Fortunately, the site itself is further up the trail, so you won't have people just walking by on the way to fill their canteens and hydration packs for the hike up Mansfield.

I love these kind of hike-in sites because they really add to the wilderness air. There are wheeled carts available for use down by the ranger station to help you haul your camping gear into the sites. Sites 6 and 7 are also hike-in sites, spread out along a walking path that winds out from the ranger station in a short loop. These two sites are a bit larger than sites 8–10. Site 7 is moderately spacious, but fabulously shrouded in dense forest.

There's a decent sense of isolation to site 6. There's a short wooden retaining wall that keeps the tent platform intact and level. This site is set beneath a grove of tall spruce trees, so there is a deep, woodsy, cool air to the site. The forest is loosely spaced enough that it lets lots of sunlight down through the woods to the site. This too adds to the unique character of this site. It's relatively close to the rest rooms, but not too close.

The Cedar lean-to, on the other hand, is right behind the bathroom building, a bit close for me. Site 5 and the Ash lean-to are also tucked in down behind the Cedar lean-to. Site 5 is set within a moderately dense forest at the edge of the woods and an open area in which the Cedar lean-to is situated. Site 5 and the Ash lean-to are at the edge of a fairly steep bank as well, which adds to the character of the sites, but requires that you be extra cautious if you're camping here with kids.

There is an open, grassy picnic area right across the parking lot from the ranger station. Sites 1–4, and the Maple, Birch, and Beech lean-tos are set around the periphery of this small field. These sites are a bit too exposed, but it is so quiet and dark here at night that it wouldn't matter much as evening fell. These sites also face a steep embankment.

Tucked off to the left at the edge of the picnic area is the tiny site 4. This site is really small. You'd have trouble pitching a tent designed for more than two people. Sites 1–3 are moderately spacious and a bit more set off. Site 1 is set up a bit higher than the others. All three are carved out of fairly dense forest surrounding the open field and the picnic area. Since all of the other sites here are hike-in sites, these sites are the most easily accessible at Underhill State Park.

Wherever you land at Underhill State Park, you won't be far from the trails that follow the spine of the Green Mountains and bring you to the highest point in Vermont.

To get there: Follow Route 15 to Underhill Center. Turn onto Pleasant Valley Road. Follow this through the town of Underhill to Mountain Road. Turn onto Mountain Road and follow the signs to the park.

KEY INFORMATION

Underhill State Park
P.O. Box 249
Underhill Center, VT 05490

Operated by: Vermont Agency of Natural Resources, Department of Forests, Parks, and Recreation

Information: Underhill State Park, (802) 899-3022 (summer) or (800) 252-2363 (January–May)

Open: Mid-May–Columbus Day

Individual sites: 11 tent sites and 6 lean-to sites

Each site has: Stone hearth, picnic table

Site assignment: First come, first served or by reservation

Registration: At ranger station as you enter campground; for reservations, call the park

Facilities: Flush toilets, water

Parking: At either of two central parking areas

Fee: $13

Restrictions:

Pets—On leash only

Fires—In established fire rings only

Alcoholic beverages—At sites only

Vehicles—Parking in either of two small lots near groups of sites

Other—Check in after 2 p.m., check out by 11 a.m., quiet hours 10 p.m.–7 a.m.; 8 person max. per site; 2-day min. for reservations

MASSACHUSETTS

BEARTOWN STATE FOREST

Monterey

Beartown State Forest is a beautiful, intimate campground set along the shores of Benedict Pond, a good-sized pond ready for fishing, swimming, and paddling. There are only 12 sites, but if there were a rating for percentage of perfect sites, Beartown would be way out in front.

Camping here is by reservation only, so plan ahead, call ahead, and try to get yourself one of the spectacularly secluded and superbly scenic pond sites. The Appalachian Trail passes right through the forest, and right next to the campground. If I were hiking the Appalachian Trail, I would think it well worth the effort to plan for a night at Beartown State Forest, especially if I could secure site 11.

There are a total of 12 sites. Sites 1 and 2 are nice spacious sites. Site 1 is huge, and has a large grassy area where you could place your tent. The sites themselves are surrounded by fairly dense forest. Sites 3 and 4 are on a small grassy field that separates the parking area from the state forest road. These sites are wide open and quite spacious, but not very private. They are also close to the pit toilets, which are the only facilities at this primitive campground. Even though sites 3 and 4 are right off the small parking area, they can still offer a secluded sense, especially since there isn't going to be any traffic traveling down the road past the campground later in the evening.

CAMPGROUND RATINGS

Beauty:	★★★★★
Site privacy:	★★★★★
Site spaciousness:	★★★★
Quiet:	★★★★★
Security:	★★★★★
Cleanliness/upkeep:	★★★★

Whether you're into hiking, biking, paddling, or horseback riding, you won't run out of things to do at Beartown State Forest. The campsites on the shores of Benedict Pond are worth the trip alone.

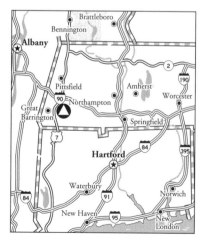

MASSACHUSETTS

Site 6 is also a very spacious site. It's set just off to the left of the rest rooms. If you're going to camp closer to the road, though, (i.e. if you couldn't score a pond site), choose site 5. There's a very short lug in from the parking area, which gives site 5 a nice, isolated feel. It's also set within a very dense grove of mixed deciduous and coniferous trees that shield the site from the state forest road.

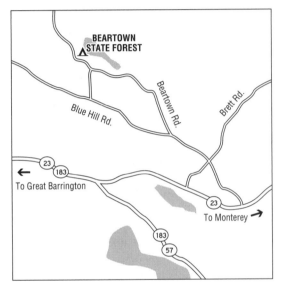

Site 7 is a roomy and private site. This site is off to the left as you start to wind down the short road that leads to the pond sites. Site 7 is also right across from the water fountain. The dense wall of woods surrounding the site gives it a nice wilderness feeling.

All of the sites have a picnic table and fire ring, although some of the slightly larger sites have two picnic tables. From both sites 8 and 12, you'll have easy access to the footpath leading to the shore of Benedict Pond. Site 8 is a bit more open than the other sites in the pondside neighborhood. Like site 12, it's near, but not on, the pond.

Site 12 is nicely isolated, but away from the pond. You'll still have a good pond view from your table over the waterfront sites, but you probably won't see the pond through the front of your tent. Site 12 is also set up on a small rise, which gives it good drainage as well as being a better vantage point, not that drainage is ever an issue. After all, it never rains when you go camping, does it? Sites 9–11 are situated right along the edge of the pond. Site 11 is the primo pond site. This really is a perfect, dramatically sculpted site. It sits on a small rise that looks out onto the placid waters of Benedict Pond and the rolling hills that frame the water. The pond access trail runs by just to the right of the site, but that's no bother. Besides offering a view filled with dramatic scenery, the site is also well isolated. With the pond-facing orientation of this site, and the ring of wildflowers and maples surrounding the site, you'll see the pond and the woods and that's it.

Since you're bound to spend lots of time just sitting and drinking in the view (and who knows, you may make some new friends happy to share the experience), there are two picnic tables at this site. You could take this site for a week and never have to leave once. You can paddle, swim, and fish right from your campsite. Even doing nothing in a site like this is spectacular.

Sites 9 and 10 have equally dramatic pondside locations. The two sites individually are a bit smaller than site 11, and they're a bit close together, but this would be a perfect pair for a group that needs two sites, and you couldn't ask for two more scenic sites. All in all, sites 9, 10, and 11 are classic pondside campsites. It's well worth planning way ahead for a few nights in one of these sites.

Beartown State Forest is a very quiet campground, even during the day. The only sounds you'll hear are the woodland birds talking back and forth, the soft splash of a canoe or kayak paddle out in the pond, and perhaps the whiz of a line being cast into the water.

With all this solitude, there's still plenty to do within Beartown State Forest. There's a larger beach and day use area up the state forest road before you get to

To get there: From Great Barrington, follow Route 23 east toward Monterey. Turn left on Blue Hill Road, and follow this to Beartown Road and signs for the park.

KEY INFORMATION

Beartown State Forest
P.O. Box 97
Monterey, MA 01245

Operated by: Massachusetts Department of Environmental Management

Information: Beartown State Forest, (413) 528-0904

Open: Year-round

Individual sites: 12

Each site has: Fire ring, picnic table

Site assignment: By reservation only

Registration: For reservations, contact Reserve America at (877) I-CAMP-MA (422-6762) or www.reserveamerica.com.

Facilities: Pit toilets

Parking: At sites or in central parking area

Fee: Massachusetts residents, $5; non-residents, $6

Restrictions:

Pets — On leash only

Fires — In established fire rings only

Alcoholic beverages — Not allowed

Vehicles — Two per site max.

Other — Motorized vehicles check in at forest headquarters

the campground. To hit the hiking trails right from the campground, follow the Benedict Pond Road (the paved road running through the forest and past the campground) to the Wildcat Trail, the Turkey Trail, the Sky Peak Trail, and the Airplane Trail. I've never ridden it before, but I've heard from mountain biking buddies out in this neck of the woods that the Airplane Trail is one you won't want to miss.

All the above trails are multi-use trails, so you'll see hikers and bikers. Be careful, be aware, and share the trails. Horses are allowed on these trails as well, but you might not see as many, since there is a separate bridle trail. The blue-blazed trails are the hiking trails, the red-blazed trail is the bridle trail, and the white blazes indicate the Appalachian Trail. The orange-blazed trails are open to everyone—hikers, bikers, horses, and off-road vehicles.

MASSACHUSETTS

CLARKSBURG STATE PARK
Clarksburg

Clarksburg State Park is up in the absolute northwestern corner of Massachusetts, right along the Vermont border. The sites at this moderately sized campground are carved out of a dense forest of pines, spruce, and hemlock that gives the woods a dark, cool feeling. Even on the most brilliant sunny days, the whole campground is immersed in the shade of the dense, verdant forest.

The coniferous roof of the campground also covers most of the sites with a velvety blanket of pine needles. The sites are spread out along a large, central campground loop road with one intersecting road that bisects the loop. Sites 9–14 are situated along the cross road. The rest are on the outer loops.

You can reserve most of the sites through Reserve America. Sites 1, 4, 10, 11, 12, 14, 18, 23, 25, and 29 are the first come, first served sites. The sites located along the inner side of the campground loop and the cross road have the most densely forested feel. The sites facing Mauserts Pond, although they are still quite a ways back from the water's edge and carved out of the forest, offer a bit more light coming through the trees and occasional glimpses of the pond.

Sites 1 and 2 are very spacious and have an isolated feeling. Even though the woods are quite dense, you can catch a glimpse of Mauserts Pond from site 2. Sites 6 and 7 are nice sites. These are set down from the road,

CAMPGROUND RATINGS

Beauty:	★★★★
Site privacy:	★★★★
Site spaciousness:	★★★★
Quiet:	★★★★
Security:	★★★★
Cleanliness/upkeep:	★★★★

The campground at Clarksburg State Park has a dark, cool, sylvan feel even on the most brilliant summer days.

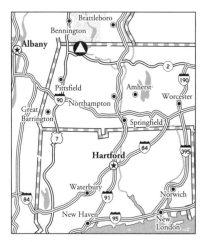

MASSACHUSETTS

which adds to their privacy and sense of isolation. Sites 10 and 11 are a bit smaller than most of the other sites at Clarksburg State Park, and they are close to the facilities.

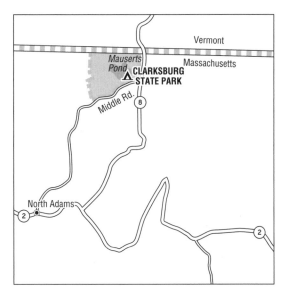

Along the stretch of the campground loop where sites 16–23 are located, the sites are quite spacious and isolated from each other and from the rest of the sites. These are all decent sites for tent camping, as you'll feel a nice sense of solitude here. There are more hardwoods mixed into the forest along this portion of the campground loop road. The brilliant green leaves of the maples in summer brighten the forest.

Moving further along the one-way campground loop road, you'll come to site 23, which is a tremendous site. This site is set way back from the road, it's quite spacious, and it has a nice sense of wilderness seclusion. The forest directly overhead is clear, so you'll also get some light filtering down to the site floor as well as a nice slice of the night sky for stargazing (once you've put your campfire out and your eyes adjust to the dark).

Sites 25 and up are a bit smaller than most of the others, particularly those situated along the outside of the campground loop road, but they're still quite nice and offer a private atmosphere, as they're set within the dense coniferous forest. The walls of pine and spruce form an effective barrier between the individual sites. Site 29 is the exception, but this is quite a large site and well suited for a group or family.

Site 31 is set within its own clearing. This would be a good site if you have smaller kids, as it will be easier to keep your eyes on them. Site 33 looks much the same way, but it's a bit smaller.

It seems that site 36 has vanished from the Clarksburg State Park campground loop. In its place is a trailhead that leads off in the direction of the Mauserts Loop. Perhaps the site was sacrificed to make a spot for the trailhead—not a bad trade off if you ask me.

Finishing up the campground loop road, sites 35–44 are smaller than some of the other isolated, larger sites and those located along the outer loop, but thanks to the deep, dense nature of Clarksburg's forest, they still provide a nice sense of privacy and isolation.

Overall, the sensation here is one of being sequestered in a dense forest. There's a hushed silence about the place, even during the daylight hours. Then, during the evening, all you're likely to hear is the snap and crackle of campfires.

During the day, you'll definitely want to check out Mauserts Pond. There's a footpath leading to the pond right across from site 25. If you bring a canoe or kayak, it might be easier to head over to the day use area, which has a boat launch and beach.

There are several fairly lengthy hiking trails winding through Clarksburg State Park. The Mauserts Loop Trail leads from the campground (I believe this is the trailhead at the former location of site 36), and crosses over Beaver Creek, then brings you up toward Vermont. The Horrigan Road Trail veers off to the west about two-thirds of the way to the Vermont border, after which the trail is called (appropriately enough) the Vermont Line Trail. The Bog Trail winds around the northern end of the pond, and brings you to the beach and boathouse.

To get there: Follow Route 8 through Clarksburg heading toward Vermont until you see the signs for Clarksburg State Forest on the left.

KEY INFORMATION

Clarksburg State Park
Middle Road
Clarksburg, MA 01247

Operated by: Massachusetts Department of Environmental Management

Information: Clarksburg State Park, (413) 664-8345

Open: Memorial Day weekend through Labor Day

Individual sites: 44

Each site has: Fire ring, picnic table

Site assignment: First come, first served or by reservation

Registration: At ranger station; for reservations, contact Reserve America at (877) I-CAMP-MA (422-6762) or www.reserveamerica.com.

Facilities: Flush toilets, beach area, boat launch

Parking: At sites

Fee: Massachusetts residents, $10; non-residents, $12

Restrictions:

Pets—Dogs on leash only

Fires—In established fire rings only

Alcoholic beverages—Not allowed

Vehicles—Two per site max.

Other—Quiet hours 10 p.m.–7 a.m.

GRANVILLE STATE FOREST

Granville

Driving down the West Hartland Road, the long dirt road that leads into Granville State Forest, you can't help but feel a reassuring sense of remoteness. The forest itself is spectacular—a relatively even mix of conifers and deciduous trees that includes a lot of maples, whose green leaves reflect the summer sun and illuminate the forest.

You'll find Granville State Forest in the southwestern corner of Massachusetts. The southern edge of the forest is actually right on the Connecticut border. There used to be two separate camping areas here—Hubbard River and Halfway Brook. While the Hubbard River area had a more wilderness feel to it, this area is currently closed, and has been for several years. If you're interested in this area, contact the ranger station and ask when it may reopen.

The Halfway Brook campsites are a bit further up the road from where the Hubbard River sites were. The Halfway Brook sites are nestled within a fairly dense forest of mostly hardwoods. It's a relatively small camping area, with only 22 sites. It's deep within the borders of the state forest, so it's nice and quiet. In the evening, all you'll hear are the birds as they settle down for the night, the soft rush of Halfway Brook, and the crackle of your campfire.

Most of the sites at the Halfway Brook camping area are available by reservation. For these and all state park and state forest

CAMPGROUND RATINGS

Beauty: ★★★★
Site Privacy: ★★★★
Site Spaciousness: ★★★★★
Quiet: ★★★★
Security: ★★★★
Cleanliness/upkeep: ★★★★

Set deep within the woods, Granville State Forest has a nice remote feeling to it. You'll fall asleep to the sounds of the forest and Halfway Brook.

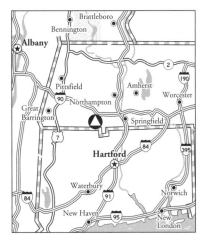

MASSACHUSETTS

campgrounds in Massachusetts, call Reserve America at the number listed in the Key Information. Only sites 8, 11, 12, 13, and 16 at Granville State Forest are available on a first come, first served basis.

Sites 1–5 are definitely worth a look if they're available. These are set off from the main campground, and actually face the West Hartland Road. Site 1 couldn't be any closer to Halfway Brook, which makes this site particularly attractive. The site sits right next to a small pond formed by the intersection of Halfway Brook and Small Brook. Sites 1 and 2 are very private, as there is plenty of forest between the two sites themselves and the rest of the campground. Adding to the sense of seclusion, sites 1 and 2 are set further back off the road. Any other sounds you might hear from the rest of the campground are obscured by the light whisper of Halfway Brook tumbling by in the background.

Sites 3, 4, and 5 are also nicely isolated, but a bit closer to the rest of the campsites in the main loop. The rear border of these sites abuts the borders of sites 6, 8, and 9 in the main campground loop. These sites are set within more open forest, so they're spacious, but a bit less private even though access to these sites is still from the West Hartland Road, not the campground loop. Parking for sites 1–5 is also separate from the rest of the campground.

Sites 6 and 7 are very spacious and next to each other. There's a fair degree of privacy between these two sites and the rest of the campground, but the forest is loosely spaced between the two sites. This would be a good pair of sites for a larger group. Site 8 is nicely isolated, nestled into the forest right where you turn off the campground road to the parking area. Site 8 is surrounded by fairly dense forest, so there is a strong sense of seclusion from the rest of the campground.

The rest of the sites provide a nice blend of seclusion, spaciousness, and privacy, set amidst the dense mixed forest that fills up the campground. Site 11 is quite secluded. There's a short drive down to the site off of the primary parking area in the center of the campground. Sites 10 and 11 are both quite close to Halfway Brook, so you'll hear that as you fall asleep.

Sites 12 and 14 are very open and spacious. They are also set up to be disabled accessible. There's a disabled parking spot quite close to site 14 as well. Site 16 is nicely isolated, set at the very end of the campground loop road on the other side of the campground opposite sites 10 and 11. Sites 19, 20, and 21 are all fairly close to each other, and a bit more open than some of the other sites at Granville State Forest. Sites 15 and 19 are near a small grassy field, out behind the rest room building. Sites 13 and 21 are a bit too open for my tastes, and they're situated right on the campground loop road.

There is an elaborate network of hiking trails winding through the rest of the forest. Across the street from the campground are trailheads for the Ordway Trail and the CCC. Trail. From the CCC Trail, you can also loop around on the Corduroy Trail, which heads out past the forest headquarters and travels through

KEY INFORMATION

Granville State Forest
323 West Hartland Road
Granville, MA 01034

Operated by: Massachusetts Department of Environmental Management

Information: Granville State Forest, (413) 357-6611

Open: Mid-May–October

Individual sites: 22

Each site has: Fire ring, picnic table

Site assignment: First come, first served or by reservation

Registration: At ranger station; for reservations, contact Reserve America at (877) I-CAMP-MA (422-6762) or www.reserveamerica.com.

Facilities: Flush toilets, hot showers, pay phone

Parking: At sites or in central parking area

Fee: Massachusetts residents, $10; non-residents, $12

Restrictions:

Pets—On leash only

Fires—In established fire rings only

Alcoholic beverages—Not allowed

Vehicles—Two per site max; off road vehicles prohibited

Other—Quiet hours 10 p.m.– 7 a.m.; Hubbard River area closed until further notice

---

To get there: From the intersection of Routes 8 and 57 in New Boston, follow Route 57 west to West Hartland Road. Head south on West Hartland Road until you see signs for the forest and the campground.

---

a wetland before reconnecting with the CCC Trail. The hiking trails on this side of the West Hartland road are fairly flat.

On the same side of the road as the campground, there's the Halfway Brook Trail and the Hubbard River Trail, which leads down to where the Hubbard River Campground used to be. You can also get out to the Woods Trail, which travels up and over a small ridgeline, and the Ore Hill Trail, which follows the eastern border of the forest. The trails on this side of the road travel along or up and over Ore Hill. The aforementioned trails are all multi-use trails, so you can hike, mountain bike, and ride horses. Keep in mind that they are multi-use trails, and exercise all appropriate cautions and courtesy. Even though you might feel like you're out in the middle of nowhere at Granville State Forest, other people may have come out to experience that same feeling.

HAROLD PARKER STATE FOREST

North Andover

Throw another log on the fire as you sit back at your campsite at Harold Parker State Forest. Look around at the woods, breath deep the scent of the forest, and remind yourself that you're less than an hour from Boston. Harold Parker State Forest offers a unique sense of remoteness, especially considering it's just miles from the biggest city in New England.

The forest enshrouding the campsites at Harold Parker is relatively uniform in its character, at least among the older trees. There are sections where the undergrowth thins out and others where it grows so dense it almost looks primeval. The forest is composed primarily of tall white pines and low deciduous trees. Huge, open sites characterize the campground itself.

Most of the sites are very spacious, and some are downright enormous. The size of the sites and the character of the forest add to the open sense at the sites, but they still feel nicely secluded by their distance from each other and distance from the road.

Sites 7, 8, and 9 are all very open and quite close to the bathroom. Site 8 is also disabled-accessible, as are many others at Harold Parker State Forest. Even though site 10 is moderately spacious, it pales in comparison to the massive clearing that is sites 9 and 11. You could practically build a house atop this pair of sites.

Site 13 is absolutely enormous, and quite secluded. Several 80-foot tall white pine and maple trees punctuate the site. A low

CAMPGROUND RATINGS

Beauty:	★★★★
Site Privacy:	★★★★
Site Spaciousness:	★★★★★
Quiet:	★★★★
Security:	★★★★
Cleanliness/upkeep:	★★★★

Harold Parker is unique in its feeling of remoteness and its proximity to Boston. It's great when you need a quick escape.

MASSACHUSETTS

wall of young pines, which must be the big white pines' progeny, encircles the site. The younger pines surrounding the site fill in the forest and provide an air of complete seclusion

Although it's very open to the road and sky, site 14 feels secluded by virtue of its location on the campground road. There are several hiking trails winding throughout the campground, two of which lead off into the woods just past site 14.

Site 15 is another massive site. It's set within a grove of short white pines and is elevated from the road, which adds privacy. Sites 17 and 19 are a bit small, but set within an open grove of white pines. The ground is covered with pine cones and a soft blanket of pine needles. Moderate undergrowth and young white pines surround these sites.

All these conifers give the forest a wonderful scent. It's also a very quiet place. Usually, all you'll hear is the wind rushing through the soft needles atop the forest's elder statesmen. Now is another good time to remind yourself that you're less than an hour from Boston.

Set at the corner of the campground road, sites 21 and 23 are open to the road on two sides. They're set in a pine grove like sites 17 and 19, but are more exposed to the road. Another road just past site 21 leads down to Frye Brook.

The first site within the B loop gives you an idea of what to expect from the rest of the sites in this section. Site B1 is huge. It's very open, but it's right across from the bathroom. Site B3 is similar.

Both sites B5 and B6 are wide open to the road, but they're just far enough down the road from each other on opposite sides of the road to provide a mild sense of seclusion. Sites B7 and B8 are very spacious. B7 is set up off the road, and B8 is set down from the road. The way the weather usually ends up when I'm camping, I'd tend to go for higher ground. Site B10 is moderately spacious and nicely isolated at the top of a little hill on the campground road.

There's a uniform, moderately dense character to the forest in this part of the campground. There's also a relatively dense understory of deciduous trees and young pines, with towering white pines filling in the upper layers of the forest.

Site B12 is colossal and punctuated by several massive white pines. B11 is also quite large. Nearby, you can see two former sites that were closed for restoration, part of the regular maintenance of this heavily used campground. The forest is slowly and steadily filling in the old sites.

A large, granite boulder guards site B16. This site is also speckled with a stand of towering white pines, and nicely isolated by the boulder and its location along the road. Right across from the G1 group sites, it could get a bit noisy.

While site B18 is much smaller than B16, it has a high degree of privacy, as it's encircled by dense undergrowth. B21 is also a massive, open, sunny site that is well removed from neighboring sites. Site 22 is similarly secluded.

Towering, 100-foot tall pine trees surround site B23. There's a cathedral quality and stately feel to the forest. This site is giant and has a very open feel. Site B24 is also quite large, but it's comparatively smaller than site B23. Of course, that's like saying Mount McKinley isn't quite as big as Mount Everest.

To get there: Follow Route 114 through Middleton into North Andover. Continue for several miles until you see Harold Parker Road and signs for the park. You'll drive through the park, following signs for the campground.

KEY INFORMATION

Harold Parker State Forest
1951 Turnpike Road
North Andover, MA 01845

Operated by: Massachusetts Department of Environmental Management

Information: Harold Parker State Forest, (978) 475-7972 (office) or (978) 686-3391 (forest headquarters)

Open: Mid-Apri–mid-October

Individual sites: 89

Each site has: Metal fire box, grill, picnic table

Site assignment: First come, first served or by reservation

Registration: At ranger station as you enter campground ; for reservations, contact Reserve America at (877) I-CAMP-MA (422-6762) or www.reserveamerica.com.

Facilities: Flush toilets, water spigots, playground

Parking: At sites and three additional parking areas

Fee: Massachusetts residents, $10; non-residents, $12

Restrictions:

Pets—On leash only

Fires—In established fire rings only

Alcoholic beverages—Not allowed

Vehicles—Two per site max.

Other—Quiet hours 10 a.m.–7 p.m., extinguish fires by midnight, checkout by 11 a.m.; 14-day max. stay

Sites 29 and 30 are very open and right across the road from each other. They're very spacious, but don't offer much in the way of privacy. Site 28 is like 29, in that it's very open on two sides of the road. It's set off from its neighbors, but too open to the road for me. You could characterize most of these sites by saying they're massive, open and set amongst stately white pines. That's certainly the case with site 38.

The few sites along the short C road, including sites C2–C5, are a bit open to each other, but very spacious and well spread out. On the A loop road, sites A2–A6 are very spacious and open. These sites are quite large, but exposed to each other and to the road. Further up the A loop, sites A7, A8, and A13 are also very open to the rest rooms.

Sites A15 and 48 are close neighbors, and open on two sides at an intersection of the campground road. Site 46 is huge and open. It's a bit secluded by the forest on one side, but exposed on the other to site 48.

Site 41 is roomy and encircled by an understory of young white pines and huge white pines and maples. It's also nicely secluded by its location as well. It's just a bit open to site 44 across the road. Sites 43 and 44 are open, but feel a bit more nestled into the forest due to the absence of neighboring sites on either side. A dense understory and huge white pines surround site 45, but the site is quite small, which gives it a cozy feel.

The loose trio of sites 52, 54, and 56 are way off on their own. The campground road leading past these sites cuts through a dense, mixed forest with equally dense understory and ferns filling in the ground cover and thickening up the forest. Sites 52 and 54 are outrageously huge. There's a very open air to these sites, and they're exposed to the sky.

Then you come to what is most likely the premier site at this campground. Site 56 is unbelievable. This site is completely secluded, massive, and encircled by dense younger white pines and huge maples and older white pines. It is quite far from any other site, so the sense of solitude is absolute.

There's a funky bend in the campground road a bit further down, so even though sites 59, 61, 62, and 63 are moderately spacious, they're all open to the campground road where it cuts back at almost a 45-degree angle. From this intersection, the sites along the right side of the campground road, including sites 63 and up, face Frye Pond. Sites 61–68 are very open and don't offer much privacy, but again they are close to the pond. Site 68 is set up off the road, but it's also right next to the playground area.

Of the pondside sites, site 69 is the most gorgeous. This site is set within an open forest that gently rolls down to the shore. The loose pines and maples give this site a dark, cool character. It's a very open and spacious site as well.

Sites 79 and 81 are smaller and open to the bathrooms, parking area, and basketball net. Sites 85, 86, and 87 are extremely spacious and open. There are more disabled-accessible sites in this part of the campground, including sites 61, 74, 77, and 78.

Harold Parker has some of the largest sites I have ever seen, many of which are also quite well secluded. While this would seem remarkable and welcome at any campground, it's all the more amazing when you consider this campground is closer to Boston than any other profiled within this book.

MOHAWK TRAIL STATE FOREST

Charlemont

There is an immediate sense of reverence upon entering Mohawk Trail State Forest. The woods here have a cathedralesque quality. Take a moment as you drive in to get out of your vehicle. Gaze at the tall, nicely spaced spruce and pine forest towering over you and forming a canopy, which preserves both the "wise silence of the forest," with apologies to Ralph Waldo Emerson, and the delightful scent of conifer.

This is an older growth forest, as the trees are all at least 100 feet tall, with some reaching considerably higher than that. At the forest floor level, the tree trunks are quite massive and there isn't much in the way of an understory, so the forest has an open feel to it. The sunlight filters down through the giant conifers in broken shafts, and any breeze is mostly captured by the long arms of the forest. Parts of the forest are also interspersed with mixed maple, birch, and other hardy deciduous trees, as well as the offspring of the giant evergreen masters.

The sites in the first cluster are set fairly close together. They're also fairly open for such a densely forested area. These sites are very open, clean, and spacious, but not quite as private as you might expect upon entering the forest.

In the loop with sites 36–56 down near the Cold River, you hear the sounds of the forest birds and the rushing water. The

CAMPGROUND RATINGS

Beauty:	★★★★★
Site Privacy:	★★★★
Site Spaciousness:	★★★★
Quiet:	★★★★★
Security:	★★★★
Cleanliness/upkeep:	★★★★★

The towering forest as you enter the campground at Mohawk Trail State Forest is breathtaking. If that doesn't get you, wait until you see the sites along the Cold River.

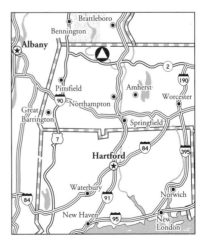

MASSACHUSETTS

sites right along the river are the best. They are set within a beautiful loose grove of mixed hardwoods and conifers. RVs are allowed in the Mohawk Trail State Forest, but you won't find any in this part of the campground, primarily because they are not able to negotiate the extremely tight turn at the end of the road leading into this group of sites.

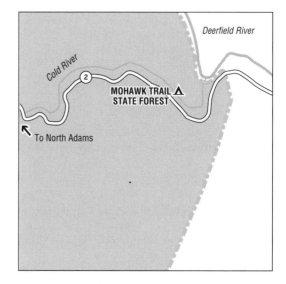

The riverside sites are spectacular. Sites 45–48 all sit right on the riverbanks at the end of the loop, so they are even more isolated than the other sites in this cluster. Sites 46 and 47 are the perfect riverside sites. Across the river from site 47 is the Mohawk State Forest picnic area, but all the daytrippers will be gone by the time you're lighting up your campfire to cook dinner.

The sites numbered in the 30s are spacious, but very open and set on a hard, dirt surface. This isn't exactly the sort of setting you would expect to find considering the character of the forest as you first drive in.

Sites 14–22 are down off a short road from the upper campground loop. Sites 15 and 16 are small, but sweet riverside sites. They are set up on the riverbanks a bit higher than the sites in the 40s and 50s. Site 22, at the end of this small loop, is the key site in this cluster, as it is very spacious and private.

The whole 14–22 loop is set beneath a grove of enormous spruce trees, so there's plenty of shade and that earthy, deep woods scent. And of course, there's the Cold River rushing by right next to the campsites as well, so all your senses are satisfied.

The main section of the campground with sites 1–12 and 23–33 is a nice section, but the sites are very open with minimal privacy. There's a nice forest canopy, so this whole area receives a lot of shade, but the minimal undergrowth doesn't give the sites much of a sense of seclusion.

When you come to camp at Mohawk Trail State Forest, look for the sites in the upper 40s and lower 50s down at the end of the campground and near the Cold River. That's where you'll want to be. If that doesn't work, go for the 14–22 loop.

Remember, this is black bear country, so all the appropriate precautions apply with food, garbage, and even any clothes upon which you may have spilled food. When you're turning in for the night, place anything that may have food scents safely in your car.

KEY INFORMATION

Mohawk Trail State Forest
P.O. Box 7
Route 2
Charlemont, MA 01339

Operated by: Massachusetts Department of Environmental Management

Information: Mohawk Trail State Forest, (413) 339-5504

Open: Mid-April–mid-October

Individual sites: 56 sites, 7 cabins, group camping area

Each site has: Fire ring, picnic table

Site assignment: First come, first served or by reservation

Registration: At ranger station; for reservations, contact Reserve America at (877) I-CAMP-MA (422-6762) or www.reserveamerica.com.

Facilities: Flush toilets, water spigots

Parking: At sites

Fee: Massachusetts residents, $10; non-residents, $12

Restrictions:

Pets—Dogs on leash only

Fires—In established fire rings only

Alcoholic beverages—Not allowed

Vehicles—Parking at sites only

Other—Quiet hours 10 p.m.–7 a.m., check out by 11 a.m., 14-day max. stay

To get there: Follow Route 2 East from North Adams until you see the signs for Mohawk Trail State Forest on the left.

MOUNT GREYLOCK STATE RESERVATION, SPERRY ROAD CAMPGROUND

Lanesborough

You won't find many other campgrounds with a deeper sense of wilderness and seclusion than the Sperry Road campground on Mount Greylock. This is true, primitive, mountainside camping. Sure, you can still drive your car to the campsite, but you are literally up on the side of a mountain within the deep forest. The campground is six miles up the auto road leading to the Bascom Lodge at the summit of Mount Greylock. Bear left off the auto road onto the Sperry Road, which leads right into the campground.

Each of these sites feels remote and rustic. There are 34 individual sites, and 5 group sites. Most of the sites are available by reservation through Reserve America. The rest are first come, first served. The sites here are very private and spread out. Some are a bit on the small side, but the rustic nature and deep wilderness sense of seclusion is perfect. The sites are spread out along the main campground road and a short loop branching off to the left after you enter the campground. Each site is nestled within the dense forest of mixed deciduous and coniferous trees.

Located at the apex where the short loop heads off the campground road to the left, site 8 is open on both sides. It's a little less private than the other sites, as it has road on two sides, but it's spacious and easily accessible. Sites 6 and 17 are a bit smaller than the others on this loop, but they're still

CAMPGROUND RATINGS

Beauty:	★★★★★
Site privacy:	★★★★★
Site spaciousness:	★★★★
Quiet:	★★★★★
Security:	★★★★★
Cleanliness/upkeep:	★★★★

The Sperry Road campground on Mount Greylock has a truly remote and rustic flavor. You'll be deep in the woods, perched on the mountainside, and close to a massive network of hiking and biking trails.

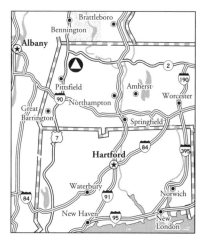

MASSACHUSETTS

quite nice and surrounded by fairly dense woods. Site 17 is set within a grove of young hardwoods and it's close to the pit toilets. Site 18 is set well off the road, so the sense of seclusion is intense. Site 21 is very spacious, and has a small grassy area for your tent. Site 22 seems a bit too open for my tastes, but it is close to the rest room if that's a priority.

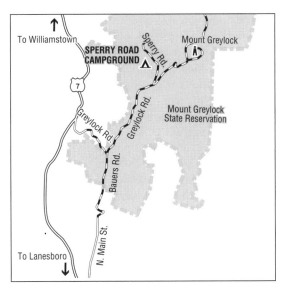

Several of the sites further down the campground road are lug-in sites. These are my favorites, as the wilderness air is predominant at these very private sites. You truly feel as if you have the woods to yourself, even though you're still car camping. Sites 23 and 26 are classic walk-in sites. They require about a 50-foot hike into the site, so they are very private. When you set up in one of these sites, you won't even see your car from your campsite, much less any neighbors.

Site 30 is small, but very isolated and private. Sites 25, 26, 27, and 29 are some of the other lug-in sites. These sites provide a tremendous amount of privacy. Site 28 is right off the road, not quite a lug-in site, but still well isolated from its neighbors. The walk-in sites offer the deepest sense of solitude imaginable. You won't see or hear anyone else around you.

Site 33 is another lug-in site, on the other side of the road. You can barely see your site from the campground road. Overall, the remote and rustic feel of the Mount Greylock Sperry Road campground provides an excellent wilderness sense and the right dose of solitude. It's absolutely silent, save for the natural sounds of the forest and your own campfire.

Sites 34 and 35, down on the end of the campground road, are also walk-in sites. These are quite spacious and distant from the rest of the campsites. These sites are remarkably secluded and set within a dense forest of mixed hardwoods and conifers, younger trees and old, so the variety of the forest is visually stunning. After the sun goes down, the thick forest reflects the light from your campfire, making the trees look like a wall surrounding your site.

During the day, there will be plenty to do. Camped right on the side of Mount Greylock as you are, you're right in the midst of a giant network of trails for hiking and mountain biking. The Appalachian Trail cuts through here as well, so you may run into some through-hikers in your travels up and around Greylock.

A number of trailheads lead right out of the campground. There's a Nature Trail loop that leads around behind sites 13, 14, and the Chimney group site. It eventually intersects with the Hopper Trail and the March Cataract Trail. The Hopper Trail starts right next to site 16. Down by the end of the loop with sites 4 and 5, there's the Roaring Brook Trail and the Deer Hill Trail.

Then there's always the classic Thunderbolt Trail on the other side of the mountain. I have somewhat fond memories of this trail. I've only descended the mighty Thunderbolt once so far. I brought out my telemark skis for the occasion, and it was downright ugly. The dense late winter snow would grab your skis and refuse to let go. The mountain won that day, but it was a blast nevertheless.

To get there: Follow Routes 7 and 20 North through Lanesborough, then follow signs to the Mount Greylock State Reservation headquarters. The campground is located on the Sperry Road, which is several miles up the auto road heading toward the summit.

KEY INFORMATION

Mount Greylock State Reservation
P.O. Box 138
Lanesborough, MA 01237

Operated by: Massachusetts Department of Environmental Management

Information: Mount Greylock State Reservation, (413) 499-4262/4263

Open: Mid-May–mid-October

Individual sites: 35 sites

Each site has: Fire ring or stone hearth, picnic table

Site assignment: First come, first served or by reservation

Registration: At ranger station; for reservations, contact Reserve America at (877) I-CAMP-MA (422-6762) or www.reserveamerica.com.

Facilities: Pit toilets

Parking: At sites

Fee: Massachusetts residents, $5; non-residents, $6

Restrictions:

Pets—On leash only

Fires—In established fire rings only

Alcoholic beverages—Not allowed

Vehicles—Parking at or near sites

Other—Quiet hours 10 p.m–7 a.m., check out by 11 a.m., 14-day max. stay

MASSACHUSETTS

MYLES STANDISH STATE FOREST

South Carver

CAMPGROUND RATINGS

Beauty: ★★★★
Site Privacy: ★★★★
Site Spaciousness: ★★★★
Quiet: ★★★
Security: ★★★★
Cleanliness/upkeep: ★★★★

Myles Standish State Forest has several distinct camping areas. The place is massive, so give yourself plenty of time to explore.

Myles Standish State Forest is huge. In fact, it's the largest publicly owned recreation area in southeastern Massachusetts. It terms of square mileage, it's big enough to be its own city. You could actually think of it as a city, with the campsites separated into "neighborhoods." There are actually several campgrounds within Myles Standish State Forest.

Myles Standish State Forest is easily accessible from Boston, the Cape, and the South Shore. There are plenty of places for hiking, biking, paddling, and fishing. No noisy off-road vehicles, though, as they are prohibited throughout the park.

All the campgrounds are located on or near the kettle ponds that punctuate the park's landscape. Barrett Pond is one of several campgrounds within the park. Site 1 is tucked off to the right as you enter this area. Like many of the campsites within Myles Standish State Forest, it's very large and well isolated.

The rest of the sites at Barrett Pond are very clean, spacious, and fairly well isolated from each other, which is good since the forest here is quite open and loosely spaced. The forest cover is comprised of tall, stately pines and spruce, and there is very little undergrowth, so the feeling is open and airy. A soft blanket of pine needles covers the campground floor, so you'll always have a good surface on which to pitch your tent.

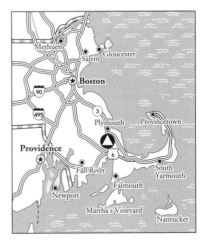

MASSACHUSETTS

Site 19 is particularly fantastic. It's set up off the campground loop road overlooking the pond. It's also right next to a small beach area. Sites 24 and 25 are also right on the pond's shore. Sites 43 and 44 are very open, but also very close to the pond. The open character of the forest is welcoming. There's a hush about the area.

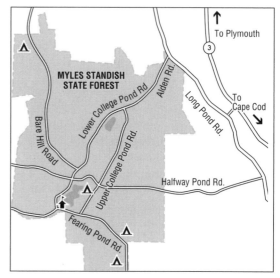

Charge Pond provides the greatest concentration of sites. The campground road forms a loop around the pond. Off this main loop, seven distinct camping areas are located. The different camping areas surrounding Charge Pond are designated by letters. The A loop sites seem a bit more spacious than the other loops. The A sites are slightly more open, and surrounded by a forest of tall white pines. This is especially true of the sites along the outer side of the A loop road. The inner loop sites are about the same size and offer a similar sense of seclusion as the C, D, E, and F loop sites. There are 49 sites within the A loop.

The group sites are located within Area BN, for B North. As opposed to large open group sites at other campgrounds, the group sites at Charge Pond are actually several contiguous sites you can reserve all at once. This can be nice for a group with several families, as you can designate quiet sites and sites where people may want to stay up around the fire. The sites within the group areas are similar in size and seclusion to the individual sites in the other loops.

The BS (for B South) loop sites are for horse camping. The sites are huge, to accommodate horse trailers. Even though the individual sites are huge, they are still isolated from the neighboring sites by the dense forest.

Within the C area, the sites are moderately sized, and very uniform. Be sure to mark which site you've occupied, as it can be tough to tell them apart. The sites are fairly well isolated, as they're surrounded with short dense undergrowth. The site surface is firm and sandy—very reminiscent of nearby Cape Cod.

Loop D looks very similar to loop C, with moderately spacious, very clean, and isolated sites. The privacy is enhanced by the short, dense undergrowth and thick, scrubby pines that seem to thrive in that coastal combination of salt air and sandy soil. The sites on the outer side of the loops have an even more defined sense of privacy since there's more space in between them.

Area E has more of a woodsy, pine-forest feel. The trees are a bit taller and more developed, but still mixed in with the dense undergrowth that separates each site to provide a pleasant degree of isolation. Some of the sites with larger or more numerous white pines along the border have blankets of pine needles on the site floor. With 59 sites, the E area is the largest collection of sites around Charge Pond.

There is an area F at Charge Pond, although it was not on the map I obtained from the ranger station. The 32-site F loop is similar in character to the rest of the Charge Pond areas, with moderately spacious sites. All the sites have a nice sense of privacy, surrounded by dense undergrowth, white pines, and scrubby brush.

The Fearing Pond area 1 is similar in character to the Bartlett Pond area. The

To get there: From Route 3, take Exit 5. Head west on Long Pond Road to the signs for Myles Standish State Forest on the right.

sites lie in a gently rolling forest, covered with a lush blanket of pine needles. The loosely spaced forest of spruce and white pine lets a lot of light and breezes through the campground.

Overall, the Fearing 1 sites are a bit more private than the Bartlett sites. The forest is indeed quite open, but there is a bit more undergrowth here. Site 4 is set up off the campground road and offers a nice sense of isolation. Sites 10–15 are a bit closer to each other and not quite as private as some of the nearby sites.

The pond sites are the sites to look for here. Site 23 is wonderfully isolated. There's a short hike down to the tent space from the campground loop road, so the site is truly set off from the rest of the campground, and it overlooks Fearing Pond. Sites 24 and 25 are also pondside, fairly isolated from the other sites if not from each other. Sites 40–43 are quite open, but face the pond for excellent views.

When I was researching this guidebook in the summer of 2001, the Fearing Pond area 2 was closed due to a bridge that had washed out. Look for details on the Fearing 2 area in the next edition, or call the park for details in the meantime.

The Curlew Pond area is one my favorites at Myles Standish State Forest. There are a total of 81 sites set within the gently rolling forest surrounding Curlew Pond. The sites are fairly spacious, but not too private. The forest is nice, an even mix of deciduous and coniferous trees.

Site 12 is the site to reserve. This is a delightfully isolated site at the water's edge. Site 17 also provides a nice sense of seclusion. It's set up on a short hill with an open view of the pond. Actually, sites 17–36 are all set along the campground loop road as it winds along the shore of the pond. All have killer pond views. The sites themselves aren't too spacious, but that doesn't matter all that much when you consider the setting and the sense of privacy from the other sites.

Another exceptionally nice site is site 24. This is set down from the road and has a small grassy area for your tent. It is right on the pond, so you can fish or take a dip right from your campsite. Site 27 is another classic pondside site. There's a huge white pine hanging over the site, which provides a nice protected and secluded feel.

Although sites 31 and up along this end of the road aren't quite as private, they're right on the water. Sites 43 and 44 are set up on a small hill. They're also a bit more open, but very spacious, with a nice site layout and a blanket of pine needles. Sites 52–54 are small, but offer commanding views of Curlew Pond.

Sites in the upper 50s of this loop are set within a grove of tall white pines with a few deciduous trees mixed in. Thanks to the open sense of the forest and the pond view, this is a very quiet and peaceful corner of the campground.

Myles Standish State Forest is a heavily used area, so from time to time you'll see individual campsites closed and signed "Site Restoration." It's nice that the rangers let the forest reclaim these well-worn sites, as it beautifies the campground.

While the kettle ponds are some of the main attractions at Myles Standish State Forest, there should be plenty to do for everyone in your group. There are miles of trails designated for equestrians, mountain bikers, and hikers. Plus, the place is big enough that it could take a solid week to fully explore the forest.

NICKERSON STATE PARK
Brewster

It's no secret that Cape Cod gets packed during the summer. Just look at Route 3 leading toward the Sagamore Bridge or Routes 495 and 25 leading toward the Bourne Bridge on a summer Friday night, and you'll see lines of cars waiting to get on the Cape. What may be a secret though is that you can still find some solitude and wilderness on the Cape. Nickerson State Park is one of those rare and remote spots.

Part of the reason Nickerson is such an incredible refuge in the midst of the Cape Cod crowds is its size. It is huge. At 1,955 acres with 418 campsites, you can find all sorts places to quietly lose yourself in the rolling pine forests that blanket the park. This is one of the most densely forested areas on the Cape. The forest itself is beautiful, with loosely spaced balsams, firs, and pines. Once you've decided on a spot to pitch your tent, take a quiet moment for a deep breath. When there's an onshore breeze, you can smell the earthy scent of the coniferous forest and the salty tang of the nearby ocean in the same breath.

There aren't any sites within Nickerson specifically set aside for tent campers, but several of the eight discrete areas lend themselves particularly well to tents. Look for sites in areas 2, 3, 5, or 7. Areas 2 and 3 are about a mile from the main entrance, and are set up in open loops. Each has its own rest room and several drinking-water spigots.

CAMPGROUND RATINGS

Beauty:	★★★★
Site Privacy:	★★★
Site Spaciousness:	★★★
Quiet:	★★★★
Security:	★★★★
Cleanliness/upkeep:	★★★★

Nickerson State Park is quite large, but it's also one of the few spots on the Cape where you can find a slice of wilderness for yourself, even during the busy summer season.

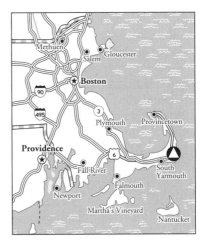

MASSACHUSETTS

Area 5 is about a half mile from the entrance on the way to Flax Pond. Several of the sites here are open and loosely spaced, especially 12, 14, and 16–18. A few pathways lead off the bluff down to Flax Pond, where you can swim, fish, paddle, or just enjoy a few moments walking along the water.

There are also some loosely spaced sites in area 7. Of the 46 sites in area 7, the clusters of 27–29 and 30–36 are particularly isolated, especially if you're with a group and can secure them all. The sites in the low 30s are closest to Higgins Pond. Some of these sites (especially those closest to the water) have some sandy areas, so if you have a set of those extra large tent stakes for securing your nylon dome in loose surfaces, bring them along.

Several sites are available for reservation from late May through early September. These include sites 24–67 in area 1, sites 113–122 in area 2, sites A-83 and 93–104 in area 3, sites 30–78 in area 4, sites 16–23 in area 5, sites 46–98 in area 6, sites 110–144 in area 6X, and sites 8–17 and 27–44 in area 7. All other sites are first come, first served.

Even if you take the last site in the park (which is not outside the realm of possibility if you come during July and August), you're still in for some sweet tent camping. Even on those sticky summer nights when the weather is hot and muggy, there are often cool breezes blowing through the forest and over the bluffs.

The several kettle ponds (glacial ponds fed by groundwater or precipitation) dotting the park are among Nickersons' main attractions, especially for the day use visitors. Cliff Pond is the largest, and the only pond in which waterskiing is allowed. Nevertheless, it still makes for beautiful paddling and swimming. Electric trolling motors are allowed in Flax Pond, if you want to drop a hook in the water in hopes that you'll find a hungry trout. The others, Higgins Pond, Eel Pond, Little Cliff Pond, Ruth Pond, Keeler's Pond, and Triangle Pond are just for paddling, swimming, fishing, or pond-gazing.

You could spend days exploring the trails that wind throughout Nickerson before you crossed them all. You can hike, bike, roller blade (on the paved paths), and in the winter you can cross - country ski and snowshoe. It's an amazing network of trails, and even on the busiest summer weekend, you can still discover a little slice of wilderness solitude. Some of the trails end up in the park's neighbor's backyards, so if you end up on something that looks like private property, be respectful, turn around, and hike back into the park.

More than 8 miles of the 25-mile Cape Cod Rail Trail pass through the park, making it the perfect launch pad for trips on the trail. You can pedal all the way to Dennis to the west of Nickerson State Park or South Wellfleet to the east. There are several businesses along the rail trail that rent bikes and helmets, if you didn't bring your own.

The Namskaket Sea Path also runs along the shoreline where Nickerson State Park faces Cape Cod Bay. It extends for two miles from Linnell Landing in

To get there: Follow Route 6 East to Route 6A West. Follow Route 6A West for a mile or so to the entrance to the state park and campground on your left.

KEY INFORMATION

Nickerson State Park
3488 Main Street, Route 6A
Brewster, MA 02631-1521

Operated by: Massachusetts Department of Environmental Management

Information: Nickerson State Park, (508) 896-3491

Open: April–October

Individual sites: 418 throughout 8 areas

Each site has: Fire ring, picnic table

Site assignment: First come, first served or by reservation

Registration: At main entrance on Route 6A Monday–Friday, 9 a.m.–3 p.m. or call (508) 896-4615; for reservations, contact Reserve America at (877) I-CAMP-MA (422-6762) or www.reserveamerica.com.

Facilities: Rest rooms, hot showers, pay phone

Parking: At sites and day use areas

Fee: Massachusetts residents, $12, non-residents, $15

Restrictions:

Pets—On leash only

Fires—In fire rings only, do not leave unattended

Alcoholic beverages—Not allowed

Vehicles—Parking at sites only

Other—Quiet hours 10 p.m.–7 a.m., 14-day max. stay

Brewster to Skaket Beach in Orleans. This is well worth exploring, especially at low tide, when you can walk across the mouth of Namskaket Creek. The Namskaket Sea Path passes through an intertidal zone, where you'll see seashells, hermit crabs, sea birds, and all sorts of seaweed and driftwood at the high water mark.

While you're out there on the ocean side, take some time to explore the Brewster Flats. At low tide, it looks as if you could walk all the way to Provincetown at the end of the Cape. It's especially fun with kids, who tend to notice things adults might otherwise pass by. As peaceful as a stroll along the sandbars of the Brewster Flats can be, make sure you pay attention and exercise caution. When the tide turns and starts coming in, it comes in ferociously fast, rolling up and over the sandbars and advancing on the shore with startling speed. I was caught out there once in February (of all the times to be overtaken by the tide) and came back wet from the knees down.

Whether you spend most of your time at Nickerson State Park hiking the trails, biking along the rail trail, relaxing by the shore of the ocean or one of Nickerson's ponds, or just enjoying the last embers of your campfire, you'll discover a Cape Cod that isn't quite as crazy and crowded as you imagined.

SAVOY MOUNTAIN STATE FOREST
Florida

You could separate the 45 campsites at Savoy Mountain State Forest by character into two very different groups. Most of the campsites are set within the woods bordering the campground, but there are many in a pastoral setting atop a hill covered by an open grassy field, which is punctuated by several large oaks, apple trees, and lilac bushes. This open orchard-like field in the center of the campground affords a nice view of the open sky. That unfettered view even extends to most of the sites set into the woods on the outer perimeter of the campground loop road.

The first three sites at Savoy Mountain State Forest are tucked off on their own short road leading off to the right after you pass the ranger station at the campground entrance. Sites 1–3 are quite isolated from the rest of the campground, and considerably more private than most of Savoy's other sites, especially site 1, which is located at the end of this short road. Site 3 is very spacious, set off on a slight rise at the beginning of the short road leading down to sites 1–3. Sites 1 and 2 are the best sites in this part of the campground, however. They are spacious and isolated from each other, as well as the rest of the campground. They're also set in a grove of tall maple trees.

The forest framing the campground at Savoy Mountain State Forest is a dense mix of mostly deciduous trees, so there's a strong sense of shade and privacy to the wooded sites. In these sites, light filters

CAMPGROUND RATINGS

Beauty: ★★★★
Site Privacy: ★★★★
Site Spaciousness: ★★★★
Quiet: ★★★★★
Security: ★★★★★
Cleanliness/upkeep: ★★★★

Savoy Mountain State Forest has a fascinating blend of sites, some tucked into the woods, some set upon a grassy hill, and others nestled among apple trees.

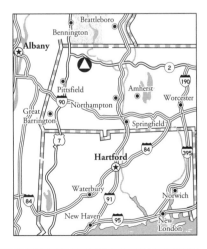

MASSACHUSETTS

down to the forest floor in fractured shards.

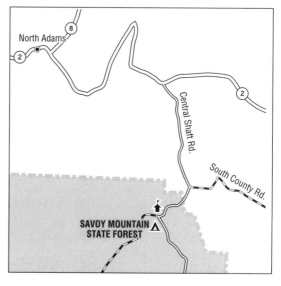

The sites set up on the grassy hilltop at the center of the campground, including sites 34–45, are breezy, spacious, and open, but not quite as private as the wooded sites. While I'm almost always a fan of more secluded forested sites, many of these central sites have a fabulous pastoral feel about them, as if you were camping in an orchard. The openness of these sites makes them perfect for some intense stargazing, or even leaving the tent packed and sleeping under the stars. What sites 34–45 may lack in seclusion and privacy, they more than make up for in the pastoral setting. In close proximity are the large trees that break up the field as well as several bunches of brush and wildflowers. This part of the campground would make a perfect setting to film a remake of *The Sound of Music*.

On the outside of the campground loop road, sites 29–31 are set within the forest at the edge of the field. They share the benefits of the forest and the field, in that they are open but also feel somewhat secluded.

If these sites had nicknames, site 32 would be called the orchard site, as it is framed with several small apple trees. Site 31 is also nicely isolated with a couple of apple trees maintaining a vigil at the entrance. If those are the orchard sites, then site 39 is the lilac site. This site, set high on the open field, is right next to a huge lilac bush.

Sites 8–21 are spaced out along the other side of the campground loop road. These sites are close enough to the forest to have a sense of solitude, but also face the field to view a dramatic spread of the hilltop, wildflowers, trees, and a sweeping expanse of sky. Most of these sites also give you a combined view of the field on the hilltop out the front of the site and South Pond out the back. The pond isn't too close, but you can catch glimpses of it through the trees. The trail to the South Pond Beach starts right between sites 17 and 18.

The spacious site 21 is tucked into a clearing in the dense forest at the end of this part of the campground loop road. Its position at the end of the road and the thick forest encircling the site gives you a nice sense of solitude. The forest is also clear directly overhead, giving you a good view of the night sky.

Perched right on the corner where the campground road loops around, site 22 is a bit more open, but is still roomy and nice. Site 23, next door, is large and scenic. A grand old maple hovers overhead, offering a comfortable roof to the site.

Nestled into a grove of small apple trees and wildflowers off the outer perimeter of the campground loop road, site 29 also has an orchard quality. The other sites along this stretch of road are spacious and accessible, but set apart and tucked into the woods enough to offer a bit of privacy.

The day-use area, just down the road from the campground, has a beach and boat launch, giving you access to North Pond. Because of the easier access, expect North Pond to be a bit more crowded than its sibling to the south. While there is a small beach area on South Pond, you can only get there through the campground. Both ponds have excellent hiking trails that loop around them and off toward the rest of Savoy Mountain State Forest's trail network.

To get there: Follow Route 2 East into Florida. Turn right onto Central Shaft Road and follow the signs to Savoy Mountain State Forest

KEY INFORMATION

Savoy Mountain State Forest
260 Central Shaft Road
Florida, MA 01247

Operated by: Massachusetts Department of Environmental Management

Information: Savoy Mountain State Forest, (413) 663-8469

Open: Mid-May–Columbus Day

Individual sites: 45 sites, 4 cabins

Each site has: Fire ring, picnic table

Site assignment: First come, first served or by reservation

Registration: At ranger station; for reservations, contact Reserve America at (877) I-CAMP-MA (422-6762) or www.reserveamerica.com.

Facilities: Flush toilets, showers, water spigots

Parking: At sites

Fee: Massachusetts residents, $10; non-residents, $12

Restrictions:

Pets—On leash only

Fires—In established fire rings only

Alcoholic beverages—Not allowed

Vehicles—Parking at sites only

Other—Quiet hours 10 p.m.–7 a.m., 14-day max. stay

WINDSOR STATE FOREST

Windsor

Windsor State Forest is a very small, unassuming, quiet campground. It might not be the sort of place you'd identify as a destination for hiking, biking, or other activities, but it's perfect for spending a quiet night in your tent. There are 22 primitive campsites here, set beneath a grove of massive conifers. Most of the sites are tightly packed in a small loop, but there are several key spots spread out along the banks of Westfield River.

Overall, the campground is very quiet and peaceful, especially since it's fairly small. Even though your neighbors will be close, there won't be many of them. The sites are clean and quite spacious, although the arrangement of the sites precludes any real privacy. Because of its size, none of the sites are too far from the pit toilets.

The first group of sites is located within the only loop in the campground. While the degree of privacy within this cluster isn't the highest, it is sometimes nice to meet your temporary campground neighbors. Also, the loop sites are set beneath a fantastic grove of towering spruce and pine trees. When the conditions are right, the forest scents in this grove are unbelievable.

Sites 1–9 are set up along the inside of the small loop. There is virtually no undergrowth, and the sites are right next to each other. On the outer side of the loop, furthest from River Road that runs through the state forest, you'll find sites 10–16.

CAMPGROUND RATINGS

Beauty:	★★★★★
Site privacy:	★★★★
Site spaciousness:	★★★★
Quiet:	★★★★★
Security:	★★★★
Cleanliness/upkeep:	★★★★★

Windsor State Forest is a primitive, intimate campground. Several of the best sites here are located right on the banks of the Westfield River.

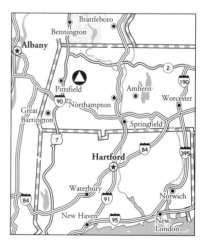

MASSACHUSETTS

The sites within this group are nice, they're just too close together without much in the way of undergrowth or forest separating them. There is a sense of isolation from above, as the forest canopy is fairly dense. When night falls, the campground grows quite dark, except for the shimmering lights from the ring of campfires. The effect at night is that of a Civil War encampment or a wagon train en route westward. The campfires are all uniform and evenly spaced along this small loop of sites.

For a greater degree of privacy and isolation, choose from one of the sites situated right along the riverbanks, or across the campground road from the river. Windsor State Forest campground is another case where two privacy ratings apply: one for sites 1–16 and one for sites 17–22. The former would get a 1 or 2, and the latter a solid 5.

Site 19 is beautiful, and set right on the banks of the river. It's the first site you'll come to on the road leading through the state forest. It's set within the dense forest growing along the riverbank. This site is very quiet and has a nice, isolated feel, especially at night. The only sounds you'll hear are those of the campfire and the steady rush of the river.

Site 18 is also just off the main road, but it's further back. It's on the opposite side of the road from the Westfield River and it's surrounded by trees, so it's a bit quieter. As the daylight wanes, all you'll hear is the river gurgling by in the background. This site is also fairly open and spacious.

A beautiful spruce grove enshrouds site 20, so this site feels a bit darker, but you can't beat the location. Site 22 is similar to site 18, in that it is spacious, carved out of the dense forest, and opposite the river. The site itself is a bit more open that the other sites along the riverbank, but it is enshrouded in a grove of deep green spruce.

Site 21 is the second site situated right on the banks of the Westfield River. Like site 19, this is an artfully sculpted, very spacious, and secluded site. Windsor State Forest is worth looking into just for the chance of camping in sites 19 or 21.

The campground and the rest of Windsor State Forest may be small and unassuming, but the sense of quiet and isolation are welcome. The forest is close to Monroe State Forest, Savoy Mountain State Forest, and Mohawk Trail State Forest. It's not even that far from Clarksburg State Park. So if you've come to the northern Berkshires for whatever outdoor adventures suit your tastes, and you want a quiet, comfortable campground to call your home, check out Windsor State Forest. You'll be especially pleased if you get the chance to pitch your tent along the riverbanks.

To get there: From Adams, follow Route 116 west through Savoy to River Road on the right. Follow River Road to the campground.

KEY INFORMATION

Windsor State Forest
River Road
Windsor, MA 02170

Operated by: Massachusetts Department of Environmental Management

Information: Windsor State Forest, (413) 684-0948

Open: Late May–early September

Individual sites: 22

Each site has: Fire ring, picnic table

Site assignment: First come, first served or by reservation

Registration: At forest headquarters; for reservations, contact Reserve America at (877) I-CAMP-MA (422-6762) or www.reserveamerica.com.

Facilities: Pit toilets

Parking: At sites

Fee: Massachusetts residents, $10; non-residents, $12

Restrictions:

Pets—Dogs on leash only

Fires—In established fire rings only

Alcoholic beverages—Not allowed

Vehicles—Parking at sites

Other—Quiet hours 10 p.m.–7 a.m., 14-day max. stay

CONNECTICUT

CONNECTICUT

DEVIL'S HOPYARD STATE PARK: CHAPMAN FALLS CAMPGROUND

East Haddam

CAMPGROUND RATINGS

Beauty:	★★★★★
Site privacy:	★★★
Site spaciousness:	★★★★
Quiet:	★★★★★
Security:	★★★★
Cleanliness/upkeep:	★★★★

If you're wondering how this state park came by its name, you're not alone. There are a variety of "theories" as to how the name Devil's Hopyard came about. One thing folks do agree on is that the name refers to the numerous holes bored into the rock at the base of Chapman Falls. The most oft repeated explanation is that these holes are the result of the Devil hopping from rock to rock to avoid getting his feet wet. His hooves burned these holes in the rock. If you can think of a better or more entertaining theory, feel free to share it with your fellow campers.

The Chapman Falls campground at Devil's Hopyard State Park has 21 sites spread out in a wooded grove right near the campground's namesake. The falls provide not only a beautiful spot to relax and enjoy the view right outside the campground, but the constant rush of the water is a welcome addition to the forest's soundtrack for your stay.

The 21 wooded sites at this cozy little campground are arranged on either side of the short campground road. The sites are open and very spacious, but not too private. On one side, the sites are set along the barrier of scrub brush that separates the campground from the waters above Chapman Falls. On the other side, the sites are set against the edge of the woods.

The sites along the water are the nicest. The sites at the end of the loop are nicer

Devil's Hopyard is small and scenic. The cozy group of campsites is located just a few steps from Chapman Falls.

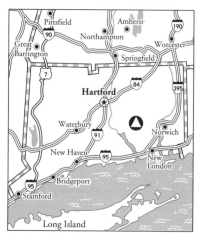

CONNECTICUT

still, plus they have the added benefit of being a bit more private. Site 8 is probably one of the most secluded sites within the campground. Sites 10 and 11 are also set off from the rest of the campground, but not from each other. This would be a good pair of sites for a larger group.

Site 15 is a desirable site, as it's situated right along the water leading to the falls. Sites 16, 17, and 18 are all incredibly peaceful sites right along the water. Site 16 is the key spot for anglers. You could fish right from your campsite.

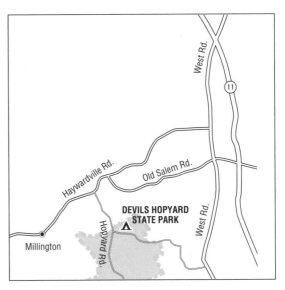

Because of its small size and remote location, the campground is very quiet, except for the welcome sounds of the woodland birds and the light, incessant rushing of Chapman Falls. The loosely spaced forest of mixed deciduous and coniferous trees lets a lot of light down onto the campsites. The forest at the border of the campground and within the rest of the park is much more densely packed.

Chapman Falls is a spectacular series of waterfalls that cascade downward for nearly 60 feet, continuing on as the Eight Mile River. The river flows past the Devil's Hopyard picnic area a bit further downstream from the campground. This day use area is popular with anglers. It's also a very scenic place to walk around or just relax by the river. Except for the campground, Devil's Hopyard State Park is closed from sunset to 6 a.m.

This area of Connecticut is just north of the town of Lyme. If that name sounds familiar, it should. Lyme has the unique and unwelcome distinction of being home to the first diagnosed cases of lyme disease. While the area in which lyme disease has been reported has spread over the last several years, it's still well worth paying extra attention to the risk posed by ticks in this area.

Deer ticks are the culprit. The nymph (or baby) deer ticks are particularly toxic. They're also extremely small and difficult to find. This doesn't mean you should stay inside all summer long. Just check yourself over very carefully, especially your head and hair. If you do find one, don't panic. Generally, the tick has to be embedded for 24 hours to pass on the disease. Just remove the tick completely with a pair of tweezers, and sterilize the bite. Okay, end of tick lecture.

KEY INFORMATION

Devil's Hopyard State Park
366 Hopyard Road
East Haddam, CT 06423

Operated by: Connecticut Department of Environmental Protection

Information: Devil's Hopyard State Park, (806) 873-8566

Open: May 26–Labor Day

Individual sites: 21

Each site has: Fire ring, picnic table

Site assignment: First come, first served or by reservation

Registration: At ranger station; for reservations contact Reserve America at (877) 668-CAMP (2267) or www.reserveamerica.com

Facilities: Pit toilets

Parking: At sites

Fee: $9

Restrictions:

Pets—Not allowed

Fires—In established fire rings only

Alcoholic beverages—Not allowed

Vehicles—Two per site max.

Other—Quiet hours 11 p.m.–7 a.m., check out by noon, visitors allowed 8 a.m.–sunset

To get there: Devil's Hopyard is right off Route 82, three miles north of the intersection of Route 82 and Route 156.

CONNECTICUT

HOUSATONIC MEADOWS CAMPGROUND

Cornwall Bridge

The statuesque forest and the Housatonic River flowing by make for a dramatic setting at this western Connecticut campground. Many of the sites at Housatonic Meadows are spread along the banks of the river. There are two main areas within the campground, the Riverside Area off to the left as you enter the campground, and the large loop off to the right where the majority of the sites are located.

The Riverside sites are very open and set right on the riverbanks beneath a loosely spaced forest of tall conifers. They're also packed in fairly tight. The sites are beautiful. It's a delight to camp next to the river, but you'll be as close to your neighbors as you are to the river. What the sites offer in peaceful, relaxing scenery and proximity to the river, they lack in seclusion and privacy. You run the risk of being near a trailer or RV, but you could also set up your tent so that the first thing you see and hear in the morning is the Housatonic cascading by.

There are a few sites in the Riverside Area that are more private than the others. Sites 23 and 24, at the end of the Riverside Area road, are the most private sites in this section. They're at the end of the cul de sac, and being off on their own little loop provides them a better sense of isolation. Sites 1 and 2, at the beginning of the Riverside Area road, also offer a welcome sense of solitude. This is especially true of site 1, which is separated from the rest of this

CAMPGROUND RATINGS

Beauty:	★★★★
Site Privacy:	★★★
Site Spaciousness:	★★★★
Quiet:	★★★
Security:	★★★★
Cleanliness/upkeep:	★★★★

Between the high forest canopy and the riverside setting, Housatonic Meadows is a beautiful spot.

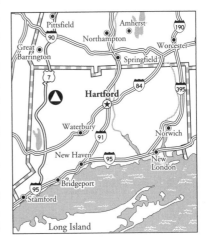

CONNECTICUT

row of sites by a short line of brush.

The forest here is a beautiful mix of tall pines and maples. Closer to the river, the forest is mostly pines, so there's a deep shade over this part of the campground. Between the shade of the forest canopy and the proximity to the river, these campsites remain cool even on the steamiest summer days.

While the sites here are close together, they are large and very neat. You might not have much privacy, but you are right on the river. You can fly-cast or launch canoes and kayaks right from your campsite, although it's probably best to drive upriver and launch from there. Then you can enjoy a leisurely paddle back to the campground. The Housatonic is fairly wide here, and the water is moving right along. It's relatively safe for these activities, but as always, be prudent when entering the river, especially if you are with children. Swimming here is not permitted, as the current is often swift.

The Knob Hill Area is off to the right as you enter the campground. The loop off to the left within this area has some very nice sites perched high along the riverbank. These sites afford a somewhat obscured view of the river through the forest. The sites are fairly open, but set on the border between the woods and a more open grove of tall conifers that shade the rest of the sites.

Generally speaking, most of the sites along the left side of this loop (the side facing the river) are the best for tents. These sites are neatly tucked into the forest, and while they're not right on the riverbanks like the sites in the Riverside area, they offer a bit more seclusion, and you can still catch glimpses of the river through the loosely spaced forest. You can also walk down through the forest to just sit and watch the river flow by, one of my favorite things to do.

In the first part of the loop on this side, sites 25–27 are a bit too open for my tastes. These sites are set facing the ranger station. Sites 31, 32, and 33 are isolated sites, set within a dense pine grove. If you're going to set up your tent on this side of the campground, check to see if any of these sites are available.

The furthest end of the loop on this side is called the Pine Bluff Area. The sites numbered in the 80s here are nice. These sites face the river and are set on the edge of the forest and the open meadow. They're a bit more secluded than the other sites in this area, particularly those sites set within the open grassy field. The sites in the grassy field (numbered in the 60s, 70s, and 90s) are spacious, but not too private. The rest of the Pine Bluff sites are a bit too open, set up on a grassy hill without much privacy and no woods separating the camping area from view of Route 7.

The river is clearly the main attraction, but there's also some nice hiking nearby. You can hike up and over the 1,120 foot high Pine Knob from the campground. You can pick up the trail across Route 7 from the campground, or drive south a short distance to the trailhead. Follow the blue blazes and hike the entire 2.5-mile loop over Pine Knob and Ridge Crest. You'll also be on the Appalachian Trail for a time. The southern leg of this loop follows the Hatch Brook back down to the river, which makes for a cool, relaxing hike.

To get there: Follow Route 7 North, approximately two miles north of the intersection of Routes 7 and 4. Look for the campground signs on the right, heading north.

KEY INFORMATION

Housatonic Meadows Campground
Route 7
Cornwall Bridge, CT 06754

Operated by: Connecticut Department of Environmental Protection

Information: Housatonic Meadows State Park, (860) 672-6772 (camp office) or 927-3238 (park office)

Open: May 2–Labor Day

Individual sites: 97

Each site has: Fire ring, picnic table

Site assignment: First come, first served or by reservation

Registration: At ranger station; for reservations contact Reserve America at (877) 668-CAMP (2267) or www.reserveamerica.com

Facilities: Flush toilets, showers, water spigots, pay phone

Parking: At sites

Fee: $12

Restrictions:

Pets—Not allowed

Fires—In established fire rings only

Alcoholic beverages—Not allowed

Vehicles—Two per site max.

Other—Quiet hours 11 p.m.–7 a.m., check out by noon

MACEDONIA BROOK STATE PARK

Kent

Deep in the forests of western Connecticut, Macedonia Brook State Park is grand in both size and character. Following the long access road leading into the campground (or more accurately, campgrounds, as there are several distinct areas within the park), you'll pass some stellar picnic areas set beneath the towering forest and right next to the pristine waters of Macedonia Brook. You'll also pass the sites of the Old Furnace, the Gorge, and the Lower Falls. Myriad twists and turns in the brook invite you to spend hours casting a line in the tumbling water to coax out a brook trout.

There are four separate camping areas within Macedonia Brook State Park: Birch, Hickory, Maple, and Overlook. Some of these areas are further subdivided. These four areas are spread out along the long and winding road leading through the campground. The remote wilderness character of the forest combined with the widely dispersed camping areas give the entire campground a quiet, secluded feeling.

You'll pass the day-use pavilion and volleyball net as you drive toward the camping areas. The Silver Birch Area is the first group of campsites you'll come to as you drive deeper into the campground. Sites 1–4 in Silver Birch are open sites set within a grassy loop right by Macedonia Brook. While these sites don't offer much privacy from one another, they are completely separate from the rest of the campground.

CAMPGROUND RATINGS

Beauty:	★★★★★
Site privacy:	★★★★
Site spaciousness:	★★★★
Quiet:	★★★★★
Security:	★★★★
Cleanliness/upkeep:	★★★★★

Macedonia Brook State Park is magically scenic. There are many sites along the river that are quite isolated, perfect for fishing or just watching the river flow past.

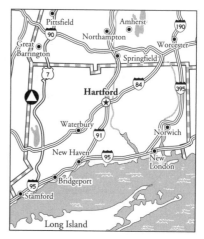

CONNECTICUT

Their riverside location is their best aspect. You could fly-fish right from your site.

The Upper Birch Area includes sites 7–17, which are open, spacious, and neat, but not particularly private. They're set within an open grassy hillside with sporadic trees, but surrounded by dense woods. Many of the sites are set against the border of the forest. The open field gives sweeping views of the night sky for an intense stargazing experience. The constant whoosh of the stream rushing by is peaceful and relaxing.

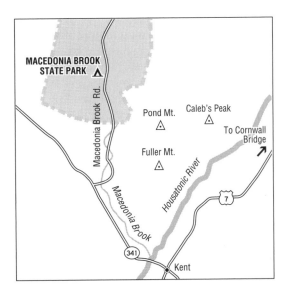

There is a water pump located near site 17. Also, sites 16 and 17 have huge stone hearths for your campfire instead of the typical fire ring, which seems diminutive by comparison.

The Lower Hickory Area includes sites 18–23. These sites are close to the river and fairly isolated, although the forest is quite open within this area. Upper Hickory is home to sites 24–30. These sites are even more exposed, set on the border between the forest and an open, grassy area.

The Red Pine Loop, with sites 32–37 is a nicely isolated loop. I especially like this corner of the campground. There's not a bad spot in this loop. The woods here are a bit more dense, so these sites offer a great sense of seclusion. There are more deciduous trees mixed into the forest here, and the added shade gives these spots a nice, deep woods feel. Site 33 is tucked off on its own at the top of the loop. Site 32 is another nicely isolated site.

Perched on the banks of Macedonia Brook, sites 38 and 39 would be well suited for a group of fly-fishermen. These two sites are together on a small grassy field right next to the brook. They're wide open, set between the brook and the campground road, but they're actually quite private later in the day, as they're entirely separate from the rest of the campground.

The Overlook Area includes sites 42–64. The upper sites on this wide open grassy hillside have a spectacular view of the forest, the sky, and the surrounding hillsides of South Cobble and Chase Mountain. Generally, the sites within this loop are large, but not too private.

The sites in the Maple area are numbered in the 70s. These sites are beautifully isolated in a dense grove of varied tree species. This loop is just past the Overlook Area on the right as you drive along the campground road.

The camping areas within Macedonia Brook State Park seem to offer a choice between an air of seclusion and sweeping views. Also, the sites on the grassy hillsides are more open to breezes, so they are often cooler and less buggy than the sites set deep within the woods.

There are numerous hiking trails winding throughout the state park, and plenty of places to drop a hook in the water. Most of the trails are called (and marked) simply by colors. The Blue Trail follows a ridgeline to the east of the camping areas. The Yellow trail intersects the Blue Trail just west of the pavilion. The Green Trail, leading out from the Upper Birch Area, also intersects with the Blue Trail. The Orange Trail runs from the Upper Birch Area to the Maple Area. Lastly, The White Trail takes you from the pavilion to the top of nearby Cobble Mountain.

To get there: From Kent, follow Route 341 to Macedonia Book Road on the right. Turn right here and follow this until you see signs for the park.

KEY INFORMATION

Macedonia Brook State Park
159 Macedonia Brook Road
Kent, CT 06757

Operated by: Connecticut Department of Environmental Protection

Information: Macedonia Brook State Park, (860) 927-4100 (campground) (860) 927-3238 (park office)

Open: April 14–Labor Day

Individual sites: 80

Each site has: Fire ring or stone hearth, picnic table

Site assignment: First come, first served or by reservation

Registration: Contact Reserve America at (877) 668-CAMP or www.reserveamerica.com/camping

Facilities: Pit toilets

Parking: At sites

Fee: $9

Restrictions:

Pets—Not allowed

Fires—In established fire rings only

Alcoholic beverages—Not allowed

Vehicles—Parking at sites only

Other —Quiet hours 11 p.m.–7 a.m., check out by noon

ROCKY NECK STATE PARK

Niantic

Rocky Neck State Park is a big place. Its 700 acres include the campground, a beach area, picnic areas, and a beautiful salt marsh. Bride Brook flows into a good-sized marine estuary that is a haven for wildlife viewing, bird-watching, crabbing, and fishing.

The campground itself is moderate in size, and set near the center of the park. Don't get too dismayed when you start seeing RVs and trailers through the trees on your drive in. There are several tent-only loops at the southern end of the campground.

The loop with sites I–P is right next to the bike trail leading down to the beach. You could walk down this trail as well of course. If you've brought the bikes along with you, though, hop on as it's a fair distance to the beach. If you've got a handful of small kids or a huge pile of beach toys, you can also drive down and park closer to the beach.

When you cross over the bridge leading to the picnic areas and the beach, you'll pass the salt marsh. Don't rush to get to the beach or back to your site, because it's worth spending a few moments looking out over the marsh. You may luck out and be treated to a heron sighting. Besides loading up on the view, you can also fish or break out the crab nets and try to scare up some blue crabs. Check the rules and regulations regarding crab size and number of catch before plunging in.

CAMPGROUND RATINGS

Beauty:	★★★
Site Privacy:	★★
Site Spaciousness:	★★★
Quiet:	★★★
Security:	★★★★
Cleanliness/upkeep:	★★★★

Rocky Neck State Park only has a few tent sites, but they are pretty well separated from the flotillas of RVs.

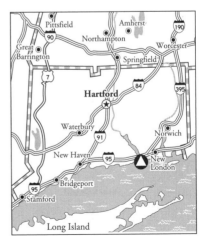

CONNECTICUT

The tent loop sites within Rocky Neck State Park are spacious, but not very private. The feel is more like camping in an open field near the woods. Still, it's pretty quiet down at the tent-only end of the campground. Plus, you're that much closer to the beach, the marsh, and the rest of the park. There are three loops, broken into sites A–H, I–P, and Q–X.

For access to all the tent sites, you park in a small parking area, then lug your gear in a short distance. The

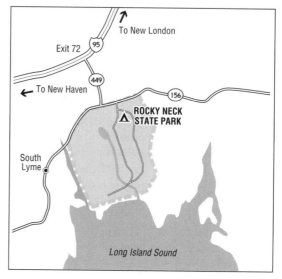

tent loops surround the nature center, so if there are any interpretive programs on the schedule, they'll be happening right in your back yard.

Each site has a picnic table, but no place to set up a fire. There is a central, community fire ring over by the I cluster, which is a neat idea. You still have a place to sit around the fire, and you might make some new friends in the process.

The tent clusters are set on a grassy field punctuated by a loose grove of scrubby conifers, mostly hemlock and juniper. The A–H cluster is nicely situated. There's an open field in the middle of the cluster, but the sites are set in the woods surrounding the loop. This is the only cluster set up like a loop. The clusters with sites I–P and Q–X have sites arranged in two rows across from each other.

Rocky Neck State Park is a good spot for bird-watching. Between the proximity to Long Island Sound, the salt marsh, and the forest, you'll see a sizeable variety of feathered friends. In fact, the other site loops within the campground, many of which have a few select sites that are more private than the rest, are named for shorebird varieties, like Osprey, Heron, Egret, Seagull, and Crane. For the most part, however, you'll want to camp in the tent areas described above. Most of the sites within the "bird loops" are a bit too open and too populated with RVs and trailers to appeal to the tent camping crowd.

The big open grassy areas are great for playing Frisbee or tossing a football around. There are also lots of people just walking about, biking, or in-line skating. Consequently, please drive extremely cautiously on the campground roads. There will be lots of people, large and small, rolling or walking around.

Rocky Neck State Park seems fairly quiet and cozy for such a large state park. The loops named for birds are a bit too open, but the tent clusters are well worth a look. You'll still be able to see most of your neighbors in the tent clusters, but at least it will be a quiet neighborhood of kindred spirits. You'll also be hard pressed to find a softer surface on which to pitch your tent. You'll sleep soundly on the thick, grassy field that's home to the tent clusters.

To get there: From Route 95, take Exit 72 and follow the signs to the park.

SELDEN NECK CAMPGROUND

Haddam

There is absolutely no way you'll find an RV at the Selden Neck State Park campground. There are no designated tent-only areas, no inherent rules or regulations prohibiting them, but until someone invents an RV that floats, Selden Creek is just for tent camping. You can only reach the park and the campground by boat.

This fabulously peaceful little state park is perched on the northern corner of a small island separated from the banks of the Connecticut River by Selden Creek. The campsites are right on the river, and there are no docks, moorings or facilities other than fireplaces and pit toilets. You'll have to approach the campsite with a small craft. Whether you choose a small sailboat or motorboat, or better yet, a canoe or kayak, is entirely up to you.

There are four discrete camping areas on Selden Neck: Hogback, Springledge, Quarry Knob, and Cedars Camp. Those are listed roughly in order of my personal preference. The first three areas are situated right along the banks of the Connecticut River. The main channel runs down the river right next to Selden Neck, so on a busy summer day, there will be a lot of boat traffic, including some ferry boats and sizable powerboats. Consequently, it can be a bit busy during the day and there may be a bit of chop on the river and splashing up against the banks of Selden Neck. Secure your boat adequately, or pull

CAMPGROUND RATINGS

Beauty:	★★★★
Site privacy:	★★★★★
Site spaciousness:	★★★★★
Quiet:	★★★★
Security:	★★★★★
Cleanliness/upkeep:	★★★★★

Selden Neck has some of the most spectacular and accessible island camping in New England.

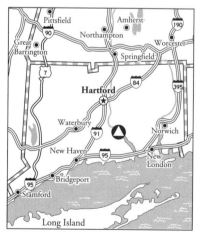

CONNECTICUT

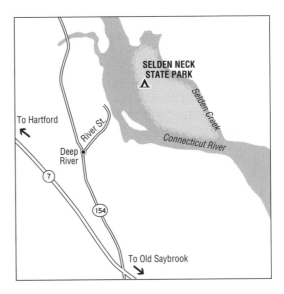

your canoe or kayak up onto the shore to keep it from
getting bashed around, or
worse, slipping off onto the
river without you.

The Hogback, Springledge,
and Quarry Knob areas are
similar in character. There
are small, grassy areas upon
which to pitch your tent.
You'll be fairly close to the
riverbanks, and behind the
sites there's a short, steep
hill that rises in the center
of the island. Hogback is
the smallest of these areas,
with room for 6 campers.
Springledge accommodates
8 campers and Quarry Knob has room for 12.

You can really immerse yourself in a sense of wilderness and solitude,
despite the fact that you're camping right on the Connecticut River, which can
sometimes feel like the maritime equivalent of an Interstate. The small, densely forested camping areas, the way they are set off from each other, and the
fact that you're on an island all contribute to the atmosphere of solitude on
Selden Neck. This becomes even more apparent toward the end of the day as
the river traffic quiets down.

The Cedars Camp area attracts a lot of day use, as it's tucked into a corner of
Selden Creek off the main branch of the river. If the weather or winds are a bit
rough, this would be a good choice because the small beach where you arrive
is more protected. It's also a good choice if you happen to be camping with a
larger group, as this area of Selden Neck can accommodate up to 20 people.

The nearest boat ramp is the Deep River public boat launch, which is right
across the river from Selden Creek and the island on which the campground is
located. It's a fairly short paddle in a canoe or kayak, and a snap in a small

motorboat or sailboat. The only trouble is parking at the boat launch. Parking right at the boat launch is only for Deep River residents who have purchased a sticker. Get dropped off or park just outside the boat launch parking area, if there's room.

Keep this in mind as you're packing and preparing for your trip. You are traveling to an island to camp. There are no stores on this island. You need to bring with you everything you will use—all your food, water and camping supplies. Running out to a store because you forgot batteries or hot dogs is not impossible, but it's not going to be very easy. The flip side of that coin is that you must also pack out everything you've used and any trash you've generated. The camping areas have pit toilets, but there aren't any garbage cans. Live by the pack it in, pack it out mantra.

One trick for packing meals I've always appreciated when kayak camping (equally applicable for canoes or other small boats) is to prepare something you can freeze. Take a frozen Tupperware container out with you and by the time dinner rolls around, your meal will have mostly defrosted. Then all you have to do is heat it up and you're ready for dinner.

Once you make landfall and set up your camp, you'll probably want to take off in your boat to do a little exploring. Selden Creek, which winds its way around Selden Neck island, is an absolutely delightful area to paddle. The

> **To get there:** To Deep River boat ramp, take Exit 4 off Route 9. Follow Route 154 into Deep River. Turn right at the four-way intersection downtown (Route 80 heads off to the left). Follow this road to Deep River boat launch.

KEY INFORMATION

Selden Neck Campground
Gillette Castle State Park
67 River Road
Haddam, CT 06423

Operated by: Connecticut Department of Environmental Protection

Information: Gillette Castle State Park, (860) 526-2336

Open: May 1–September 30

Individual sites: 4 sites that accommodate total of 46 campers

Each site has: Fire pit, pit toilet

Site assignment: Reservations required

Registration: Make reservations at least two weeks prior to visit by mail to Gillette Castle State Park Supervisor (address above)

Facilities: Pit toilets

Parking: Boats only

Fee: $4

Restrictions:

Pets—Not allowed

Fires—In established fire pits only

Alcoholic beverages—At sites only

Vehicles—Boats only

Other—Visitors must leave by 8 p.m., campers must pack out all trash

water is often as still as glass, even on days when the wind has churned the main channel of the river into a swirling froth. Selden Creek casually winds around through swampy marsh and overhanging trees past some cliffs and the forested hills of the mainland. At times it feels like you're paddling through a bayou, other times through a northern fjord, but it always feels like you're a million miles from anyone.

There's one important caveat you might not expect. Beware of the swans. They are beautiful birds, there are plenty of them, and they are fiercely territorial. I have been charged by swans on three separate occasions while paddling through Selden Creek. It's kind of ridiculous from a human's point of view. I was in a 17 foot-long, bright yellow kayak. Still, this stubborn, ornery swan charged me broadside. Besides the fact that it's always best to view wildlife from a respectful distance, such that your presence has as little affect on their behavior as possible, it pays to be mindful of how close you are to the swans. If you get too close and they attack, they could poke a hole in a fiberglass canoe or kayak, or worse yet, break your arm or wrist. Those long, slender necks are solid muscle.

Swans are indeed beautiful birds, but they can be aggressive. So be cautious and respectful. It's the right thing to do and it's the safe thing to do. If a swan starts posturing, appears agitated, or tucks its wings up into attack mode so it looks like a Romulan Warbird, simply continue on your way and they'll eventually leave you alone to enjoy the otherwise peaceful and pristine solitude of Selden Creek.

With a campfire crackling in the fire pit, a full belly from dinner, a warm glow on your face from spending the day on and around the river, sit back at your campsite and admire the river as it slows down for the night. Looking west across the river from the Hogback, Springledge, and Quarry Knob sites, you'll have a beautiful view of the opposite riverbank and the top of Gillette Castle. When the weather is right, you're at one of the best spots in Connecticut from which to admire the sunset.

RHODE ISLAND

BURLINGAME STATE PARK

Charlestown

Burlingame State Park is like a megalopolis of campgrounds. The park itself encompasses 2,100 acres. Even though it's easy to get overwhelmed by Burlingame's 755 sites, there are lots of spots within the park that make for some nice tent camping. That's not a typo, by the way. They really do have seven hundred and fifty-five sites!

Much like cities (and with a campground this huge, it's an applicable metaphor) have good areas and not-so-good areas, so too does Burlingame. That's not to say that there are any dangerous areas or places you shouldn't be after sunset, just some places that are better for tents.

There aren't any tent-specific neighborhoods within Burlingame State Park, but there are individual sites set aside for tents. These designations are based primarily on site size. There aren't any hookups within Burlingame State Park, but the open spacious nature of the sites can be inviting to RVs as well as our tent-bound brethren. Still, there are several areas you should check out that are well suited for tent camping.

Generally speaking, the further off the main loop throughout the park you get, the more secluded and quiet your campsite will be. Most of the sites are fairly open and certainly spacious, but the airy forest doesn't provide much of a barrier between the sites. Most of the sites are set beneath a mixed forest of pine, spruce, and balsam,

CAMPGROUND RATINGS

Beauty:	★★★★
Site privacy:	★★★
Site spaciousness:	★★★
Quiet:	★★★
Security:	★★★★
Cleanliness/upkeep:	★★★★

The campground at Burlingame State Park is massive—the largest in New England—but there are still a few spots where you can find a slice of wilderness for yourself.

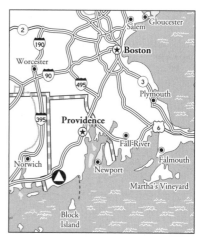

RHODE ISLAND

with a smattering of hardy deciduous trees. The salty air and the sandy soil keeps the forest from growing in too densely. However, the sandy soil also makes it easy to drive in tent stakes.

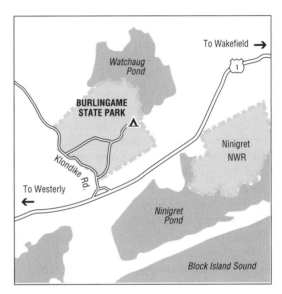

Right near the entrance to the campground, check out the Mills Camp Area. This is your first left as you drive into the campground. Mills Camp includes sites A–U and AA–UU, all of which are fairly open sites set within a loosely spaced forest of low conifers.

Continue deeper into the campground, and you come to the upper 500 sites. These sites, especially site 565, are nicely isolated and wooded. Sites 554–559 within this area are set up where the forest is a bit more dense. This offers these sites a deeper sense of isolation. The sites themselves are perfectly open, there's just more woods in between you and your many neighbors.

Further along the outer campground loop road, some of the lower 400 sites are nicely isolated, especially site 424. On this section of the road, which is the part of the loop furthest to the left looking at the campground map, you should check out the grouping with sites 408–426. This cluster offers a nice degree of privacy and quiet.

Sites 201–211 are fairly open and not quite as private, but they're set beneath a cathedralesque grove of spruce trees. Sites 214, 216, 218, and 219 in this area are also nice, plus they're convenient to the rest rooms.

The Main Camping Area, as indicated on the map and including sites 18–131, is where you want to be. It's much like its own campground within a campground. It's more wooded and secluded and quiet. Site 143 is a particularly nice site, as it sits well off the loop road. The even numbered sites in the upper 130s and lower 140s are also nice, with a moderate sense of seclusion.

The 131–150 loop in the Main Camp area also has many sites you'll want to check out. The outer loop sites within this area in the 160s and 170s are worth a look. Again, here the forest is a bit more dense, although there are a few sites here on the inside of the loop that are fairly open.

The other more densely packed portion of the Main Camp Area, which encompasses the first 90 sites, is close to the shores of Watchaug Pond and some of the boat rental facilities. The sites here are tightly packed beneath an open forest canopy, but the whole area still has a nice, woodland feel.

There are many clusters where two or three sites will be angled in towards each other. These would be good sites for large groups or families needing a couple of sites bunched together. Mention this when making your reservation if you'd like contiguous sites.

Burlingame State Park is on the shores of Watchaug Pond, and it's just a few miles from Rhode Island's renowned beaches. You'll have plenty to do both within and outside of the park when you come here.

If Burlingame State Park was any bigger, it would practically cover the state. I can see it now, the park ranger would be running for governor. I still can't help but think it's ironic that the largest campground in this book, both in terms of acreage and number of sites, sits in Rhode Island, the smallest state in New England.

To get there: Follow 95 South to Route 4 South to Route 1 South. Follow Route 1 to Charlestown, and turn right at the Burlingame State Park Campground sign.

KEY INFORMATION

Burlingame State Park
1 Burlingame State Park Road
Charlestown, RI 02813

Operated by: Rhode Island Department of Environmental Management

Information: Burlingame State Park, (401) 322-7337 or 7994

Open: April 15–October 31

Individual sites: 755

Each site has: Fire ring or stone hearth, picnic table

Site assignment: First come, first served

Registration: At campground headquarters

Facilities: Flush toilets, showers, camp store, pay phone

Parking: At sites and other parking areas

Fee: Rhode Island residents, $8; non residents, $12; visitors, $2 per car

Restrictions:

Pets—Not allowed

Fires—In established fire rings only

Alcoholic beverages—Not allowed

Vehicles—Parking at sites and other central areas

Other—14-day max. stay

FORT GETTY RECREATION AREA

Jamestown

Fort Getty Recreation Area will appeal to history buffs and anyone wanting to combine a little paddling or beach-combing with their camping experience. It's also a perfect spot to capture a bit of island camping mystique without actually loading up a boat, canoe, or kayak and blasting off across the water. Set on a wind swept bluff near the southern tip of Conanicut Island in the middle of Narragansett Bay, this is a beautiful oceanside campground. Even though this camp-ground is on an island, rest assured, you can get there by car. What it lacks in privacy and distance from the nearby flotilla of RVs, it makes up for in salty sea breezes, sunrises and sunsets to die for, rocky beachfronts worth hours of exploring, and a fantastic spot to drop a kayak in the water.

There is a modest-sized tent camping area, which is set off as much as possible from where the RVs roam. I say as much as possible because there isn't a whole lot of room within the campground proper. The scenery and setting compensate quite nicely for the site density, though. Here's a hint, once you've found your campsite, set up your tent so the opening faces out toward the bay. That way, when you wake up, your first views will be of the new day rising over the water.

As you drive into the park, the long access road leading into the campground

CAMPGROUND RATINGS

Beauty:	★★★★
Site Privacy:	★★
Site Spaciousness:	★★★
Quiet:	★★★
Security:	★★★★
Cleanliness/upkeep:	★★★★

Fort Getty Recretion Area's campground is fairly wide open, but the panoramic vistas of Narragansett Bay and the sea breezes can't be beat.

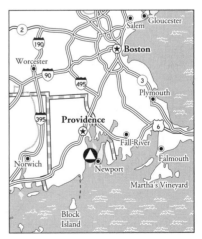

RHODE ISLAND

passes by a couple of residences, so it feels like you're heading up someone's driveway, but rest assured, this road does in-deed lead to Fort Getty Recreation Area. You'll come to a pay station in the middle of the road. Check in here, then keep cruising. The road winds around to the right, and the campground is ahead on the left, toward the end of the peninsula.

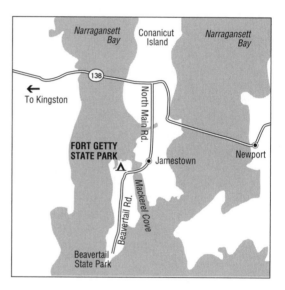

As you drive in, you'll pass the Fox Hill Salt Marsh on your left. This is a great place to walk around, or just find a cozy spot to take in the scenery. If you're into bird-watching, you'll particularly enjoy training your eyes and binoculars on the various shorebirds found here.

You'll quickly realize this campground doesn't embody the forest-bound sense of solitude you'll find in most other New England campgrounds, but the waterfront setting can't be beat. The tent-only area is toward the top of the small hill off to the left as you reach the campsites. The tent area includes sites 1–14. The sites are all very open and fairly tightly packed, but the parking for all the tent sites is along the periphery, so the cluster of sites feels like a little tent village.

Right next to the camping area is a big open field—a tremendous spot for picnicking, kite flying, Frisbee throwing, you name it. There's also a sand volleyball pit nearby. This open area for casual play and hanging out reinforces the laid-back, island mentality that predominates at Fort Getty.

Camping with some little kids? The rocky beaches surrounding the park offer endless hours of rock-hopping and beach-combing. Some of the cliffs and larger rocks are a bit steep, so you'll have to keep a sharp eye on the younger ones, but I can guarantee your kids will be tuckered-out after a day spent prowling around on these rocky shores.

For the historically minded, there are a couple of bunkers remaining from when Fort Getty was an ammunition depot during World War II. These are also cool little spots for older kids to play in.

The land on which the campground is perched is surrounded by several other small islands dotting Narragansett Bay. In a place like this, the environment is captivating, regardless of the weather. It's brilliant on bright sunny days, cool and refreshing when the mainland is sweltering. The stars at night are absolutely crystal clear, and you'll see deeper into the universe since there isn't much in the way of light pollution out there. Even in the fog or light rain, the islands poking in and out of the fog give the place a sense of mystery, as if you'd almost expect to see a pirate ship emerging from the mist to bury it's treasures on one of the islands.

If you're planning to have a large family reunion, wedding reception or some other sort of huge bash, you can reserve the Lt. Col. John C. Rembigas pavilion for such functions. This is off to the left of the campground, the open field, and the volleyball pit.

Fort Getty Recreation Area is a scenic and centrally located spot, well suited to

KEY INFORMATION

Fort Getty Recreation Area
P.O. Box 377
Jamestown, RI 02835

Operated by: Town of Jamestown

Information: Fort Getty Recreation Area, (401) 423-7211 or 423-7264

Open: May 18–October 1

Individual sites: 14 tent-only sites, 103 trailer sites

Each site has: Fire ring

Site assignment: First come, first served

Registration: At ranger station

Facilities: Flush toilets, showers, water spigots, pay phones, boat launch, fishing dock

Parking: Near sites, additional parking at day use area

Fee: $17, $22 for trailers

Restrictions:

Pets—Dogs on leash only

Fires—In established fire rings only

Alcoholic beverages—At sites only

Vehicles—Park near sites

serve as your base camp for fishing, paddling, SCUBA diving, and beach-combing adventures. It's also an amazing place to fly a kite. Charlie Brown would have loved it—steady winds and barely a single kite-eating tree to be found. Those winds also make Fort Getty Recreation Area the place to be on those steamy summer afternoons. While those camping deep within the forest are sweating bullets and slapping bugs, you'll have a strong, cool breeze keeping your temperature down and the bugs away.

Fort Getty Recreation Area is near Beavertail State Park, so named for the shape of the point of land. Look at a map. It really does look like a Beaver-tail. Goddard State Park is also nearby in Warwick. Additionally, there's a nice sandy beach right outside the park off Beavertail Road. You need a res-ident sticker to park there, though. You could walk to it from the camp-ground, but it's a healthy walk and perhaps a bit much for younger kids. You could also ride your bike, but be extra careful crossing and riding on Beavertail Road. It's not that busy, but there's a big curve in the road right by the beach and the temptation to gaze out over the bay has to be over-whelming for people driving by.

I love places where you can take a deep, healthy breath and get the scent of a campfire and the ocean in the same breath. Fort Getty Recreation Area is def-initely one of those places.

GEORGE WASHINGTON MANAGEMENT AREA

Glocester

You'll be tempted to check your map as you drive into the campground at the George Washington Management Area. Did you somehow take a wrong turn and end up in Vermont or New Hampshire? Nope, this is indeed Rhode Island, but it's far from the wind swept beaches, sandy soil, and short, scrubby pines and beach roses you might expect from Rhode Island topography. As soon as you enter the campground, you are enshrouded by a canopy of conifers. The tangy pine and balsam scents mixed in with earthy wisps of wood smoke make for quite a welcome.

The entire George Washington Management Area and the contiguous Pulaski Memorial State Forest are both densely wooded areas with a gently rolling forest floor. The area is free of really steep hills, uneven terrain, and heavy undergrowth. This makes for many nice places to pitch a tent. Stop to pay your fee at the ranger station as you drive into the campground, and you're ready to go.

The campground wraps around the shores of Bowdish Lake. Down by the beach area, there's a beautiful stone Recreation Hall built by the Civilian Conservation Corps. A plaque set in stone in front of the building honors the members of the CCC who built the hall. The beach is the perfect spot to go for a quick swim, to spend the day with the kids, or kick back on a blanket and read a book. You could

CAMPGROUND RATINGS

Beauty:	★★★★
Site Privacy:	★★★★
Site Spaciousness:	★★★★
Quiet:	★★★★
Security:	★★★★
Cleanliness/upkeep:	★★★★

The entire George Washington Management Area is a lush, dense forest redolent of northern New England. It's quite accessible, yet has a pleasant remote feel.

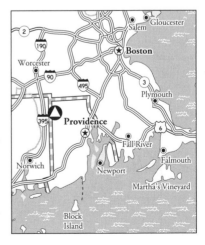

RHODE ISLAND

also drop a hook or a paddle in the water (or both!) if you're so inclined.

Sites 26, 27, and 28 are quite spacious and close to the lake. These are some of the prime spots at the George Washington Management Area campground. The loop with sites 34–45 is another good area in which to pitch your tent. These sites within this loop are a bit smaller than some of the others located along the main campground road, but they're nestled within a dense pine grove and fairly

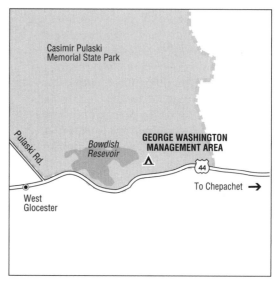

close to the lake—both attractive aspects. This loop is the first left off the main road once you're in the campground.

Further down the road, sites 5 and 6 are well worth investigating. They're good sized and set off with plenty of space in between them and the other sites. Sites 11 and 14 are right on the border of the campground proper and the rest of the George Washington Management Area. These are also nice sites, as the forest becomes more dense here on this end of the campground. Site 12 is also particularly secluded.

Follow the main campground road past all these sites, and past the loop for Shelter 1 off to the left, and you'll be heading off into the rest of the George Washington Management Area. This is a great area to explore when it's time for a hike or bike ride.

The entire campground has plenty of space and forest for everyone. However, several sites and sections along the main road are a bit too open for my tastes. Sites 7, 9, 12, 17, and 18 aren't quite as private as some of the other sites located along the main road and those tucked off in the side loops.

If you've come with a large group, or have several members of your group who would rather not sleep on the ground, check out one of the two AMC-type lean-to shelters. These have a wood floor and are open on one side. If you're going for one of the shelters, try to secure Shelter 1. It's set up on a small rise at the end of its own loop. There's a nice sense of privacy to this site. It's at the far end of the campground road, and right on the border between the campground and the rest of the expansive George Washington Management Area.

Shelter 2 is also in a fairly nice spot, quite separate from the rest of the campground at the end of a short road leading off to the right from the main campground road. However, it's right next to a large, open sandy lot that looks like overflow parking. While it may detract a bit from the scenery, if you have a large group all arriving in their own vehicles, you won't have any trouble finding parking. This is the site to choose if you're camping with 100 of your closest friends, all of whom insist on driving their own cars!

One restriction worth noting is that possession of alcoholic beverages is grounds for expulsion from the campground. They must have had some problems with ebullient revelers in the past, as they seem quite serious about this one. This restriction is clearly stated in several spots on the campground literature. If you like to kick back with a beer or a glass of wine after dinner, wait until the next campground. Try a cup of tea instead.

To get there: From Route 295, follow Route 44 West through Greenville and Chepachet into Glocester. Keep an eye open for the campground sign on the right.

KEY INFORMATION

George Washington Management Area Campground
Route 44
Glocester, RI 02814

Operated by: Rhode Island Department of Environmental Management, Division of Forest Environment

Information: Rhode Island Division of Forest Environment, (401) 568-6700

Open: April 13–October 15

Individual sites: 45 sites and two shelters

Each site has: Fire ring

Site assignment: At registration when you pay for permit

Registration: At pay station near campground entrance or office in recreation hall.

Facilities: Toilets, water spigots, boat launch

Parking: At campsites, additional parking available near recreation hall and Shelter 1

Fee: Rhode Island residents, $8; non-residents, $12; shelters, $20. Visitor fees: residents, $2; non-residents, $4; seniors, half-price.

Restrictions:

Pets—Not allowed

Fires—In established fire rings only

Alcoholic beverages—Not allowed

Vehicles—Two per site max.

Other—4-day max. stay, visitors must be out by 10 p.m., quiet hours 10 p.m.–7 a.m.

Another point to ponder is the wildlife. Let them remain wildlife. Don't feed them or otherwise tempt them by leaving food or dirty dishes around your campsite. The George Washington Management Area campground is wild and scenic, but it's also very accessible. Once otherwise wild animals become acclimated to human presence, they often have to be relocated or exterminated, and you don't want to be responsible for that. Plus, there are general safety considerations. Raccoons are occasional carriers of rabies, so report any incidences of raccoon or other animal bites or scrapes. It's also not a bad idea to report any strange or aggressive animal behavior.

At 3,500 acres, the George Washington Management Area is big enough to be a one-stop–shopping type of place for outdoor adventure. Bowdish Lake is right there for swimming, fishing, and paddling. The network of trails winding through the George Washington Management Area and Pulaski Memorial State Forest will keep the hikers and mountain bikers in your group busy for days.

The Walkabout Trail, marked by orange and red dots, is an eight-mile hike that passes by Wilbur Pond, a beautiful hemlock grove, and some wetlands. The trail leads right out of the campground. There are several alternate-trail options along the way for those who don't want to go the full eight miles. The blue dot–marked cutoff makes it a two-mile hike, and the red dot–marked cutoff makes it a six-mile hike.

There's a tiny sign hung at the apex of the roof on the backside of the ranger station that sums up the friendly nature of the George Washington Management Area. Look closely, drive slowly, look up and you'll see it as you're leaving—"Have a Nice Day" with the classic yellow smiley face.

APPENDICES

APPENDIX A
Camping Equipment Checklist

Except for the large and bulky items on this list, I keep the essentials of car camping together, so that they're ready to go when I am. I make a last-minute check of the inventory, resupply anything that's low or missing, and away I go!

Essentials
tent (with rainfly)
sleeping bag
sleeping pad
pillow (of some sort)
flashlights (one large flashlight and one headlamp)
stove (either multi-fuel backpacking stove or Pyramid folding stove)
fuel for stove (either gasoline for backpacking stove or charcoal for Pyramid)
mess kit, including:
large and small pots
frying pan
griddle
spatula
plates
bowls
mugs
knives, forks, and spoons

spices
cooking spray
can opener
corkscrew
matches
candle
first-aid kit
duct tape

Extras
camp chairs (some may consider these essential)
hammock
binoculars
canoe or kayak with all related gear (although there are a few campgrounds in this book where paddling gear really isn't optional)
mountain bike with all related gear (again, sometimes this is not an option but a necessity)

APPENDIX B
Sources of Information

Maine Bureau of Parks and Lands
22 State House Station
Augusta, ME 04333
(207) 287-3821
www.state.me.us

Acadia National Park
Box 177
Bar Harbor, ME 04609
(207) 288-3338
www.nps.gov/acad

New Hampshire Department of Resources and Economic Development
Division of Parks and Recreation
172 Pembroke Road
P.O. Box 1856
Concord, NH 03302-1856
(603) 271-3628
www.nhparks.state.nh.us

Vermont Department of Forests, Parks & Recreation
103 South Main Street
Waterbury, VT 05671-0603
(802) 241-3655
www.vtstateparks.com

Green Mountain National Forest
231 North Main Street
Rutland, VT 05701
(802) 747-6700
www.fs.fed.us/r9/gmfl

United States Department of Agriculture Forest Service
White Mountain National Forest
P.O. Box 638
Laconia, NH 03247
(603) 528-8721
www.fs.fed.us/r9/white

Massachusetts Department of Environmental Management
251 Causeway Street, Suite 600
Boston, MA 02114-2104
(617) 626-1250
www.state.ma.us/dem

Rhode Island Department of Environmental Management
Division of Parks and Recreation
2321 Hartford Ave.
Johnston, RI 02919
(401) 222-2632
www.riparks.com

Connecticut Department of Environmental Protection
Bureau of Outdoor Recreation
State Parks Division
79 Elm Street
Hartford, CT 06106-5127
(860) 424-3200
www.dep.state.ct.us

INDEX

A B O U T   T H E   A U T H O R

A lifelong New Englander, Lafe Low spends nearly all of his free time out-side—skiing, camping, skiing, mountain biking, skiing, kayaking, and skiing. He first started camping in grade school, when he and his best friend Dan Quagliaroli would head off into the southern Connecticut woods every Saturday afternoon with lofty ideals, indomitable spirit, and ridiculously heavy backpacks.

On the professional side, Lafe earned a Bachelor of Arts degree in Journalism from Keene State College in 1984. From there, he immediately went to work in the magazine world. After working for a variety of comput-er magazines, he decided to launch his own magazine, *Explore New England,* in 1995. This was truly the crossroads of his personal and professional pas-sions. After *Explore New England,* he went on to be the editor of *Outdoor Adventure* and an acquisitions editor for The Globe Pequot Press. He is now an editor with *CIO* magazine. *The Best in Tent Camping: New England* is his first book, but probably not his last. He currently lives in the Boston area.